Praise for
Why Couples

"*Why Couples Fight* is a compassion[...] guide for helping couples end destructive cycles of conflict."

—Janis Abrahms Spring, PhD, author of *After the Affair* and *How Can I Forgive You?*

"Relationship expert Mira Kirshenbaum once again has written a relationship book that has the potential to save troubled marriages with practical advice based on personal wisdom and the insights gleaned through many years of treating couples from all walks of life. Mira explains through case examples the negative consequences of fighting for power when needs are unmet while giving the reader a clear path to utilizing honesty, compassion, and kindness to overcome nonproductive means of managing conflict. Read this book with your spouse, do the exercises, and you both will likely regain the love that has been remaining dormant in your marriage."

—Arthur P. Ciaramicoli, EdD, PhD, author of *The Soulful Leader*

"*Why Couples Fight* offers couples wise and easy-to-follow advice as well as some great stories, a lot of humor, and Mira's down to earth, tell-it-like-it-is style. Read the book and work with her '1, 2, 3' strategy and you will listen better, see more options, and increase the likelihood of finding solutions to whatever the issues are."

—Dr. Dorothy Firman, *New York Times* bestselling coauthor of *Chicken Soup for the Mother and Daughter Soul*

Praise for the previous works
of Mira Kirshenbaum

"A great book! A must-read for everyone today who cares about their relationship. Simple, powerful insights for getting more than you imagined from the precious time you have together."

—**Jack Canfield**, *New York Times* bestselling author of *Chicken Soup for the Soul*

"What a useful book! Kirshenbaum's insights and suggestions will be of much assistance in bringing more intimacy and peace of mind to us all."

—**Gay Hendricks, PhD, and Kathlyn Hendricks, PhD**, *New York Times* bestselling authors of *Conscious Loving*

"A wise, compassionate, and very readable book. It will bless many lives."

—**Harold S Kushner,** bestselling author of *When Bad Things Happen to Good People*

"If you want to find your way back to the people you love, this book is a must-read."

—**Michelle Weiner Davis,** author of *Divorce Busting*

"An uncommonly wise and practical book—I really couldn't put it down. I kept finding useful insights and new paths to follow."

—**Pepper Schwartz, PhD,** author of *Love Between Equals*

"Brilliant."

—**Shere Hite,** author of *The Hite Report*

Why Couples Fight

Why Couples Fight

*A Step-by-Step Guide
to Ending the Frustration, Conflict,
and Resentment in Your Relationship*

Mira Kirshenbaum

CITADEL PRESS
Kensington Publishing Corp.
www.kensingtonbooks.com

ISBN-13: 978-0-8065-4044-3
ISBN-10: 0-8065-4044-3

First Citadel trade paperback printing: January 2021

10 9 8 7 6 5 4 3 2 1

Printed in the United States of America

Electronic edition:

ISBN-13: 978-0-8065-4045-0 (e-book)
ISBN-10: 0-8065-4045-1 (e-book)

To my daughters Rachel and Hannah . . .
I'm so proud of you and I love you beyond words.
You make me so happy.

And to my grandson Nick . . .
You are a great gift to me
and it's a joy to see you grow into a fine young man.
I love you so so so so much.

I've just finished writing the last chapter, and now, finally,
I feel at peace. At last I've kept a promise I made to myself
when I was ten, and that I made again and again over the years.
A promise I made with tears: to find an answer to the question
"Is lasting love possible, and if so, how in the world can we
make it happen?" I've given my life to this question,
and you hold the answer in your hands.

Contents

A Note to My Reader

Let's face it: you're not holding this book in your hands because you're totally happy in your relationship. In fact, you may be pretty unhappy in it.

Maybe you're not getting a lot of your needs met in your relationship. And this has led to a lot of conflict. Or open warfare. Or maybe the coldness of underground warfare.

And no matter how strong you are as a person, you may often be astounded at how frustrated your partner makes you feel when the two of you try to work out the slightest issue.

I know how you feel because I've felt the same way all too often in my own long-term marriage. I know the pain of that frustration since I was a little refugee girl. Since I watched helplessly as my parents struggled in their terrible marriage.

Life is all about having the right tools. Just ask any cook or carpenter. If you have the right tools, you can do anything. If you don't, you're dead in a ditch. This book is about giving you the tools you need to put an end to painful, unproductive conflict and instead talk to each other like two people who actually care about each other so you can both get your needs met in your relationship.

I also know how you feel because I've worked with countless people just like you for over forty years and seen all your struggles to get your needs met, to overcome your awful sense of helplessness, and to find your way back to the love that still lives, however deeply buried it may seem at times.

There is a way to save love from drowning in a sea of bitterness, even if it doesn't feel that way right now. However helpless you may feel, you are not helpless. And you and your partner can become the couple you always thought you were and always wanted to be.

A note on gender identity and sexuality in this book

I've written this book for everyone. Whoever you are and however you see yourself in terms of identity—man, woman, neither, fluid, non-conforming, questioning, queer, in transition, two-spirit—you're in this book and I honor you all equally.

And it's the same when it comes to your sexuality. I can't think of a variety of human sexuality I haven't worked with and embraced in my desire to help you in your own terms and based on what you yourselves want.

But while you are all here in spirit, it's possible that you might not find a couple I talk about within these covers that reflects your exact situation. And I apologize for that. I won't say it was unavoidable: everything is avoidable. But these days, the variety of gender and sexual expression is endless.

But the conflict and struggles you've had with your partner over who you are and who you want to be and how the two of you fit together—they *are* here. And you are here, in these pages and in my heart.

Why Couples Fight

PART I

Understanding Why Things Have Been So Hard in Your Relationship

1

"What happened to us?"

*"I want us to be happy . . . but I don't know
if that's possible anymore."*

Honeymoons come to an end all too soon, and we accept that. It's the natural order of things. What we're hoping for, though, is to go from the honeymoon to a more stable, solid, enduring love.

Instead, we too often end up pretty far from anything like the land of love. It's more like a quicksand of conflict.

Elise and Brad waited a long time before getting married, wanting to make sure their careers were launched. Now here they are, in a committed relationship for twelve years, with two kids.[*] They, like a lot of people, confuse their lifestyle—pretty good, with friends, family, vacations, a nice but small apartment—with the quality of their relationship—*not* so

[*] All the cases here are composites based on real people in real relationships. I've either seen them as patients or gotten to know them through our research. They include people of all racial and ethnic backgrounds and all sexual orientations and gender identities, and in varying forms of committed relationships. I've written them as composites to protect their privacy.

good, with a pretty big falloff in affection and intimacy and a steady rise in distance and conflict. Still, since they see the wheels coming off some of their friends' marriages, they think theirs must be more or less okay.

But if you asked them, and I did, they'd say that a lot of their needs weren't being met, and when they tried to get them met it was a big hassle. But *why*? That was the mystery.

Take one random evening for example, when the kids were at a school thing and were going to be coming home after dinner.

Elise comes home from a long day in the office—meetings, calls, crises, confrontations—walks into the living room, and steps out of her high-heeled shoes, kicking them out of the way as she dumps her three bags on the couch. She takes off her jacket and tosses it on a nearby chair—but misses so the jacket falls to the floor. She tells herself she'll pick it up later, and plops on the couch where she starts flipping through the mail. Most of it is junk mail—catalogs and credit card offers. She throws it all on the coffee table and hauls herself up to go into the kitchen to pour herself a glass of wine.

Soon her husband Brad comes home, his feet stumbling over her shoes in the entranceway where they landed, his stressed-out nerves stumbling over the general mess that greets him. He knows that Elise knows that her mess will set him off. She knows that Brad knows that she knows he'll be thinking she did it deliberately to annoy him. Why else?

There's almost no point in fighting. They could just say, in unison, "Fight number seven. Check," and be done with it.

But that would be too simple. Too much of a betrayal of their feelings.

Brad opens with, "You just couldn't do it, could you—figure out a way for me to not come home to a mess."

"So, I left a few things around. That makes me a monster? Of course you couldn't possibly just roll with it, could you?"

That's how it starts, and it ends with an exchange of hearty *fuck-yous*.

For some couples, fifteen minutes later one partner is saying to the other, "Hey, what do you want for dinner?" For others, they're not talking for days. For some, this just might have been the last straw.

So, what's going on here? First of all, it's not "just a fight." And what I mean by "just a fight" is when two people disagree and eventually work things out except that maybe things get a little heated in the process. No, it's more than that. It's a battle in the midst of a long history of resentments and disappointments and frustrations and unmet needs. Such as? Oy, where to begin . . . They have two boys. Good kids. But Elise wanted a girl, and wanted them to try one more time, just one more, and that would be that. But Brad not only said *no*; he said *no* to even talking about it, saying to her face that there was in fact nothing to talk about. No money, no room, and absolutely no interest on his part. Case closed.

Let's not make Brad the only bad guy in this. Elise did everything she could to make his life miserable in an attempt to change his mind.

And that's just one example of the many issues they have. Something millions of couples struggle through as well.

So let's ask the question again. What's going on here

with these two people having so much conflict and so much trouble getting their needs met? They are, after all, bright, articulate, caring people. It's time to eliminate some of the usual suspects. If you want to pull your relationship back from the bad place it's in, you have to identify the *real* problem. You can't blame bad toast on your bread when the problem is your toaster.

Rounding up the usual suspects

Is it that there's a bad fit between Brad and Elise? You know, that a neat freak should never marry a sloppy Joe? But the fact is that most people are different from their partners with respect to things like how neat the house should be or how many kids they should have.

Do Brad or Elise—or maybe both of them—have deep psychological issues? Sigh. "Deep psychological issues" are like tiny bugs in houses. You can always find them if you look for them. Everyone has them. So let me just say this. Out of the thousands of couples I've worked with over the past decades, the individuals in those relationships were no more burdened by psychological problems than the population as a whole.

And what about stress? Well, they sure had a lot of it, what with money issues ("If only Brad made more money!"), health issues (both kids had serious allergies, which added stress to the family), the small apartment, and the fact that they had noisy neighbors. Okay, but the issue is whether they are more stressed out *than other couples*. And that I doubt. We think of ourselves as more stressed out than other people we compare ourselves to because we see ourselves when things are at their toughest—the car suddenly needs a major repair, one of the kids has suddenly started punching other kids in school, a promotion at work just fell through, and hubby's spent all evening farting as if his life depends on it—while we see our friends showing themselves at their best (who's going to post the crappy stuff on Instagram?), to say nothing of their not mentioning some of the toughest things they're dealing with.

We—along with Brad and Elise—may quite rightly say we have it bad. But we're far less often justified in saying we have it worse than others.

And speaking of Brad and Elise's kids with allergies punching other kids in school, is it having kids *in and of itself* that lowers the quality of marriage? Oh, for sure. No one doubts it. Kids are a kind of anti-romance, anti-intimacy, anti-peace-and-quiet stress machine. They're essential for family, and family is great. But family is not the same thing as marriage. In any case, every marriage with kids is in the same boat.

So is it marriage *itself* that's the problem? Kids + time + routine + boredom + habit + accumulation of resentments = a relationship on life support?

"Marriage is just too damned hard."

A lot of people these days say that marriage is too damned hard. And I know a lot of people feel that this is true. What they're also likely to say, looking straight at their partner, is "What the hell is wrong with *you*?" I know that in my own marriage I could always bypass looking at my relationship and my role in it by simply blaming my husband and fantasizing how wonderful things would be if he weren't the selfish, insensitive jerk he seemed like at the moment.

Then some therapist tells them to stop making "you" statements and start making "I" statements, and so they say something like, "*I feel* you're a selfish, insensitive jerk!" Wow, that made a huge difference. (I'm being sarcastic, just in case you weren't sure. But not all that sarcastic . . .)

Then they meet with friends who complain about their own relationship but also say maybe it's not all "his" fault. *That's* when you might hear a big sigh and people saying, "Marriage is just too damned hard."

And then, if they're at all thoughtful, you'll hear them ask, "Why?"

So, if marriage is so hard, why do we even bother?

Look, it's not marriage itself that's the problem. That would be like saying that the reason a lot of people have health problems is the body itself. And this is a far-too-negative view of marriage. It completely ignores the enormous benefits from being with someone you know and who knows you, whom you can trust, whom you genuinely like, with whom you have a long, shared past, with whom you have overcome so many challenges, with whom you can grow old. Plus, if you're being honest with yourself, you'll admit that you love each other and you love being married . . . when you're not fighting.

So then, whatever the mysterious force that gets us into that not so great place, we find ourselves there. Certainly there are unmet needs. Almost certainly conflict of one sort or another. And a sense of distance and resentment. Worst of all, things seem to get worse, not better, no matter what we do.

The turning point

Of course even once the honeymoon is over, it's not all fights, not even mostly fights. Soon enough, with a longing backward glance at the honeymoon days, some of us find we're quite content with a nice walk around the block after dinner with our partner.

But for too many of us, even that can feel out of reach. And at some point, inside ourselves, we reach a turning point. It's not that sex gets to be routine and affection scarce. It's not that we've had our first fight, and then many more, and have gotten used to a hot climate of conflict or an all-too-cool climate of avoiding conflict and each other. It's not even that we've come to realize that too many of our needs just aren't being met in this relationship, and, if we can believe our partners, the same is true for them.

That's not the turning point, because these days so many of us have hardened ourselves to the thought that marriage is hard and likely to be far from perfect.

The turning point for so many of us is when the D word creeps into our heads. D for divorce. Or maybe the B word: B for breakup. Not as in "That's it! I want a divorce!" We may still be a long way from that. It's more the sense that divorce or breakup or separation is not only suddenly a possibility but even—just maybe—something that might be a good idea. Scary as hell, but a good idea. Maybe. It's more like this:

> *I'm at the point where I think about divorce all the time. Is it what I want? No. Of course not. I want us to be happy, the way we were. Close. Feeling like we have each other's backs. But I just don't know if that's possible anymore. So ... I try to work on my marriage, but in the middle of the night I think about ending our marriage.*

Most of us have been in this place. I know I have. It doesn't necessarily mean you have a bad marriage or that your relationship is doomed or that deep down you really want out. But it sure as hell means that you feel like the two of you are in trouble, and *that* means you probably are. You're jumping around hard on pretty thin ice.

You know how to make conflict happen, but you don't know how to make love happen anymore. But hang in there. You'll soon learn how.

The look of love gone bad

The trouble we get into in our relationships, where we're haunted by the D word, can look very different from one couple to another. Tolstoy was right when he wrote, "All happy families are alike; each unhappy family is unhappy in its own way."

Take Debra and Mike.

Debra and Mike met in college and *bam!* None of their friends got why these two belonged together, but Debra and Mike got it, and they got it bad. Mike was getting a degree in music and in fact was on track to becoming the successful bad-boy rock musician he looked like. Debra was pre-law, but she was the cool chick, loved to party, and dreamed of a career in poverty law, and Mike liked the idea of that. Mike's music career took off right away and he supported Debra all through law school. Debra went to work; Mike's career kept going, but kept staying short of any kind of stardom.

You know . . . life. Then more life: a baby, less money, and both Mike and Debra growing dissatisfied with their careers, their incomes, their lifestyles (Mike on the road a lot, for example), the whole way everything was fitting together. The cool chick and the hot guy were struggling.

Now I happen to know that they were good people and really cared about one another. But still, there were a lot of sources of conflict. Money was always going to be an issue, the fact that it's tough to make a living as a musician or a poverty lawyer. Lifestyle. Parenting turned out to be a huge issue: Mike (!) turned out to be the strict one, but he was never around enough to have much say.

After their second child came along, Debra started losing some of her interest in sex. Part of it was fatigue, part of it was Mike's off-and-on presence at home and in her heart. Mike didn't help things by too often coming home in a bad mood from a bad tour.

This was all normal stuff, what people go through in so many marriages, regardless of who the people are or what they do for a living. Debra and Mike descended into a tangle of struggle and anger and discouragement and resentment, mixed with hope and attempts at plugging the leaks in their ship.

But what exactly did that state look and feel like to

Debra and Mike? And where are the most common places that leaky ship takes people?

A lot more places than you might think! The conflict-filled, D-word-haunted relationship comes in a number of different flavors.

War and peace. Sometimes people find themselves in a relationship where there are long periods of quiet, but then trouble starts brewing and at some point people lose their shit. There's a huge fight, so scary that you both pull back and smooth things over. Nothing's been resolved, just smoothed over. And so things stand, until the next blowup. In case you were curious, that was Debra and Mike.

Endless warfare. Sometimes conflict and struggle take people exactly where you think it would. Quite simply, they fight a lot. Sometimes huge blowouts, but sometimes lots of sniping, bickering, arguing. And always there's the feeling that if ever they should try to discuss an issue it would be sure to end in a fight.

Shrunken lives. People don't necessarily decide to do this. It just works out this way. Some parts of their lives continue to work well. For example, you always enjoy going out, and talking, just the two of you. So you continue to do that. Traveling together works, so you do that. But let's say sex—whether to have it or not—has turned into a battlefield, so you just X it out of your lives. And over time you X out all the other bits that don't work well. Your relationship has shrunk down to a small fraction of what it had been. You have the illusion that things are working well, like a hapless employee who has the delusion that things are fine because he's been stripped of most of his responsibilities.

Winter. Here in Los Angeles people think it's cold when it's, like, 59 degrees out. Hah! Back in Boston, cold was more like 29 degrees, and up in Utqiagvik, Alaska, –9 degrees would be considered just kinda cold. But whatever your reference point, it can always get colder. Sometimes the conflict between two people is so dismal and all-pervasive that few connections are left besides habit, which is a powerful connection indeed. Millions of couples shiver together in the feeble warmth of a relationship's embers. While they can't stand to struggle anymore, they can't stand to split up. So winter sets in. Politeness reigns. They spend their time together walking on teacups. Emptiness masquerading as harmony. And it feels okay as long as they don't think about it or until someone better comes along.

And finally, there's this.

It is what it is. For some people this is the best possible outcome when you can't let go of your needs but the struggles to get them met are not working very well either. Many people rate these relationships as satisfying, not because they really are, but because they want to be grown-ups about the whole thing. The relationship is actually not horrible. But it's not great. This isn't what you bargained for, and you dream of something better, but you're still together and a lot of your friends aren't. If divorce were easy, if you knew you could find someone better, then maybe . . . But . . . it is what it is.

A way forward

When it comes to relationships, the *why do we fight?* is really *why do we set off in the wrong direction when our partner— to our shock—resists meeting our needs?* We respond to our partner not meeting our needs, they respond to what we do, and then we, in turn, respond again. And round and round it goes.

It's not that we "fight." It's that in our frustration we end up treating each other in cruel and contemptuous ways.

It's something we get sucked into, no matter how smart we are. That's why watching very smart people fight is so funny, as well as being so very sad. They're not even people anymore. They're just what people become when they're caught up in this desperate, unproductive struggle to get their needs met.

And really that's all they want: to get their needs met. But they don't—in the most painful way possible. And how horrible is *that*? It's like you're trying to swim with the current, because that's so much easier, except that the more you swim, the more you make the current go against you, to the point where you exhaust yourself and the only place you go is backwards.

And this points us to the answer. What if we could figure out why it is that you and I and our parents and cousins and most of our friends have so much freakin' trouble resolving the conflicts we have with our partners? What if there was a solution that we all could use to resolve these conflicts, so the pain and resentment would go away, needs would be met, and instead of living with a mess of unsolved problems, we'd have a much better life because we'd have so many good solutions to those problems?

There's something—which we'll nail down in the next chapter—which makes it very hard for nice, normal people to avoid running into conflict when it comes to getting their needs met. And the things they do to deal with each other make the problem worse, not better.

So, why can't two smart, loving, caring people work out all their problems? Why do they get tangled up in unproductive fights?

2

The *Real* Reason Marriage Is Hard: Power Struggles

*"I don't want power. I just don't want
to feel disempowered."*

The stuff two people who live together can struggle over can be *anything*:

- Over where to set the thermostat. "I'm dying of cold at sixty-nine degrees!" "You could wear a sweater!" "If I wanted to live in a sweater, I'd have moved to Sweden!"

- Over how to parent our kids. "You're going to spoil him at this rate!" "Children need love!" "You think I don't love my kids!?"

- Over what "getting our spending under control" really means. "Let me try to wrap my head around this. You spent three thousand dollars on Christmas presents for your family?! Are you crazy?" "No, you're totally right—I should be a stingy hateful person like you, I suppose!" "Oh no, *you're* right—trying to buy love from a bunch of ingrates is always a smart move! I'm sure they'll be so grateful they'll drive down and fix our roof for us now!"

- What to do about a huge student loan obligation. "Look, I'm sorry you have all this money you have to pay back, but you took it on before we met." "Yeah, but what about our pledge that we have each other's backs?" "Yes. Yes! But you totally lied to me about how much you owed." "I told you I owed a lot!" "You sucker-punched me! I never realized 'a lot' meant two hundred and thirty thousand dollars!"

- Over what you would do "if you really loved me." "If you really loved me you'd find time in your sooooo busy day to call me and see how I was doing every once in a decade!" "Maybe I should show you my love by quitting my job altogether!" "You don't even try to understand me!" "Do you have even the slightest clue about what *my* day is like!"

- Over something having to do with sex. "You never want to have sex anymore!" "Well, you always wait for the perfect moment: when we've finally climbed into bed and we're tired and it's perfect for you to get away with a quickie!" "With you there's never a right time! You're always going, doing—you can't even sit through a meal without getting up and down."

- Or this: "I give you BJ's all the time. Without your even asking! But you won't go down on me even if I beg you to. It's not fair and it's really hurtful." "Listen, I've explained why it's hard for me. I can't keep repeating that." "I think you're just being a big fat spoiled baby and I think deep down you hate women. That's what I really think."

- Or boundary issues. "You keep saying you're just friends with Miranda from the lab. I think you're full of it. Those texts from her like '*you mean sooo much to me*' or when she signs off *xoxox*? I think she's taking you down, if she hasn't taken you down already, and I want you to dial this all the way back to a strictly professional relationship." "You are so far off base it isn't even funny. She is my most important professional relationship. But that's all it is. It's just that we work closely together and she's an affectionate person. She's like that with everyone. Ask around." "Oh, I get it. This colleague is more important to you than our relationship and my peace of mind. Good. Thanks sooo much for making that clear."

And on up to the most complicated, painful, difficult conflict you can imagine.

So here it is: There's a conflict. The two of you want different things and—ah! the great tragedy of life—you both can't have them. (Or at least you think you can't.) Now let's track the storm as it develops.

Very often, the conflict starts as something that goes on inside the individuals involved. For hours, days, years sometimes, you just go around hating the way your partner drops their wet towels around the bathroom, but you don't say anything about it.

Then words are exchanged. Not necessarily a fight.

Maybe just a comment. Maybe just "You know, it would be nice if you put your wet towels in the hamper once in a while," and your idiot partner takes that as, "Oh, my little darlin' would think it nice if I tossed my wet towels in the hamper *on occasion*. Well, bless her heart. I should try and do that sometimes."

So there's typically a ramp up from a "comment" like the above to a conversation, to an angry conversation, to full-scale, scary-ass blowup, to a state of total rage and frustration. Or to a state of surrender, resentment, and despair.

Endgame? There rarely is an end game. Just pseudo-endgames. More like waiting games.

Maybe someone caves in. "Fine! You want to live like a pig? Fine! If you want to live like a pig, I'll treat you like a pig." Whatever the hell that means! Except it's a fake surrender. It's not acceptance; it's exhaustion and postponement of the struggle to another day.

Or else there's a compromise between two exhausted people that doesn't really please anyone—"Okay, I'll try to remember to put my clothes in the hamper and you'll try to not get bent out of shape if I forget." "Trying to remember" never satisfies anyone, nor does "trying not to get bent out of shape."

All this is exhausting and it makes you feel, "Why bother?" Of course. It's not as if all that struggling produced good solutions.

And that's the thing. It's not just that we end up with an atmosphere of hurt and anger and resentment. There's a growing buildup of unmet needs.

> **Every unresolved conflict, every conflict that's not resolved with patience and understanding, means your relationship is burdened with more and more unmet needs. And more resentment.**

How can we all be moving backward like this when we're trying to move forward?

I just talked with a young woman who wanted to start having kids, like, now. Her guy wanted to wait five years, which would have been feasible for the woman biologically, except that she didn't want to wait. And he didn't want *not* to wait.

I know this isn't an easy problem to solve, but still, there were all kinds of possible solutions—I'm sure you can come up with many of them—and I've helped plenty of couples find these solutions. The solutions are there. And ordinary, everyday people can find them. On their own. Just the way you can almost always find your car keys if you've left them lying around the house somewhere.

But it's not the problem itself that's the problem. It's the very dynamics of their struggle that gets them, and the rest of us, in trouble. The way they said things like, "Well, if you're going to be that way about it, then I might as well . . ." or "You ask me to care about you, when you clearly don't care about me" or "I think *you're* selfish? Wouldn't anyone think someone is selfish who . . . ?" And so they go, hacking their way at each other all the way to a total breakup.

The worm in the apple

The reason two people who fell in love and who are halfway sane and intelligent have trouble resolving their conflicts lies in the things we do and say to make each other feel disempowered as we try to work out our differences.

You feel disempowered because of something your partner did or said, or maybe even because of something about who your partner is. And that something made you feel disempowered on your side because it felt like your partner's taking power on their side.

And in case you think I'm going to let you off the hook, uh-uh. Your partner feels disempowered because of something you did or said, or maybe even because of something about who you are. Please don't clutch your pearls and say, "*Moi!?*" I'm not saying you're a bad person. I'm just saying you're a person. As you'll see, this is just what people do.

Here's an example: Suppose you really, really want to move to a bigger house, and so you put that out there as a possibility. You say to your partner as nicely as you can, "I'd really love it if we could move to a larger place." Objectively, a perfectly reasonable thing to put on the table. After all, you just said "place," not "palace."

But there's nothing to prevent your partner from hearing your statement, which is as innocent as a newly hatched baby duckling, as something dark and sinister as a newly hatched black mamba snake. Maybe it was the "I'd really love it if . . ." that made him feel his legs were being cut out from under him. "Oh boy," he thinks, in near panic, "she's starting with this and she's never gonna let it go. I'm doomed, unless . . ."

Unless he strangles the baby in the cradle. Which means saying something disempowering.

Think of disempowerment as the difference between your partner saying loudly, "Are you kidding? There's no way we could afford that now" versus saying calmly, "Let's talk about it."

The difference between those two responses would lie in how they'd make you feel. The second response—"Let's talk about it"—would not only feel good in a general way—hopeful and encouraging. It would also feel *em*powering. It would be saying that you have a voice and it's a voice worth hearing and respecting. Yeah, you may have assumed that. But it makes a huge difference to hear that your partner feels the same way.

But the first response . . . well, I don't know. Maybe you've gotten hardened to this kind of thing over time, the way you get hardened to people shoving in the subway. But to my well-honed clinician ears "Are you kidding?" sounds dismissive. I would feel someone was trying to brush me aside if they responded to me that way. And "There's no way we could afford that" just plain old sweeps the entire issue off the table.

And responses like that make me—most people, actually—feel disempowered. If I know my partner would prefer not to move to a bigger place but is wide open to talking about it, I don't feel disempowered. I feel I have a fair hearing. Whatever makes the most sense, whatever is best for both of us—we can figure it out. But making me feel dismissed and shut down, which is how so many of us feel two minutes into talking to our partners about difficult issues, just makes me feel helpless.

In any case, saying, "Are you kidding me? There's no way we could afford that now," is just the beginning of the drama. No one is going to stay feeling disempowered for long. Even if my partner didn't mean for any of this to happen—maybe he just thought he was being "honest" with me—I'm going to have to climb back into the ring. I'm going to have to re-empower myself. I'm going to have to make my "not so fast, buster" move.

And let's say I do that by getting emotional. Angry. Intense. Crazy, scary angry. To my partner, it's as if I'd just burst into flames and was throwing those flames right at him. And of course my anger seems disempowering to *him*, all the more so if he thought he was just being "honest."

So he has to re-empower *himself*. And whatever the hell he does next, it makes *me* feel disempowered, and 'round and 'round we go, down and down into greater depths of frustration, anger, and opposition.

And there's no good way for this to end.

So what just happened?

There are two more or less ordinary people with more or less normal needs. → There's a conflict between their needs. → There's something about the needs themselves or the way the needs are expressed that makes the other person feel disempowered. → The other person has to do something to feel re-empowered. → This goes back and forth and escalates. → The conflict goes unresolved and the need goes unmet. → There is an atmosphere of resentment and discouragement in the relationship.

> It's not that anyone wants power. It's just that no one wants to feel disempowered. But from the outside, and from the inside as well, it looks and feels like a struggle for power.

Power goes with love like a fish goes with a bicycle

It seems really weird to talk about power in the context of love. What does one have to do with the other? Power is what evil people hold over others. Mad scientists. Dictators. Slave owners. Abusers. Oppressors. Not well-intentioned folks who just want to get along with their partners. Not you and me.

Right?

Wrong. Sorry, but wrong.

A lot of people just don't think of using the word *power* to describe what goes on in their relationship. Many people have said to me, "No one has power over me." Or, "Yeah, my partner might raise his voice or get all macho or stubborn or something, but he can't control me unless I let him." Or, "Well, I might feel very frustrated sometimes, but I don't feel disempowered."

And most of us wouldn't say that power is the thing we want in our relationships. Power might be at the *bottom* of many of our wish lists.

But, hey, most people have distorted body images, even though they have full-length mirrors at home! Well, just the way many of us think we look much worse than we do, many of us think we're much more innocent when it comes to using power in our relationship than we are.

Maybe the word *power* itself is the problem. Look, I don't think all this should hinge on the use of a single word. You can use whatever word you feel comfortable with. Control. Dominance. Bossiness.

But let me tell you where I'm coming from. It's my work with *help-seeking couples*, or *individuals seeking help* because of relationship issues. In other words, my patients. Regular folks, like you and me. It's just that fear, frustration, and pain have caused them to seek help.

And for these people it's immediately clear to me that they really do feel disempowered in their relationships, and they know it. If you ask them, they have no hesitation saying they feel that most of the time their partner seems to be more powerful than they do. They will say that they have a great deal of trouble getting their needs met in the face of the way their partner responds to them.

There's an exercise I've done with my couples over the years. Each writes down "*How empowered I feel in this relationship*" on a scale from 0 to 10 and "*How powerful my partner seems to me to be in this relationship*" on a scale from 0 to 10.

Over 93 percent of the time, *both* people think the other partner is more powerful than they are. What better evidence could you have of relationships being a kind of mutual disempowerment machine?

Let's be clear. None of this means that there's anything wrong with you or your partner. Neither of you has to be unusually interested in power or power hungry to any degree at all. Neither of you has to have controlling or domineering personalities. None of that.

All you need is to be normal people who get frustrated like everyone else, and hurt, and scared, when the things you care about feel threatened. Which in most relationships happens all the time.

"This *can't* be us . . . can it?"

To look at the role power has played in your relationships, try to answer these questions:

1. For your current relationship, which statement is truer:
    a. "Most of the time, I feel I have less power than my partner."
    b. "Most of the time, I feel more powerful than my partner."
2. For most of your past relationships, which statement is truer:
    a. "I generally felt disempowered."
    b. "I generally felt I had the upper hand."
3. For your current relationship, which statement is truer:
    a. "We each of us probably spends more of our time trying to get our own needs met."
    b. "We probably spend more of our time trying to keep the power equally balanced between us."

4.   For your current relationship, which statement is truer:
   a.   "When my needs aren't being met I get frustrated and I'll do things I'm not proud of to try to get my needs met."
   b.   "When my needs aren't being met, even though I'm frustrated I won't do anything that puts my partner at a disadvantage."

Your answers to questions 1 through 4 should make things pretty clear to you. The more often your answer was option "a" to a question, the more likely it is that something having to do with power is causing trouble in your relationship, and it's not all your partner's fault.

What is power? In general, it's something neutral: the ability to make something happen or to prevent something from happening. I have the power to pick up a pillow; I don't have the power to pick up a car. I have the power to turn off a lamp; I don't have the power to turn off the sun. (Or a two-year-old's tantrum, for that matter.)

Power in a relationship can be a very good thing, like the relationship between a parent and an infant. The baby is helpless—totally adorable of course—so thank goodness there's an adult around with the power to take care of the baby. It's a rare baby who complains that its parents are too controlling.

But in a relationship between two adults who are in love and are committed to living their lives together, power is the ability to make happen what you want to happen more easily than your partner can make happen what they want to happen. If I can prevent you, generally speaking, from getting what you want and instead get what I want—if the thermostat is generally set the way I want, if the windows are open or closed as I prefer, if the throw pillow situation is more to my liking than yours—then I have more power. That's just the fact, Jack. And that's not a good thing. My power means more of my needs get met. And fewer of yours. And you're thinking the exact same thing.

Right now you might be saying, "Hold on there a minute. All this talk about fighting and conflict. I'm not sure that describes my relationship. Yeah, a lot of my needs aren't being met. But most of the time we're pretty calm. So does all this apply to us?"

Well . . . probably.

Not everything is what it seems like, oh no

Power struggles—love-strangling power struggles—often don't look like what you might think. Which is why it can be so easy for people in an unhealthy relationship to think that power issues don't apply to them.

Chris and Melissa *hated* fighting. Like lots of couples. So when there was conflict, here's what would happen, generally:

First, nothing much is said. At the last minute, before they were supposed to go away for a long weekend at Melissa's parents' house, Chris announced he couldn't go because of "work stuff."

"Oh," Melissa said coolly. "I wish you'd told me. What am I supposed to tell them?"

"Well, like I said, I had work stuff come up."

Melissa sighed. "Fine."

Second, after a number of incidents like this, Melissa announces they "have to talk." "You really need to tell me about your plans in advance so we can discuss them. You can't just drop them on me like you're the boss."

And then, typically, Chris will plead helplessness. "I'm sorry, Mel, but I'm doing the best I can. I tell you as soon as I know, and if I drop things on you it's 'cause they're dropped on me. I don't know what to tell you . . ."

And they go a couple of rounds of this until they both feel utterly helpless and quite sure the other has no clue about what's going on. Then someone gets a bit intense—maybe Melissa starts crying because she feels Chris is lying to her, or Chris's voice gets harsh because he feels Mel just totally doesn't understand—but instead of escalating they quickly decide to drop it.

Third (in one version of how this goes anyway), Melissa just gives up. One day after they have this "discussion" she just says, "Look, fine. Fine. It has to be this way. I'll just have to adjust."

Peace? Harmony?

Sometimes! Sometimes people just accept and let go. But too often they're just surrendering out of exhaustion and lack of ideas. And that's not surrender at all. The real name for it is "Lying in Wait."

When it comes to power in relationships, no one ever really wins, and no one ever gives up. This is like a law of physics for power struggles:

> **When it comes to the power struggles in relationships, there is rarely a final victor, and rarely a final victory.**

And so Melissa "adjusted" by planning her life without Chris, just the way, from her point of view, he'd been planning without her. Chris gradually became aware of occasions where he was just not expected to be there. Sometimes he was relieved. But a lot of the time he was disconcerted. And he had a strong sense that the overall temperature in the marriage had gotten turned down quite a bit.

Make no mistake: this is an *escalating* power struggle. It will continue to escalate over time until Chris and Melissa are as far apart as they can be without actually not being in a relationship at all. And then the next step will be divorce.

It escalates because whatever Chris or Melissa does to respond to the other's needs will result in new or renewed distance. Perhaps measured in the increasing length of time between when they make love.

"Oh, Melissa, do we have to deal with this now?"

"Well, just when do you suggest we do deal with it?" Melissa says, sharply putting the knife down on the kitchen counter.

"It's always something with you, Mel. I mean . . ."

"Look," Melissa says, "I have to go put on a sweater. But fine, you're right. It doesn't always have to be something with me. You can go back to your phone."

And Chris can feel the sexual chill in the air. All without a harsh word being spoken. It's just like when you have a friend you gradually have less and less to do with.

Sure, escalation can mean crazier and crazier fights. But it can also mean *fewer* and *calmer* fights but a growing sense of estrangement.

One wants to fight, the other doesn't. Lots of times you have one person quite comfortable with confrontation and the other quite uncomfortable with it. What in the world does that look like? Fighting? Not fighting? What?

It looks like fighting about fighting. But they're still in a disempowerment struggle. David loved a good fight—he never saw an issue he wasn't ready to rip wide open. He'd go from zero to furious in no time flat.

"Jessica, what the *hell* is going on with your relationship with Gabe? Isn't he supposed to be your ex? But you spend all this time yackety-yackety back and forth. I'm *fed up*!"

Now watch what Jessica does.

"Oh my God, David, why are you taking that tone with me? If you have something you want to discuss, let's discuss it like two adults. You don't have to start out by attacking me."

"The attack started with your in-my-face being all pally-pally with Gabe. *You've got to cut it out.*"

"David, when you can figure out another way to talk to me, I'll listen to you. In the meantime, what I have to say is, Fuck you and bye-bye . . ."

You see what's happening here. They're not talking to each other about the same thing at all! David is yell-talking to Jessica about her being close with her ex, Gabe, which threatens David. A reasonable enough issue. Jessica is talking to David about the way David is talking to her.

When a confronter and non-confronter tangle, things can go to hell pretty quickly, and the disempowerment struggle can be intense. That's precisely because they are not talking about the same things, so both feel ignored, dismissed, and ultimately humiliated. And while the confronter has, of course, loads of power moves at their command, the non-confronter has loads of quieter but just as effective power moves at their command. The confronter yells, the non-confronter sighs, cries, or runs and hides. One way or another, it's still blow for blow if you measure it by the feeling of disempowerment each inflicts on the other.

And that's the right measure. My intentions don't make something a power move. But if what I do or say—even if I just sigh or roll my eyes—results in your feeling disempowered so that at some point you need to re-empower yourself, then what I do or say is a power move.

A power move is anything we do or say that makes the other person feel disempowered.

We'll have a lot more to say about power moves later.

There are wars, and there are wars. You may have in your mind an image of a marriage beset by power struggles and think, *Hmmm, we don't fight like that.* Like *what*?

Even if both people in the relationship are out and out confronters, things may not look like what you'd think is a power struggle. I'm thinking of two movies: *Who's Afraid of Virginia Woolf* and *The War Between the Roses.* Yes indeed, those are all out, knock-down, drag-out, day-in, day-out fights to the finish. But they're not the power struggles most of us live, because they're unsustainable. If the fighting is too intense for too long, you quickly end up in divorce court or criminal court.

So real-life power struggles simmer along with a lot of sniping and bickering. They explode into huge fights, which then submerge into long, uneasy truces. There can be a lot of crypto-fighting: doing things like "analyzing" each other in ways that put the other on the defensive.

In fact, fighting itself is no measure of how dug into a power struggle you are at all. Some people who "fight" are just loud, vocal negotiators.

The ultimate test lies simply in whether either of you—and in most cases it's both of you—generally feels disempowered in the relationship, or in some significant aspect of the relationship (sex, money, parenting, household responsibilities, in-laws, and so on). If so, then you are caught in a dangerous disempowerment dynamic.

Blame-storming

James and Vanessa had a big problem. Vanessa's mom, Hester—a widow—was starting to develop dementia. This kind of thing is a crisis for any family. And every family will say, "Yeah, and it's particularly a crisis for us because . . ." But in fact every family has its *because*. Let's face it, if you take any random family with, let's say, a couple of teenage kids and the parents are in their late forties, there are going to be plenty of difficulties already without Grandma or Grandpa getting dementia.

The problem was what to do about it. Vanessa didn't like her mom very much, but felt she had a duty to do all she could to care for her. James actually did like Hester, but he didn't want her in their lives: everyone was too busy. Plunking Hester down in the middle of things would be the straw that breaks the camel's back. Plus, James and Vanessa could not agree about what they could afford to do financially.

But most important, they'd had a long history of not doing well with conflict. They were both sweet people; it's just that conflict did something to them. James would turn into Mr. Know-it-all. He'd begin sentences by saying, "Look, . . ." or "The fact is that . . ." or "It should be obvious to anyone that . . ." To Vanessa, almost every what-should-we-do discussion felt like an experience of being talked down to.

And that made her mad. And bitchy. So she'd respond with putdowns. When James turned into Mr. Know-it-all, Vanessa turned into Ms. Viper-tongue. If verbal terrorism were a thing of beauty, then it was lovely to see how quickly James and Vanessa could go from sweetness and light to the horror of a verbal knife fight in mere minutes whenever they tried to deal with a conflict. And this one was a doozy. Instead of brainstorming solutions, they blame-stormed their way into a sheer impasse.

The thing is, though, that James and Vanessa—like all of us—are caught in a deep illusion. What they thought was that they were each married to someone very, very different from themselves. That their marriage was a walking text-book of irreconcilable differences (except when there wasn't a conflict, in which case everything was fine!). And that the person they were contending with was a dirty fighter.

None of this was true.

Yes, it *seemed* true. And any sane person in their shoes would have thought it was true. But it is a fact of psychology that when things go wrong, or we anticipate them going wrong, we blame some characteristic of the other person or the situation. This is called the *Fundamental Attribution Error* by psychologists. If I'm frustrated and resentful in my relationship, if my needs aren't being met, it's you! It's gotta be! Or something else. Whatever. But it sure as hell isn't me.

The last thing that occurs to people is to say, "We're in a mess. It must be because we are doing something wrong."

And what exactly do James and Vanessa—and the rest of us—have so much trouble seeing? When it comes to conflict, we don't see that we have trouble because we've been using the wrong *tool*. Feeling disempowered and reacting to it is just a tool, and it's the wrong one for the job of fixing a relationship.

How to ruin a good relationship by using the wrong tool

If you wanted to take a daily pill guaranteed to turn a good relationship to crap, then, boy, do I have the pill for you. Because it's one almost all of us bring with us into our relationships and take every day.

Here's what's in the pill: *frustration*. This is made up of the feeling that you won't meet my needs. You won't see things my way. You don't do what I want you to do. *Belief in your own good intentions*. We all do this. And we're right! We are, mostly, well intentioned. The thing is, though, that, first of all, we judge others not by their intentions but by their actions and, second, they judge us not by our intentions but by our actions. What does this add up to? That's the next ingredient: *blame*. So if I'm judging myself by my good intentions, then the problem here can't be my fault. (Even people who are pretty self-aware still over weigh their good intentions and under weigh the effects of their actual actions on their partner.) So if it can't be my fault, it has to be your fault. *The story.* And if it is, in my view, your fault, I have to come up with a story—an explanation—of how it's your fault, and I do. We all do. It's the easiest thing in the world. As simple as: "Men!" Or "These bitches be crazy." Or "What a narcissist [or whatever psychiatric diagnosis is in the news a lot]."

And that's it! *I'm frustrated, I know I'm good, so you must be bad, and it's as easy as falling off a log to figure out why you're bad.* Boom! Done.

And of course "me good, you bad" can also be "me smart, you idiot" or "me sane, you crazy." Whatever the case, you try to take power away from the bad, crazy idiot. You'd be a bad, crazy idiot not to! Which takes us straight—do not pass Go, do not collect $200—into the hell of escalating power moves.

This, of course, is connected to the fundamental attribution error, where we blame the lobster for it being hard to eat if we're dumb enough to come at it with a knife and fork. But as a longtime New Englander, I can tell you lobster is not hard to eat if you have the right tools, and a knife and fork aren't the tools you start with. A nutcracker is, even though a lobster is not a nut.

Well, in the same way, James and Vanessa were convinced that their conflicts were unresolvable because, (1) each thought the other was a bitch/bastard when it came to working things out; (2) because they imagined that they had to be very, very different people to get so stuck so often in conflicts; and (3) because they'd come to believe that conflicts themselves were these monstrously difficult mountains to climb.

All along, we think the other person has been the problem, or the issue itself has been the problem, when in reality we've only been experiencing what life is like when you use the wrong tool.

The wrong tool—and the real reason marriage is so hard—is that we get caught up in that dynamic of feeling disempowered and then trying to re-empower ourselves.

But—and this is crucial—for all this to work, to make your relationship be great again, to bring back the love, to end the deeply discouraging power dynamics, you and I need to do one thing to make the right tools work:

You have to be willing to change. You. Yourself. To see that your way of being you is contributing something to the way things are. To not only stop blaming your partner but start seeing your own role in things being the way they are.

All I'm stating is a simple *fact*: when couples come to me for help, whether in person or, like now, in the pages of a book, the big difference between couples who make progress and those who don't is that for couples who thrive, *both* partners are willing to look at their role in how they are in the mess they're in and *both* are willing to make changes to improve things.

The good news is that you have choices, all kinds of things you can do or say that won't disempower your partner and won't disempower you either. Stay tuned. You'll see!

It's really all about having the right attitude. It's not about being right or turning out to be the better person. It's about each of you being willing to face your role in maintaining the situation as it is now, and to make whatever changes are necessary for your relationship to be healthy.

And so this book is all about my sharing with you what I've come to understand—along with all the thousands of couples I've worked with—about how to get the power dynamics out of your relationship and about the **1, 2, 3 Method** I will teach you that you can put in their place. Just think! Almost every couple with almost any issue could resolve their conflicts, come up with good solutions, get their needs met, prevent resentment from ever creeping into their relationship, and, well, make love not war for their entire lives together. And without being special people in any way.

So, bye-bye power? Yes. But as a woman, I know it's not something that's easy for many of us to say goodbye to.

Women and power: A complicated relationship

The whole #MeToo movement, in fact the whole women's movement going back to the nineteenth century, is all about women *taking* power. But we frame this for ourselves not as hunger for power in itself, but as, first, hunger for opportunity, the chance to be part of things, not shut out of things, and if that means being president of the United States, then so be it. It's the kind of power that enables us to break through glass ceilings and to elbow our way to the table where decisions are made or into the workplace where things are made.

And these days many of us grow up into womanhood wanting this kind of power so badly we can taste it.

Second, we want the power to be safe. In other words, some of us may want to produce films. And many of us don't. But those of us who don't want the power that legitimately comes with being in the movie business also want the power that would prevent some producer from messing with us in any way.

But that's not power *for*. That's power *from*.

So let's stand here cleansed from the guilt of being hungry for power in and of itself. That's not what's going on when we and our partners descend into a vortex of mutual disempowerment and our own attempts to re-empower ourselves.

But what about our need for power, our need to be in control, when it appears in our primary relationship? Can we say, to paraphrase Scarlett O'Hara and shaking our fists at the heavens, "As God is my witness, I'm never going to let a man take power away from me again!"?

Well, we can certainly feel this way! And who would blame us? Certainly not the vast majority of the women I know. We've seen too many relationships in which women are overpowered by men. Maybe our own parents' relationship. Maybe even our own.

Now I know full well that our personal experiences are all over the place on this. Some of us feel like we'd never let a man control us. We wouldn't let it happen. I get it! There are a lot of tough, strong women out there—me among them— and in fact there always have been. Our heroines are women who—from Joan of Arc to Nancy Pelosi and Elizabeth Warren—refuse to back down.

And I'm one of those women. I brought up my daughters to be two of those women—and they are!

There's only one teensy weensy itsy bitsy problem. It's a recipe for disaster in relationships.

Now here's what I'm *not* saying. I'm *not* saying a woman shouldn't be a strong advocate for her needs. Each person in every relationship *should* know what they want, *should* feel empowered to advocate for what they want, and *should* actually advocate for what they want. Certainly no less than her male partner. Or female partner for that matter.

But if I stand face-to-face with my partner and use my full power to get my needs met in a way that makes my partner feel disempowered, then it's just a fact of nature that my partner will try to re-empower him- or herself, and we will soon be caught up in a cycle in which the two of us—in effect—collaborate in strangling our relationship to death.

And by the way, because I see this all the time, guess what happens when one person ramrods some need of theirs through against what their partner wants? It is, at best, a very short-term victory. We talk a lot about sustainability these days, and victories in relationships that are won through power are unsustainable. Your partner's resentment will last longer and grow in force long after your delight in your victory has passed.

The alternative to this—which this book is all about—isn't for anyone, particularly women—to strangle *our own* needs to death. The alternative is a process in which we stay out of the quicksand of power dynamics entirely and yet nonetheless make sure our needs, both of our needs, get a full and fair hearing and the best possible chance for arriving at the best possible solution.

So, be the strong woman in the world that you want to be. Take control to the full extent that makes sense for you. Never let anyone shut you up or shut you down. But in your relationship, keep your strength, keep sight of your needs, but, I beg of you, let me show you how you can get your needs met without the power moves that would otherwise kick the crap out of your relationship.

As for love . . . No one—no matter how strong they are—goes into a relationship hoping for a brawl. We all hope that love will be enough. So how, *how* does power ever come to play a role in any relationship when it's the last thing people would say they'd want?

Let's figure this out.

3

What *Are* We Really Fighting About?

"Is there room for two whole people in this relationship?"

Well, let's not overlook the obvious. We really are fighting about the thing we are fighting about. If you're upset with me for always being late, that's why we're fighting. There's probably not some "real" problem that my always being late is just a cover for, like your not having worked through your parents' divorce. Even if you haven't worked through your parents' divorce—whatever that means!—you still really, really don't like that I'm late all the time.

But haven't you wondered, "Hmmm, why does this bother me *so much*? It's like, yes, I'm entitled to want such and such, but it gets me so fired up when we talk about it . . . Something's wrong there. Sometimes I don't totally understand why I get so worked up about these issues."

Yup. That's the very thing. How worked up we get. And how we deal with each other from that base of worked-up-ness. That's how we go from mere disagreement to conflict to breakdown to breakup. And if we can understand that—what exactly are the gasoline and the matches of unproductive conflict—we can understand just how to resolve conflict painlessly and productively.

So let's start with how it begins, the basis for why some issues *matter* so much to us.

The eight core experiences of love

The conflicts we get into are all too real to most of us. And we care about what we're fighting about. But we're also grown-ups who know we can't have everything we want. So the intense feelings we have about the things we fight over must *also* come from something deeper.

And in my experience they come from our deeper, more powerful hunger for *the eight core experiences of love*. These are the experiences that make us seek out love, that we dream we'll find when we and our partners say "I love you" to each other:

Attention. In the world of relationships, we know the answer to the age-old question: If a tree falls in the woods and there's no one around, does it make a sound? No. Not if the tree is like us. We need to feel seen and heard to feel we exist, much less feel loved. Most of us are starving for the attention of someone we really care about. If we're starving for that while we're in a relationship, we know something's really wrong.

Affection. Love without affection is like a sun without warmth. Or food without flavor. And food without flavor would make you wonder if it really was any kind of food at all. Affection—words, touches, kisses, hugs, any token of love—is the tight hull that keeps the ship of love afloat. Lack of affection: that's what we get from strangers.

Support. When you can't cope, I pick up the slack. When the wind has been knocked out of your sails, I breathe new life into you. When you're not okay, I find out what you need and do that. And you do that for me. And it's not even so much the doing of all this as the being able to count on the other to do this that makes all the difference. It's like walking along knowing there's solid ground under your feet. When we have this, we take it for granted. When we don't, we're starving for it.

Fairness. Well, really, it's blatant unfairness that feels like a knife in the heart. I've been home from work for three hours and you get home after a hard day only to find I've been lost on Facebook since I got home and the house is a mess and nothing's been done to start dinner. It hurts! But if two people feel the other is generally trying hard to make sure things are equitable, then that usually feels a lot like love.

Validation. People don't just fight over needs. It's also about our views of what's real. "I said I was sorry." "No, you didn't." "But you heard me!" "I barely heard you, but you didn't mean it." "But I *did* mean it." "You don't mean it. You're not really sorry." "You can't tell me how I feel!" "I can tell you're not sorry, because if you were really sorry you'd . . ." Aarrgghh! The exquisite emotional pain of having your truth denied is unmistakable. And I'm not even talking about being lied to! I'm just talking about someone very close to you having a very different memory or perception from you. "I thought our wedding went off without a hitch!" "Did we get married at the same wedding? Do you even know me at all?" This is a big deal. Especially when falling in love is so often about blissful "me too!" moments like, "I don't think your friends were very nice to you back there." "I know! I don't know what was up with them." There is much comfort in seeing things the same way and having our perceptions validated.

Respect. In a relationship, respect has a special meaning. There are things about you that you take pride in and things you feel sensitive about. Respect is what you feel when your partner actually conveys to you that they value what you're proud of and do not disrespect the things about you that you feel sensitive about. So if I put a lot of effort into working out—whatever the results!—I'll feel good if my partner notices and values how I work at it. And if I still have a fat ass in spite of all that, and feel badly about that, my partner will respect those feelings by never making me feel even worse.

Feeling cherished. We all want someone to think we're wonderful beyond our ability to justify that. We want the person who says they love us to think we're wonderful and cherish us just for being who we are.

Passion. What's the truth about passion when it comes to long-term relationships? Is passion like a flower? Something that, no matter how glorious and beautiful it is, will inevitably wither up and die? Or is it like sunsets? Some are glorious and some are beautiful, and some are just meh, but ultimately there is no end of glorious sunsets? The truth is that passion over time is like both. Of course it fades a bit with time and age, and of course it varies according to personality. All true. But this is also a core experience of love, a sense that in some consistent, meaningful way you and your partner are hot for each other. And that, like beautiful sunsets, can keep going forever.

How we get on the path to mutual disempowerment

If you were asking yourself why these eight core experiences of love deteriorate over time in a relationship, well, bonus points for you. Good question!

The less important reason, though still really important, is that we're lazy and easily distracted. In chapter 2 of my book *Our Love Is Too Good to Feel So Bad: The 10 Prescriptions to Heal Your Relationship*, I talk about what's needed in all relationships for daily maintenance and the cost of not doing it. It's exactly like the importance of properly maintaining your car if you want it to reach one hundred thousand miles.

But a much bigger deal when it comes to eroding the eight core experiences of love is the damage done by the hurt and resentment that grow out of the power dynamics in those conflicts.

Suppose you're in a difficult conflict over, let's say, whether you should take a fantastic job in a new city even though it will mean a setback in your partner's career. And this turns into a series of painful fights, a feeling of estrangement, and a relationship in perhaps serious difficulty. How did things get so bad? It's not just because you are having trouble figuring this out. Not even just because you're frustrated. It's much more because one of the core experiences of love has gotten seriously compromised in the process.

Let's face it, how bad could even a horribly difficult conflict be if you were able to maintain your ability to feel you were really listening to each other, being affectionate, supporting one another, struggling to be fair, respecting one another, making each other feel cherished, and still showing the passion you feel for each other?

Think about it!

Most people in most relationships are more emotionally fragile than they realize, because one or more of the eight core experiences of love has deteriorated. It's that, not the issue itself, that people are in conflict over, that turns conflict into something so awful, and that makes people feel they're so far apart.

So what happens to make things go bad?

It's hard to put into words, but I've seen it thousands of times. It could be something dramatic, but it's more often something almost undetectable. Let's say, just as an example, you want to take that game-changer of a job in another city and your partner in all innocence—and not a power move at all!—says, "You know, this isn't the last good job in the world. Surely you can still find something good closer to home, can't you?"

Well! What's wrong with saying that? On the face of it, nothing. You could just say, "Honey, I've tried to believe that, really. But you know how long I've been looking. And I've exhausted my contacts and my contacts' contacts. I'm starting to get really worried I won't find anything halfway decent around here, and the job they're offering me is my dream come true."

Yes, you *could* say that! But it's also very possible that what your partner said made you feel terrible and did real damage in the area of the core experiences of love.

Perhaps you suddenly feel your partner has not been paying attention to you at all.

Or you suddenly lose all sense that your partner supports you: otherwise they wouldn't have said such a thing.

Or maybe you feel your affection collapse in a heap: How can you desire someone who seems to care so little for you?

Or you could be infuriated because what your partner said felt so unfair, hugely minimizing your needs compared to their needs.

But beyond these eight core experiences of love we're also fighting about something that goes even further. Something that's essential to both people feeling loved but that gets us—at the same time—into a lot of trouble.

Is there room for two whole people in this relationship?

What do we want in a relationship? Not what do I want or you want. We each have our wish lists! But if we were to sit down with our partners when we're just starting out as a couple and say out loud what we want, we might say something like this:

"Look, you're you and I'm me. And I know we're different. What I want *so*, so much is for you to accept me for who I am and I want to accept you for who you are, and I'm sure that's what you want."

That's it, really. Acceptance.

Now if we both love bird-watching and the Boston Bruins (that's a hockey team, for those of you who are clueless about sports), well, there's nothing to accept. We're there!

But if I like staying up late and you like getting up early, and if you like having friends over a lot and I don't, and you are quite happy to get into an argument about politics and I hate things like that, and you want to be very vigilant about how healthfully we eat and I don't . . . well! Now the path to mutual acceptance has just gotten a lot steeper. Now what are we going to do, beyond getting into endless, relationship-eroding conflicts about our differences?

Let me put this more positively:

What we *want*, all of us, is for our relationship to be a container big enough, loose enough, forgiving enough to fit within it *two whole people*. All of me as I am and all of you as you are.

Time for a very brief quiz.

1. For your *past* relationships, which statement is truer?
   a. "Most of the time I felt there was room for all of me as I really am and all of my partner as he or she really was."
   b. "I most often didn't feel there was room for all of me as I really am and all of my partner as he or she really was."
2. For your *current* relationship, which statement is truer?
   a. "Most of the time I feel there is room for all of me as I really am and all of my partner as he or she really is."
   b. "I most often don't feel there is room for all of me as I really am and all of my partner as he or she really is."

If you're like the great majority of people, your answer was *b* to both questions. Not because of some quirk of one particular relationship or person, but because this is what happens to most of us in relationships.

Which means that you've been unhappy because you've felt your partner didn't want to make room (or wasn't able to make room) for important parts of who you are. And you made your partner unhappy because you didn't want to make room (or weren't able to make room) for important parts of who they are.

It doesn't have to be big stuff. If you feel I won't make room for the part of you that wants to put your feet up on the coffee table, and I feel you won't make room for the part of me that doesn't like feet on the coffee table, then at least one of us is not a whole person in that relationship. Coffee-table feet might not be a big deal in itself, but things like this all add up. And most of the time, issues like these get to the core of who you are.

There are no power issues in relationships where there's room for two whole people. But flip that around:

Power struggles come from my frustrated efforts to try to make sure that there's room for me in my relationship, and your frustrated efforts to do the same for you.

Here's a really common example.

"I'm an affectionate person. It's just the way I am. I like to express my affection, and I want to feel *you* expressing your affection for *me*. Otherwise . . ." And Lisa's voice drifted off into something like despair or perhaps a threat.

"Well, you just want me to be like you," Amanda said, "but I'm like *me*. You know I love you. I mean, after all I've done for you? My God! But you want me to run around with hugs and kisses saying *darling* and *sweetie pie* when you *knew* I wasn't that kind of person from the beginning. Maybe you should just marry yourself, instead of being in a relationship with another human being."

Good point. With much sadness in their hearts, both Lisa and Amanda were seeing that whatever dream they'd had of their relationship going in, what they had now was a relationship between two people each using all the power they have to make things be the way "I" want even if it means things being very different from what the other person wants.

"More of me, less of you." No one ever says that, but that is what we do, and too often the struggle for that is how our relationships go.

But now imagine something very different: a relationship that has room for all of who you are and all of who your partner is. You and your moods, your need to be with your friends, the things you need for sex to be sexy and special, the way things have to be in your life for you to feel safe, and on and on. And your partner with their moods, and their weird relationship with their one weird friend, and their need for frequent unsexy sex, and seeming unconcerned about being safe because everything is always going to turn out okay, right?—and on and on.

The dream is that your relationship could contain both of you, just the way a hot dog and a bun aren't at all alike but fit together perfectly. So why have you been feeling there isn't room for both of you?

Here's my take.

In most cases, differences are far, far less extreme than they seem. Mostly they're an illusion created by the way we deal with our differences—mutual disempowerment—which ends up magnifying those differences.

Now, we've been talking about "saying things that make the other person feel disempowered" for a while now. What are these "things" that we say or perhaps do that have this effect?

There's a name for them. We've mentioned them already. They're called *power moves*.

4

Power Moves

*"I imagined a lifetime of having to cry
to get him to be kind."*

Power moves. We all make them.

That's the most important thing to say. Power moves aren't things only evil, psychopathic, narcissistic, dictatorial assholes do. No one is so nice and sweet and gentle and kind and good and loving and helpless-seeming that they can't and won't make power moves. Power moves are things we do because we are or feel disempowered, and we do these things because we just don't know how else to get our needs met. That's why nature gives even little babies ways to make power moves. You know: crying. Nature's way of turning mommies into jelly.

So what exactly are power moves?

Let's say you and I are meeting downtown for lunch and we're discussing which restaurant we'd like best.

"Where do you want to go?" you say, making the opening move. It's a power-neutral move. You're being nice, but as people who've been through this before, you and I know you aren't actually conceding anything. So far we're just having a discussion.

"Oh, gosh, I don't know," I say. "Maybe some place that has fish." I mentioned fish. Was that a power move? No. Just information. I just put a fact on the table. On the giant lazy Susan of preferences we're going to have to deal with, I've mentioned a preference for fish, not a very strong preference either. I didn't say, "As long as it has really good fish." And let's face it: you can get some kind of fish almost anywhere.

But the actual test is, did my mentioning fish make you feel disempowered?

And that's the first thing to say about power moves. If I do or say X, it's a power move if it makes you feel disempowered.

To determine whether something is a power move or not, look at its effect, not its intent.

Now look at the amazing thing we've done here. We've taken a lot of blame out of the whole power thing. We don't have to look for motives. We don't have to judge morals. We don't have to label each other. If what I do is a power move because that's how it hits you, then my intentions are irrelevant. Blaming each other for our presumed intentions just makes things a lot worse.

If I suggest we might go have lunch at a place that has fish, it doesn't matter if I meant it to be a power move or not. I might very well have meant it to be nothing more than a step in a process in which we'd each mention some preferences and that way zero in on a place we'd both like.

But if you feel I'm trying to take control, if you feel my just mentioning fish makes you feel somehow swept up in my preferences, as if I'm going to just steer this whole thing the way I want it to go, then you'll respond not to my information—"Maybe some place that has fish"—but to your own feeling of disempowerment.

And then instead of joining my preference-stating move with one of your own—"Yeah, okay, and maybe a place with Italian food on the menu"—you might say, passionately, "You know, I've been *dying* to go to this Italian place I know." Your passion is trying to knock out my presumed power play.

And then I may feel swept away by your passion. Your passion will seem like a power move to me. Whether you intended it or not. I'm likely to feel, "Sheesh, if she's so all fired up about Italian food, fine! I'll just cave. I'm sure I'll find something I can eat." But of course your tiny victory came at the cost of my feeling a tiny—or not-so-tiny—bit of resentment.

Or, we could make a big to-do out of where we're going to eat, with me squashing your idea for Italian, and you squashing any other option that I come up with.

So what do we see in this silly little mini-drama? It's more than that intentions don't matter. It's also that power moves can be incredibly subtle: "*Maybe a place that has fish.*" And it's also that each power move seduces us into making one of our own.

And, it's also that we always have a choice.

If I say, "Maybe some place that has fish," and you think, *What a pushy bitch*, well, stop for a moment and consider your reaction. You *are* the world's number one authority on how you feel, but those feelings don't qualify you to assume anything about my intent. So instead, whatever you think I'm doing, and regardless of how I've made you feel, you *could* always end the power struggle from the beginning, from *before* the beginning in this case, by responding to me as if I were *not* making a power move but just stating some information.

Solution: To prevent a power struggle from ever getting started, respond to what you think might be a power move as if it were just someone supplying you with information.

I've just stated a preference. So you state a preference. No escalating. If you don't escalate, I probably won't.

We know one thing a power move *isn't*: it isn't necessarily something someone intends. In fact, it's usually truer to say that it is more like a reflex, based on that person's history of being controlled and hurt and of fear of loss, whatever that might be. The person making power moves isn't some evil, scheming villain. It's more often a person in sheer reaction mode.

Beyond that, what is a power move?

Anything.

The catalog

Just this morning I came across this Tweet: "My wife won an argument with four sighs, two eyerolls and zero words." And there you have it. The truth is that anything, *anything* can be a power move: Asking someone what time it is. Yawning.

Saying, "I don't know, what do you think?" Misunderstanding what someone said. Putting the OJ in the fridge with the label facing toward the back. Wearing your black pajamas. Not shaving. It all depends on the context, the other person, and the state of the relationship.

There's a story by James Thurber called "The Breaking Up of the Winships." It was written in 1945. At that time, Greta Garbo was a very big deal. The husband was being driven slowly around the bend by his wife's constantly talking about how wonderful Greta Garbo was. Finally he couldn't take it anymore. And he calmly said, "Well, I think Donald Duck is a better actor than Greta Garbo."

And that remark, at that moment in that relationship, was the power move of all power moves, and it torpedoed their marriage out of the water.

To open your mind to what might be an actual power move, I'm going to offer a list of suggestions. But I must make one thing very, very clear, one more time. It's not for *me* to say that these are power moves. It is dependent on whether something makes someone feel disempowered.

A power move is something a person says or does that makes another person feel disempowered and thus puts him or her on the path to re-empowerment.

It's your feeling disempowered that makes something I do a power move. If I raise my voice you might not think that's a power move at all. Maybe you grew up in a family where everyone shouted all the time anyway. But if my husband gets intimidated when I shout, then it is a power move. It's not the shouting that makes it so. It's his reaction that makes it so.

So here's a list of things people have experienced as power moves:

NONVERBAL ACTIONS
- Walking out of the room
- Eye rolling
- Finger tapping
- Knuckle cracking
- Putting on a fierce face
- Lurching back and forth, side to side, in your chair
- Glancing at your watch
- Looking away
- Smiling

VOCALIZATIONS
- Sighing
- Groaning
- Grunting
- Going *ppfffff*
- References to God: "Oh my God." "Oh, for God's sake." "Oh, please God in heaven!"
- Silence (sometimes known as giving someone the silent treatment)

QUESTIONS
- "How'd you come up with that idea?"
- "Did your sister put you up to this?"
- "You know we can't afford this, right?"
- "Do you know how crazy that sounds?"
- "What makes you think you're entitled to that?"
- Really? *Really?*

DESCRIPTIONS OF YOU

- "Oh my God—you're such a baby!"
- "That was so passive-aggressive."
- "Have you ever considered that you might be borderline?" (or any other psychiatric term).
- "Can you be reasonable for once?"
- "You're just being insecure!"
- "You need to be in control all the time, don't you?" (This is the "taking control by accusing the other person of taking control" move.)
- "I thought you were a good person. Now I don't think so."
- "You are just like your mother."
- "You are such a bitch."
- "I thought you were a man, but obviously you're not."*

THREATS

- "You know, Sally gave me the name of a really good divorce lawyer. You see . . . here's the number. He's just ten beep beep beeps away."
- "You act like you think I need you. Maybe I do act like I need you. But it's time you got real, baby. *I don't.*"
- "You know Bob [her old boyfriend] is single now. Just thought you oughta know."

---

* These last three—some version of "You're just like your mother," "You're a bitch," "You're not a real man"—are almost guaranteed to turn a heated argument into World War III.

- "You could never survive without me, so you better be careful not to go too far."
- "Fine, do what you want, but that means I can do whatever I want."

BULLYING

- "No, *you* listen to *me*!"
- "You know, I think you need to see a therapist. There's something wrong with you. Let's have this discussion after you're fixed."
- "The answer is *no*, and I don't want to hear any more about it!"
- Screaming, "You're driving me crazy!"
- "If you ever do that again, you just watch what happens"

EMOTIONAL DISPLAY

- Punching the wall / couch / kitchen counter, etc.

Note: An actual threat or act of physical violence is more than a power move. Threats or acts of physical violence are signs of real danger. In this case, you need to say something like, "Okay, physical violence is now on the table. I don't feel safe and one of us has to leave until we can meet with a therapist to decide on a course of action." And then one of you has to actually leave. If you feel physically threatened and your partner won't leave, you have to call the police.

- Weeping, crying, sobbing. Remember: *intentions have nothing to do with this.* So, to be perfectly clear. I'm not saying your tears or your partner's tears are phony. They might be as genuine and innocent as the dew on a rose. But it's not an either/or. We may authentically cry out of sadness, anger, or frustration, but *at the same time* if we learn that tears will weaken the other person's resolve, we will be more likely to cry. The more we discover tears work, the more we will work the tears. And we all know this, on some level. There's a movie in which we see a woman breaking up with a man because of just this. Her heartbreaking line is: "I imagined a lifetime of having to cry to get him to be kind."* That phrase "having to cry" didn't mean faking tears. It meant the inevitability of tears as the only power move she would have to get that man to be kind to her.
- Jumping up and screaming . . . well, anything. Such as, "I can't take this anymore." "You're driving me crazy! You know that, don't you!"
- Just generally losing it or getting upset

EXAGGERATION
- "I can't live with green walls another day. *Not another day!*"
- "This budget of yours is going to squeeze the life out of me."

---

* *The Guernsey Literary and Potato Peel Pie Society.* A great movie, by the way.

- "I just can't live without a dog."
- "You really just want me to die, don't you? That's really it, isn't it?"
- "You are totally clueless, aren't you?"
- "You're too much for me. I can't take it anymore."

DISPLAYS OF WEAKNESS

- "God, I'm so tired of all this . . ."
- "Oy, I've got such a headache from all this . . ."
- "Look, I can't deal with this now."
- "So what do you want from me?" (Not a real question: it's really just playing stupid.)
- And while I'm at it: playing stupid. Anything that conveys the idea that you're too dopey to understand what your partner wants or to be able to do what your partner needs.
- "Now I'm a nervous wreck. I hope you're happy."

INVALIDATING THE OTHER PERSON'S FEELINGS OR NEEDS

- "I *said* I was sorry!"
- "You know, you're not the only person in this family."
- "You only think you need this."
- "You just want that because you're bored." (Or " . . . because your therapist told you your daddy never made you feel loved," or some other explanation.

CHANGING THE SUBJECT

- "*Now* you tell me!" (Instead of addressing what their partner needs, they focus on how the timing of the request affects them.)

- "And I assume you don't care about the hard day *I* had." (And this change of subject also invalidates the other person's feelings.)
- "You always say that!"
- "This comes straight from your therapist, doesn't it?"
- "You just don't care about me at all, do you?"

JUST PLAIN MAKING YOU CRAZY

- "It's just not me." Meaning: "I literally don't have it in me to do this" or "It would be so against my nature to do this that it would feel like an extreme and impossible violation." This power move involves making something that may be *difficult* for the other person, or just *undesirable*, sound utterly *impossible*. "You're asking me to be a little more neat? Or a little more calm? Or to not interrupt you so often? What?! Why . . . you might as well be asking me to fly or to choke myself to death!"
- Yessing you to death. Oh, this is a bad one. It's not saying yes. It's saying yes and not meaning it. Your mouth says *yes*, but your eyes say, "Honey, if saying *yes* will get you off my back, I'll say *yes* 'til the cows come home." People will not only *yes* you to death, they might very well go overboard in supporting how you feel and what you want. "I know! It's terrible how you've been having to be the bad guy with the kids all the time and me never disciplining them. You must resent me so much. I'm so so sorry. I'll really take charge now." And after a week your partner stops taking charge again.

The unilateral move. A unilateral move is where someone tries to bypass a possible power struggle by going ahead and doing the thing they want on their own. We've all had this done to us, and sometimes we do it ourselves. It can be something big: "Honey, I was offered a big promotion: head of our Eastern European operations. I told them *yes*. We'll be moving to Bulgaria next month. Isn't that exciting?!" Or it could be something less extreme but equally a power move: "Hey, my parents called about coming to visit and I told them they could stay with us." A unilateral move becomes a power move when it's something that affects your partner or that you've agreed you'd discuss.

Wait . . . I have to ask my partner permission before I do anything?

Aaaaand here we are: the question of freedom in relationships. You might say, "Hey! I'm not going to beg my partner for permission every time I want to turn around." Well, first of all, you shouldn't ever have to beg permission for anything: that's not the kind of thing we're talking about here. And it's not for every time you turn around. Let's not exaggerate!

If I buy a pair of running shoes, I don't have to consult my husband about it. It's not a move that affects our budget. If I buy a *car* without consulting my husband, *that's* a problem. I should consult him, because for us that's a big purchase. But I knew someone who was so loaded he could buy a Ferrari whenever he wanted without talking to his wife about it, because for them the cost of a Ferrari was a negligible dent in their budget, like me buying running shoes. (We should all be so lucky!) It's only a power move when your decision has an impact on your partner.

I know you wouldn't purposely make a decision that hurts your partner (at least I hope not). You might even think you're making the decision that's in the best interest of your partner. But it doesn't matter. We can have the best intentions, but when someone feels a decision was made without their input, they're going to view it as a power move.

Let's say you have had dogs and you're known to like dogs. Suddenly one day your partner surprises you by coming home with a dog he's just adopted from a local shelter. "Look what I brought home, honey! Isn't she cute! She's called Gussie!"

Gussie, a huge, hairy, drooling dog ambles in looking like she'd just love to gobble up a couch and a couple of easy chairs for dinner.

What your partner doesn't know is that you'd been thinking about getting another dog too, *but you'd ruled it out.* Your partner dashes out of the house very early for work, so for sure you're going to have to walk Gussie in the morning. And in the evening, Mr. Exhausted-after-a-long-day isn't going to be eager to walk the dog either. It's not as if his track record was so great with staying on top of other chores. Plus you finally have some nice, new furniture and you're totally not interested in getting dog hair all over it.

But your partner thought you'd love the idea. And what about your partner's freedom to bring a Gussie into his life? What about the whole issue of freedom in relationships?

That's a huge question. A sensible answer would speak to

both our real needs and also to our hopes for a relationship that has a chance of surviving.

But let's face it: it's an almost impossible balancing act. Part of us would like to be free to do whatever we want. Otherwise, why did we ever bother growing up in the first place? On the other hand, we knew—*caveat emptor!*—that when we entered a committed relationship our freedom would be circumscribed by the very commitments we made to our partner.

So how do we balance that out? Every couple has to work out the details for themselves, but let me sketch out what I think is a pretty reasonable statement:

Declaration of Freedom in Relationships

1. **We are both free to be who we are.**
    Who I am, how I function, what I like and don't
    like . . . everything about my essential self
    deserves to be respected and left alone.
    And the same for you.

2. **We are both free to do whatever we want *as
    long as it doesn't affect the other person*.** It may
    bug me to know that you sit around cracking
    your knuckles, but as long as I don't have to
    hear that, then it's no business of mine.

3. If your freedom somehow conflicts with my
    freedom—I don't want to hear your music,
    you don't want to be financially burdened
    by my expenditures—then we have to face
    the reality that we are not two separate

individuals but rather two connected people living in a commonwealth—a commonwealth of two. And that means we have to work out a way for my freedom and your freedom to *minimally* affect each other. That's a lot of what conflict is about: how I can be as free to listen to my music as possible while at the same time you can be as free from hearing my music as possible.

So back to the dog. The thing is that a new dog in the house affects you in a big way. It changes, or threatens to change, your life. And that's why he's got to talk about getting a new dog with you first.

And that's why both of you have to talk with the other before doing anything that affects the other. Even turning the thermostat up or down a bit.

Because if you don't, it will—like it or not—be seen as a power move, a literal taking of power, and your partner will be way, *way* less interested in being generous after you have already made them feel disempowered. If I were to write a *How to Destroy Your Marriage* book, chapter 1 would be on making as many unilateral moves as you want.

You are free to want what you want, for sure. And, yes, you're free to do what you want. But you have to realize the relationship-curdling consequences of doing that. You're free to make unilateral moves the way you're free to bring termites home to your nice wooden house. And good luck with it!

So: no unilateral moves.

On getting upset

I mentioned "losing it" or "getting upset" among the power moves. Now this is something we need to look at from two completely different points of view, *both equally valid.*

The commonsense point of view is that people just get upset. We stub our toes, we get headaches, we get upset. It's a good word. Imagine a sailboat going along. It can take a lot. But even a good boat in good hands can be upset by a strong enough wind, and over it goes.

That's how we are. And like the sailboat, it's not only an inner event, it's a very public one as well. Everyone knows when Mama is upset.

Now here's the other point of view, just as valid. **Getting upset is a power move**. For example: Pam and Sam are married. When something goes amiss, Pam is more likely to take it in stride. Sam is more likely to get upset.

Sam, from point of view #1, is a relatively more fragile creature, more easily knocked for a loop by life's events. If Sam keeps Pam waiting, Pam can shake it off. If Pam keeps Sam waiting, Sam gets all shook up. Poor Sam.

But from point of view #2, Sam is a tough person to beat when it comes to conflict. It's usually a rule in conflict that the person who gets most upset wins. Period. The only exception is the rare relationship where you have someone who gets upset and the other person is someone who's impervious to their getting upset. They just stand there, arms folded, saying, "Cry and scream and throw things all you want. We're still not getting that wallpaper with purple flowers."

Of course we often try to be impervious, but people who are (view #1) really upset or (view #2) talented at being upset can usually outlast them.

So what do you do about this? Especially when the person who gets upset will almost always take the view #1 of their own upsetment: this is real, *this is just how I feel*, **I can't help it**.

The solution we offer in this book is designed not to tamp down upsetment but to bypass it. In other words, if you do things the right way—without mutual disempowerment—no one need to *ever* get upset!

But for now, as you work through this book, here's a simple tool that'll help to short-circuit the need to get upset as a way to get your way and thereby provoke your partner into getting even more upset so they can get their way.

Passion by the numbers

Remember, just because one person is more visibly upset or passionate or intense doesn't mean that they care more. It just means that they display more. Just the way if someone you both love dies, the one who cries more isn't necessarily the one in deepest grief.

So here's the tool. It's the miraculous *number technique*. Let's say you can't agree on what car to buy. One of you is screaming and yelling. "All my life I've dreamed of a bright red convertible. Now you want to take that away from me. I'll never have my dream." The other is calm. "I just think that a smallish SUV is a more practical choice." The screamer (or the crier, as the case may be) is gonna win another battle, *but* this time you try something different. You each write down on separate pieces of paper how important this is to you on a scale from 0 to 10. Writing a 0 means you don't care at all, and 10 means it's *literally* the most important thing in the world to you. (Think of 10 as being like losing your leg or your dog.)

Then you compare numbers.

If the other person is fair (and their being upset isn't a power move), then the number they provide will show how much they really care about their preference. (Of course if the other person just wants to get their own way, they'll keep putting down high numbers, even though most people's preferences for things aren't always so strong.*) And now you've found a way to test your relative preference for something without histrionics, or at least without the histrionics serving as a power move.

My husband and I use this *all the time*. There was a ballet that came up that I sort of wanted to go to. I mentioned it to my husband, who generally likes to go to dance performances. He sighed. "I don't know," he said. I could sense his reluctance.

How easily this could have turned into conflict. I could have pushed against what I *thought* was his resistance, he

---

* In the FAQ chapter at the end of the book I've included a question about what to do if your partner is what I call a Power Person. By that I mean someone who is more interested in winning than in being fair, more interested in what he or she can get than in creating a healthy relationship, more interested in domination than in love. Because if that's the case, then your problem is deciding what to do about being in a relationship with someone who's unable to function in a relationship in a healthy way. *But for most people, that's not the case.*

could have resisted my pushing, and off we'd have gone down the rabbit hole.

But thank goodness I remembered to say, in our shorthand, "Well, what's your number for how much you want to go to that dance thing?"

As he thought, my own number came into my mind. Finally he said, "Uh, I guess, six."

"Well, guess what?" I asked. "My number is five!"

This happens all the time. The way we talk about things doesn't represent our real preferences!

"So . . ." he said, "it kinda sounds like neither of us is all that fired up about it."

Indeed, because I know him, and he's an enthusiastic guy, a 6 is not his I-really-want-to-go number. And 5 is my sounds-good-but-I'll-want-to-back-down-as-soon-as-I-find-out-how-expensive-the-tickets-are number. We decided not to go. No muss. No fuss.

And that person who's screaming and crying about wanting the red convertible? You might not believe it, but I've seen it again and again: when asked to rank how important that is on a scale from 0 to 10, where 10 is something life or death, that person will say, "Well, look, yeah, I really have had my heart set on that. And yeah, it'll kill me if we get yet another car that's not a red convertible, but when I think about our kids and our budget and our lifestyle, I gotta say it's . . . I don't know . . . a seven. I just wanted you to know how important it was to me."

And I've actually heard that person's partner say, freed from being beaten up by all the yelling and screaming, "Well! Getting an SUV was just a seven for me. So it's kind of a coin toss. But look, here's the critical thing. A convertible would be fine for the four of us even with stuff in the trunk. It's just that if there were five people or more stuff or both . . . I don't know. We might have to rent a car for the occasion. I guess it depends on how often that would come up." Sigh. "You know: you decide. But if it's a convertible, we might have to rent a car from time to time."

A loooong silence. Then, "You know, we're still going to be kind of young when the kids fly the coop. It just means the world to me that you understand and are willing to work this out with me. Would you promise me we can get the red convertible when the kids are gone, or maybe even earlier if our finances work out?"

"Oh, of course!"

How lovely it is to live in a world without power struggles.

A fact is just a fact. Or is it?

Now there are some tough calls to make when it comes to deciding whether something is a power move. Here's one:

"It's my money and I can do what I want with it," you say to me. "You have no say in the matter."

Slam!

And suppose I say, "Wow, that was some power move. It made me feel incredibly disempowered."

And suppose you say, "It *wasn't* a power move. It was just a fact. A fact *can't* be a power move."

Who's right?

Well . . . It may indeed be a fact that it's your money and you can do what you want with it. And so stating a fact is, in fact, just stating a fact. Just the way if I happen to actually be as ugly as a warthog and you state that fact, you're just stating a fact.

But just because something is a fact doesn't mean it can't have a disempowering effect. Or that it can't be used deliberately or unconsciously as a weapon. "It's my money" may be both true *and* be a weapon. Think about what that statement *does*. It shuts me up and puts me in my place. That's it. I have nothing more to say; I have nowhere to go. You've got the money, so you have the say, and that's the end of it.

But that's not the end of it, nor should it be.

First of all, in the real world, in the whole *history* of the real world, people who've been disempowered almost never give up.* They just go underground. They use guerrilla tactics. Just think about what goes on in prisons. There are guards, cells, threats of solitary confinement. Who's more disempowered than an inmate? And yet, while their power has certainly been curtailed, they don't meekly give up the struggle. On the contrary, inmates spend most of their time thinking of ways to outwit the corrections officers, and they're remarkably successful at it.

And like those prisoners, a spouse doesn't necessarily give up either. So the shutdown you might have been hoping to make happen by stating that fact might just provoke more power moves in return, and more intense ones.

But stating a bare fact shouldn't be the end of any discussion either. *No* fact should be able to shut down discussion.

Suppose the two of you are arguing over which house

---

* For some great examples of this, check out James C. Scott's *Domination and the Arts of Resistance: Hidden Transcripts* as well as his *Weapons of the Weak: Everyday Forms of Peasant Resistance.*

to buy, and your partner says, "It's my money and I can do what I want with it," because they're fed up with the endless back-and-forth-ing over houses. What then? Well, then you have to suspend that conflict and go back to a more primary issue: What should be the deciding factor when the two of you make decisions in your relationship? And that *can't* be settled by someone saying, "Because I have all the money!"

Why not? Because it is totally disempowering. And there are only two reactions to total disempowerment. One: despair, withdrawal, apathy. Or two: underground warfare. And neither makes for a good relationship.

Let's say that person is a man and you're a woman. You could—and many have!—come back and said, "Yeah, you have all the money but I have all the vagina in this relationship." After all, that *is* where power struggles end up. Then your partner comes back with a nasty remark, and this can and does go on and on, back and forth, until the earth is scorched and no one can live there anymore.

Or let's look at the other possibility. Your spouse says, "Because I have all the money!" and you withdraw. You feel you have absolutely no power and what you want doesn't matter at all. So why bother even engaging with him? And if you have no say in the outcome, then do you even care what happens? Over time, this apathy leads to less and less emotional involvement until you're left with an empty shell of a relationship.

But we're not quite done.

Suppose someone says, "But we can't afford that," and the other person responds as if they're being terribly disempowered. Is that the same thing as the example we've just gone through?

No.

"We can't afford it" is a different kind of thing from "It's my money." It's a statement of *our* condition. It is, or at least it should be, an appeal to thoughtfully and thoroughly address whether or not the two of you can afford whatever it is you're talking about.

This is where working things out becomes crucial. "We can't afford it" *could* be both a fact and a power move, particularly if it's not all that clear whether you can afford it or not. Lots of times, "affording it" is a judgment call more than it is a pure fact. But it is an opening for a discussion based on facts. A discussion about household finances has to start with numbers—and numbers are numbers; there is no room for interpretation. Facts can have the ability to neutralize power and allow for unbiased discussion.

Getting rid of the power moves in your relationship

So what does it take to get rid of the power moves in your relationship?

Work? Not really. It takes less time and energy to deal with each other in a productive way than in a counterproductive way. (Okay, it does take a little practice, but maybe less than an *hour*, total! I swear!)

Desire? Well, sure, but while you always need desire to do anything, you need to want something more than the alternatives. Do I want to be a size 2? Sure, but I want to enjoy cake even more.

So what *does* it take?

_____

Let's try this: Go back and read what power moves are and look over the examples. Then try to tackle some small conflict—like whether you keep the toaster on the counter or in the cabinet, or whether Sundays are for family outings or watching football. And as you try to figure out a solution, call each other out whenever one of you makes a power move. If he says, "You're so selfish! Unlike you I work all week. The least I can do is relax and watch football on Sunday!" point out his power moves.

For example, "Can you say what you want and why it's important to you without calling me selfish and without implying that you do all the work and I don't?"

And if you say, "Must we live like pigs? What, is it too much trouble to take the toaster out of the cabinet when you need it?" he can call you out too. When you are both conscious of your power moves, you can make an effort not to use them and go on to resolve your conflict in a way that is reasonable. Then keep doing this, like, *for the rest of your life*, whenever you have a conflict. You eat chicken without eating the chicken bones. Now you have conflict without the power moves. Simple. Done.

_____

Just think of this as the Stop the Power Move Game. It has the potential to be a learning experience for both of you—one that will kick your relationship up to a new level. But I do have to highlight one crucial guideline:

Don't argue with your partner when he says, "There, that's a power move." Yes, you may very well think it wasn't one. You probably didn't *intend* it to be one. But it's crucial that you ask your partner to explain what made him feel it was a power move. Your job is simply to understand what he's saying. Then ask what you could've done differently. Most important, don't argue. If one of you points out a power move, the other just tries saying what they were saying a little differently. That's how you win the Power Move Game.

About the no-arguing with a "that's a power move" call, here's what it looks like in action: Suppose you're making soup and you offer your partner a taste. They go *schlurp* and say, "Gee, I'm afraid it's too salty for me."

What's your comeback? Nothing! You certainly can't argue with how it tastes to them.

Suppose your partner is giving you a neck rub and at one point you say, "Oh, you're pressing too hard." What's their comeback? They can't say, "No, I'm not." No! Can they say, "Well, I didn't mean to"? Well, yeah, but it's an irrelevant point. All they can say is something like, "Sorry, I'll be a little more gentle."

So if you accept each other's statement "That's a power move" and try to remember it, then over a period of a few days of doing this you'll find things are going much better for the two of you.

Expectations

I'll be honest: at first *it's hard*! My husband and I were shocked at how many times we blew the whistle on each other, and on what kinds of things we got called out on. Certainly our self-images of innocence and goodness were quickly shattered. And this was when we were on our best behavior!

And to be honest, at first it felt a bit stilted. "I think we need to go food shopping." "I think we can wait a few days." Pause. Numbers technique. And quick solution. But no zest. If arguing is where you get your zest in life.

But it was also exhilarating! We thought, *Wow, this is radical!* It was like discovering an eight-foot-long worm living inside you and pulling it out inch by inch. Gross, but great because we were making the terrible worm go away.

You can also expect that one of you will probably be better at this than the other. One of you will probably be better at noticing power moves. One of you will probably be better at stopping making them. But please, I beg of you, on my knees, *don't keep score*. This is harder for some people than it is for others, but you don't have to progress equally quickly. The victory lies in your keeping on playing the Stop the Power Move Game, whatever the score, whatever your relative skill levels. Playing, not winning, is the goal.

Now besides the how-to, the only other thing you need to succeed isn't work or desire—it's *humility*. I'm not talking about some deep spiritual concept here. Just a sense of submission to a discipline, the way you might submit to the discipline of yoga or not eating dairy. And an acceptance of the fact that you're not perfect either. You just give your ego a rest for once and go with what's good for you. In this case, you both do it.

You look at each other and say, "Power moves feel so good to make but they're destructive and hurtful and we're going to stop making them. And even though it's hard, we're going to accept each other's definition of what a power move is. If you say X is a power move, I'll find another way to express myself."

You have to put down your weapons. You have to *want* to put down your weapons for the sake of your relationship. But you're *there*. Already. I know you are.

Most people still have a bit further to go with all this. The power dynamics that most couples get tied up in are tough to escape from. *But* you and your partner might just be one of the couples who—surprise, surprise—are close to the finish line. Check it out.

5

You May Be Closer to the Finish Line Than You Think

"No power moves? No problem!"

It is realistically possible for you and your partner to end the power struggles in your relationship now. I mean, maybe even *today*. Like most people, you might need the further help this book offers (and boy, did I—and do I), but the simple exercise I'm about to show you could be just enough. For some people it is.

Of course telling people to just stop making power moves is as helpful as telling someone who's depressed to just cheer up. So instead, I'm asking you to do the following exercise. Remember: it's just an exercise, but if you can get through it . . . Well, we'll cross that bridge when we come to it.

Step 1. You and your partner sit down and see if you're in agreement that you've spent too much time in hurtful, unproductive conflict. Arguments that go nowhere, leaving too many unresolved issues. Too many unmet needs. Hot conflict. Cold conflict. Whatever. You want to end it.

Agreed?

Agreed. Good.

If so . . .

Step 2. Think of some issue you've struggled over recently. And please, not a horribly deep, dark, messy issue with a painful past. Start with a relatively easy one. My husband and I chose the issue of living room furniture. I like things very uncluttered.* He likes comfort. And now we were trying to decide whether we should buy an easy chair or a couch. Of course, as you well know, any issue can bring out pretty intense feelings. But we hoped this would be manageable.

Step 3. Now this is the big step. *Try to resolve the issue without using power moves.* FYI: it will be impossible at first. But that's okay! This is an exercise to help you learn. And so the point is . . . learning!

Whenever one of you makes a power move, the other points it out.

Let's say you and your partner are MJ and BB. The two of you are talking about what to do about your kid who has learning issues. You go back and forth a couple of times and suddenly one of you feels disempowered. Your partner has made a power move. The script may go something like this:

---

* I just Googled "extremely sparse living room" and had a shock. The images that came up were all *way* too cluttered for me. Knickknacks and tchotchkes: I don't have *any*.

MJ: You say you care about Jayden, but if you supposedly care so much how come you were leaving most of the child care to me when he was little?

BB: Hey, that's a power move. You're trying to take the high ground by accusing me of being an uncaring parent. Let's stick to what's best for Jayden now.

MJ: You felt that was a power move? Okay. Let me do it over. I'm concerned that your suggestion will leave me with most of the work for helping him with his tutorial stuff. Can we talk about the fairness issue with that?

This was great except for BB's "You're trying to take the high ground . . ." comment, which just wasn't necessary.

So what made this great? BB pointed out a power move. MJ accepted what BB said and tried a different tack. *That's it.*

And if MJ hadn't understood how what she said rose to the level of a power move for BB, BB could have explained. And all that's needed for an explanation is something like, "Because it puts me on the defensive," or "Because it makes me feel uncomfortable."

So here's the essence of Step 3:

- **Every time one of you experiences the other making a power move, say so.**

- **If you get called out for making a power move, accept the feedback without argument, be grateful, and think of it as a learning experience.**

• **If you don't understand why it's a power move, ask for an explanation.**

Step 4. Expect to be a bit confused and frustrated at first. Most people discover pretty quickly that they've been relying on power moves a lot when it comes to trying to get their needs met, especially when they run into any resistance.

And here's what flummoxes a lot of folks, including me: besides making a power move, *what do you do when you're frustrated, when you have the feeling that led to your making the power move in the first place*? Well, try exploring a variety of things to say instead of that power move. And by variety I mean, like, *ten* things. Most people feel they've gotten stuck after they've tried one.

So after you've gotten called out for saying, "You do realize you're a really selfish person, don't you?" you could try these:

"What do you think is fair?"

Or "Why is this idea giving you trouble?"

Or "What do you need to make this work for you?"

Or "How can I make this easier for you?"

Here's the secret: *focus not on winning, but on being creative.* That's what real-life successful couples do! What's more, the very process of coming up with new ways of relating will bring you closer together. And will bring a solution closer.

You might very well feel helpless without your power moves, but just hang in there and do your best. Like with so many things, the more you do it, the easier it gets! And

I promise: if you keep working on this exercise, you'll eventually be in great shape. Anything that gets you out of your power dynamics, however awkward at first, is a great thing.

Step 5. Please, remember, if your partner says it's a power move, it's a power move, regardless of your intentions. Just move on and try something different.

And if you're one of the lucky few, you *will* be able to eliminate power moves, or at least make a great start, and that *will* eliminate the horrible cycle of two people feeling disempowered and needing to re-empower themselves, and that *will* mean that you'll come up with good solutions to your problems *and* feel that your needs are being met in this relationship.

What does success look like and feel like?

Look, I ain't gonna hype you. This isn't like taking a wonder drug, and five minutes later everything is lovely and bluebirds fill the air.

But what does it actually feel like to cut down significantly in the use of power moves? Do people say it's like walking on eggshells?

No! They say it feels very comfortable once they get used to it.

Let me put it this way: *even if* the "walking on eggshells" sensation were a side effect and not using power moves were a drug, this would *still* be the safest, most effective drug on the market. And anyway, it won't feel like walking on eggshells. The fact is that once people get used to it—just a couple of days—and get a little better at monitoring themselves and each other, it not only feels like the new normal, it feels like heaven. Imagine being able to enter into a discussion without expecting to feel beaten up!

Just have some patience with yourself and your partner, and watch things get better and easier.

But what if in spite of your best intentions, the two of you get sucked into a vortex of power moves and it seems as though the whole process is going to blow up in your face?

Have no fear.

When the pot boils over

In spite of your trying to eliminate power moves, strong emotions are going to get churned up. Hurts and resentments and frustrations will always creep in.

So what do you do about them when you're working to eliminate power moves?

Well, how about not converting them into power moves in the middle of a conflict? Just that. That's all we're talking about here. It can be as simple as saying nothing until you think of something non-powerish to say. Sometimes the best approach is to walk away for a while.

Ben is bitterly disappointed with Betty for not being someone who brings home a bigger paycheck. And maybe Ben has reason for his disappointment and bitterness. When they'd started out, Betty was an up-and-coming software engineer, so the sense they had was that the sky's the limit. But Betty was too often bored with her work and with corporate bullshit. Promotions did not come her way, but layoffs did. Her career was rocky, and, to make matters worse, she didn't seem to mind. She was only too happy to be at home with the kids. After all, Ben had a really good, very demanding job himself.

Now they're arguing about money, and Betty is trying to get Ben to rein in his spending. A neutral observer would probably say she was right at least on that point, but Ben wasn't buying it. From his point of view, Betty doesn't work hard, and now she's telling him to cut back on his spending. In his frustration, he rips her a new one about what a loser she is. He implies, maybe not so subtly, that because she earns less than Ben and less than her potential, she has no standing in a discussion about household budgeting.

This is all horrible, and horribly counterproductive.

But the feelings are real, powerful, and *there*. So what do you do?

If you're Ben, you stop the attempt to work out this conflict. You just say, "Betty, I'm starting to get upset, and before I say things I'm going to regret I think we should just stop. We can get back to this later."

More to the point, if you're starting in on calling each other a loser, just call *stop*.

And an all-important rule to remember is:

Stop means stop.

Calling *stop* is not a power move. It's part of a pre-agreement between the two of you to prevent a painful escalation. It's a call for a cooling-off period. And by the way, this is not an excuse to say, "I don't want to talk about this anymore." That's a power move. Stop just means that emotions are leading to invective, which means that the chance of coming up with a smart, mutually satisfying solution is pretty darned low. And so you need to give yourselves a time-out.

The big question

So, if you successfully eliminate power moves, you should be good to go, right? Not so fast! For most people, merely *trying* to stop using power moves doesn't magically solve everything. We find it's too hard to stop cold turkey.

Why is it so hard for us to extricate ourselves from the power dynamics in our relationships? Why does power have such a hold on us, and why do we hold on to our power so tightly? These are the questions I've asked over and over, both as a professional and as a person in a long-term relationship.

We can keep asking why, but it's more important to understand this is how we are, and once we understand that, we can begin to make peace with ourselves and our partners. The mess of bitterness, distance, and resentment so many of us find ourselves in is in fact no one's fault. Then, with blame put behind us, we can get what we need to put an end to it.

So what do we do beyond trying to eliminate power moves? That's what the **1, 2, 3 Method** in the rest of this book is about.

6

Inside the Beast
The Nature of Power in Relationships

"Power is the nightmare of love."

What we're going to do here is explore a deep mystery. How in the world can two intelligent, decent, loving people end up working hard to achieve something neither of them wants? How can it be that they look at each other and say after a fight, "Why do we do this?" and yet the very next day do it all over again? *How?*

To quote Marvin Gaye, makes you want to holler. But let's face it: if this weren't a tough problem, most of us wouldn't be here right now.

It's certainly not because we want to be.

"But I don't even want power!"

Most of us, if asked, will say we don't want power in our relationship. We want to be equal partners, part of a team. Power feels like a dirty word in the context of our romantic relationship. A force that is in opposition to love. And that's true. *Power is the nightmare of love.* Working to control people destroys love.

Women, especially, are averse to being seen as overpowering in our relationships. We don't want to be a nag, a shrew, a bitch. Even more, we don't want to be in a relationship with a man we can overpower.

Because of our discomfort with power in the domestic realm, when there is conflict a lot of women hold back on our power—because of course it's unattractive and unwomanly and unloving, we think—until frustration pushes us over the brink to the point where we lose the power to hold back our power. Shorthand version: we lose it. And scare the crap out of our partners. (Just ask some men: they'll say there's nothing scarier than an angry woman!) After which we're often very sorry and apologize profusely, casting off quickly the cloak of power we've too hastily put on. And men do the same thing.

What in the world, then, is going on in our doing what we don't want to do when it comes to power in our relationships?

Getting sucked into the power dynamics

Most people don't enter into a relationship with the intent of exerting power to create a power imbalance. And most relationships start as loving partnerships. So what happens? Sure there will be disagreements. There may even be some fights. But what pushes the relationship over the edge into a power struggle?

It's rarely one event, one fight, that tilts the balance. Far more often, it's a pattern of incidents that kicks the crap out of a relationship. Even though we really don't want power, we *really* don't want to feel disempowered. I don't want more power than you. *But I sure don't want less.*

And that sets almost every relationship on a toboggan run to hell. While no one wants power, when I complain about your not being supportive, you sigh and roll your eyes, I feel dismissed, and, in the process, disempowered.

So maybe I . . . I don't know . . . *yell.* Just to level things out again, or to feel heard when I feel you're not hearing me. But your sigh, which felt oh so innocent to you, surely doesn't in your eyes warrant my screaming like a crazy woman. (And it's a rule: if you raise your voice—a little or a lot—it will sound much louder to the other person than it does to you. Because . . . power! My raised voice doesn't sound so loud to me because I have my hand on the volume knob. You don't.) Maybe you just want to match me, but you top me by stomping out of the room and slamming the door behind you, and the steam starts coming out of my ears.

I'd like to say no one wants this dynamic, the way no one wants to be overweight. But as a society we for sure eat as though we wanted to be overweight.

And what do we call it when we keep doing something we don't want to do? We call it an addiction. And we all know that addictions, if unchecked, lead to disaster.

Addicted to . . . no, not love . . . what's that other thing?

We get so used to the cycle of fighting and making up or the use of distance to manage our difficulties—like someone who gets used to limping or seeing out of only one eye—that we end up in big trouble before we know it. Any couples' therapist will tell you that couples almost always come in only after a great deal of damage has been done. If the damage were cancer instead of shredded feelings, it would be a late-stage cancer.

So how exactly do power dynamics lead to the death of a relationship?

Of course they don't always. Lots of times they don't. But the risk is enormous.

Let's begin by getting clear what love is. I love chocolate. I loved my babies. I want to eat chocolate, to devour it. I never wanted to eat my babies. Chocolate is a luxury for me. My babies were a sacrifice for me, even when they were a delight.

Now, sure, when we meet our partners, there may be some of that "Oooh, I wanna get me some of that" in it for us. There should be! Two people in love should delight in one another. But if all there is is delight, well, you and I know that when we delight in something but don't love it, then, if it stops delighting us, we just throw it away, like three-day-old leftovers.

What love is. When you love a person, it's different. The delight is there, but so is the sense that in some amazing way, in a life where maybe all we've known is selfishness, suddenly there's this other person who matters to us in some ways more than we matter to ourselves. There's this other person whose needs can easily be more important to us than our own needs.

Now, okay, maybe we're not totally in that place when we're starting out in a committed relationship, but in any halfway healthy and loving relationship both people really do care about one another.

Naming the addiction. Then we start having conflicts. Our needs don't jibe. We've talked about the different ways this plays out, from all-out battles to seemingly buried silent warfare. But however it plays out, we find we've gone from "No, whatever you want" "No, whatever *you* want!" to doing and saying things that make our partners and ourselves feel disempowered and feeling the need to take power back.

The feeling of generosity has silently disappeared, like a bored, unwanted guest slinking out of a party. Except that we're not bored at all! We are enthralled in this battle to win, and we get just enough short-term victories to keep us in there fighting.

And this is crucial to why the power struggle is addicting. It's precisely those wins in the power wars that keep us fighting even when the fighting doesn't make sense. That's because of the Principle of Intermittent Reinforcement, one of the most powerful psychological forces. This principle says that if you want to get a pigeon or a rat or a monkey or a person to keep on doing something over and over and over again, just reward him with something meaningful at random intervals.

The entire gambling industry is based on the power of this Principle of Intermittent Reinforcement. People would never gamble if they never won. They'd never gamble if every time they bet $100 they won $97. But if someone can devise a game—and most casino games work exactly like this—where you lose $100, lose another $100, lose another $100, and then somewhere along the line win $700, then a bunch of losses, then you win $1,200, then another bunch of losses . . . Well! Even if net, net you're losing, you'll feel so tantalized, so led on, so close to the big killing, that you can't stop playing. "Yeah, I'm down thirty-nine hundred dollars but I keep winning so I know I'll be back in the black if I just hang in there."

It works this way in Hollywood. People come here to "make it." If they totally fail, well, they get the point and go back home to Peoria. If they hit big, no problem. But the worst thing that can happen to them isn't failure but that they get the occasional call back and out of those call backs they get the occasional small role. They may be starving to death with what they make from this, but it keeps them hooked. Just enough small wins to keep them from leaving the game.

People hang in there with businesses that are losing propositions because every once in a while they have a good day, a good week, a good month, and that keeps them hooked.

This is a true psychological addiction. And so is battling for power. Let me make that clear:

**Battling for power is psychologically addicting
to both partners.**

And so here's the thing: battles for power mean falling out of love with your partner because they become someone you see as your rival in a battle for a scarce resource. If you go to *their* parents' house over the holidays, you won't be going to *your* parents' house. Win for them, loss for you.

Oh, yeah, and there's something else that keeps us in the power game as if it were an addiction.

"I've got him this time"

I recently read a book about how wars get started—wars with guns and bombs—and one conclusion there was striking. Folks who start wars almost always overestimate their own power and underestimate their enemy's power. The Germans in World Wars I and II? Check. The South in the American Civil War? Check. America in the Vietnam War? Check. Napoleon in his wars? Check. It goes on and on, all these war starters who overestimated their own power.

And it's the same with bar fights.

So now imagine the exact same thing in a relationship. A power move is supposed to empower me and disempower you. It's supposed to make me one up so I have a better chance of getting my needs met, or at the very least you have a worse chance of getting your needs met. So let's say I give you the silent treatment. Oooh, that'll drive you nuts and before we know it you'll cave in and agree that my mother is a fine woman who means well.

Except we've been down that road before, and I can flummox you once or twice, but then you start to figure it out. All you have to do is not go nuts! Now we're both silent. Now we have a war of silence. It's like a staring contest. I overestimated my power by assuming I would necessarily drive you nuts by giving you the silent treatment.

There is no power move, *none*, that will be eternally disempowering. But there are tons of power moves that will give us enough short-term victories that we'll have the illusion that the power game is worth playing. And so when one power move fails—"Gee, my silent treatment seems to make him *happy*!"—there are always more power moves to try.

You might win a lot of battles, which makes battling seductive, but both of you will always lose the war.

After every single exchange people walk away loving each other just a little less, because they have just treated one another in a less loving way and have come to see the other as less loving and have come to feel seen as less loving. They've said unloving things to one another. They've treated one another as opponents. As enemies. And they keep doing it in the hope of winning.

Except that power is the nightmare of love.

But doesn't "making up" make everything all right? Yes. At first, in the beginning of our relationships. But its magic healing power soon loses its magic and its power. The will to make up and the effectiveness of our increasingly unenthusiastic attempts at making up diminish.

Another reason we are so wedded to power dynamics is that they've been with us for a long, long time. We're just dancing a dance that's been choreographed for us long before we were born.

The power dynamics are there before the beginning

Time for some generalities—that is, things that are true a lot of the time but not all the time.

For example, a lot of the time in male/female couples, more than enough to make a big difference, women over and over tell me that something they look for in a man is strength and confidence, someone who projects power, competence, assurance, because a man like that makes them feel safe. A man who can take care of himself will be able to take care of her, she thinks. It could come in handy should she become pregnant.

And men look for a woman who is "lovely," which means all kinds of things—like "pretty" of course—but in part means someone who doesn't project power. "Lovely" in large part means "nice," and "nice" means "compliant," and "compliant" means not making too big a deal about her needs so she doesn't come across as a whiny, selfish ball-busting bitch, which is not lovely at all. And to the guy all this loveliness means: easy sailing! A lot of the mating game involves projecting these things from the beginning, the idea being that you win the other person if you project the right image.

Now, there are plenty of strong women. And "lovely"

might not be the first word young women today would want to describe them. Still, when it comes to getting a guy to like you, most women would say being "lovely" is going to work better than being a ball buster.

And similar games go on with same-sex couples. There are always ways to signal you are more easygoing than you really are or more okay with the other person's assertiveness than you really are.

One way or another, the dance begins! The strong, confident man too often turns out to be an asshole, and the lovely lady too often turns out to be someone who was hiding her power and is now seen as hard as nails. Welcome to my waiting room!

Now here's the thing. Notice what *didn't* happen. *We didn't look for the person most skilled at balancing power in a fair way.* We didn't choose someone on the basis of how we could prevent future conflicts down the road by minimizing sources of conflicts. Nope. Mostly we just looked for someone who looked good and was good in bed and shared a couple of key interests with us and who didn't have a couple of big red flags waving us away. Ooh! We both like black-and-white movies and old-school Chinese food and flannel sheets, and we smell good to each other, and neither one of us is glued to their iPhone, so . . . *good to go!*

But it's not only as if we failed to plan to prevent a power struggle. It's as if we actually did plan to set one up: that's how careless we are about the factors that lead to conflict and to power dynamics.

And look at what happens once things start going.

Jamie and Blake sitting in a tree,
k-i-s-s-i-n-g

Being a typical early-twenty-first-century couple, Jamie and Blake aren't quite as young as their ancestors were when they started out in marriage. This doesn't mean they haven't been in relationships before. In fact, it means that they've been in perhaps many relationships, all of which haven't worked out, many of which ended badly.

Contemporary commitments are the triumph of hope over experience. But whatever our hopes, most of us, like Jamie and Blake, come into a new relationship wondering how badly we're going to be hurt this time.

This *alone* sets up an important power dynamic. What do you do if you want to love and be loved, but you don't want to be hurt? Well, in that case, it's far safer if you know that you are loved before you give out your guarantee that you love the other.

So here, Jamie will try to be as much like the person Blake wants as possible, as far as Jamie can tell. It's not being phony. It may be largely unconscious. It may be mostly "just wanting things to work this time." But it certainly leads to a power struggle, because Blake is doing the same thing.

The power struggle is over who can get the other to be committed first. More head over heels over whom. Jamie wins if she can get Blake more committed first. And this is very important because at the very beginning of a relationship a lot is at stake. Where you live. Who moves in with whom. Who pays for what. Who makes the greater lifestyle concessions. Who gives away how much when it comes to décor. Who sets the rules right off when it comes to burping and farting.

Now what determines who wins this power struggle is who's going to be willing to make the most sacrifices starting out.

Lots of factors come into play, of course. If Blake is just a little more open and transparent than Jamie, then that gives Jamie an advantage. If Jamie is actually far more smitten than Blake, advantage Blake. But there are other kinds of power that play a huge role here.

"Whatever you say, Mr. President." Sometimes one person brings into the relationship certain somethings that tilt the scale way in that person's favor, regardless of the other dynamics. No matter what else is going on, if Blake just happened to be a huge movie star, or a moving-and-shaking billionaire, or, let's even say, the president of the United States, well, you *know* that Jamie would have to make a lot of concessions about how they lived.

But the advantages don't have to be that extreme. All that's needed is for Blake to have a more demanding job than Jamie does. Or to make significantly more money than Jamie. Blake doesn't even have to be more successful than Jamie to be more powerful on the job front: if Blake's job is more insecure then it'll be all hands on deck to prevent Blake from losing his job. If they're both rushing to get out of the house in the morning, it'll be Jamie more likely to get out of Blake's way, so Blake won't be the one who's late.

"He, or she, who pays the piper calls the tune." Or, to put it another way, money talks.

Money differences make everything weird, and it's not because of money itself but because of power.

I knew a young guy named Teddy who was making millions a year on Wall Street. Teddy was terrified of getting involved with someone. First of all, he was afraid of never ever knowing *if* someone was marrying him for his money. He lived in a luxury apartment in the best part of town. Since that was the only clue to how much money he really had, his MO was to never tell the women he was going out with where he lived.

Now don't tell me you can't guess how that played out! As the days and weeks went by, it progressed from being a non-issue, to being a mystery, to being creepy, to being infuriating to the women he was seeing. He creeped out these women way before he could find out whether they were thinking about whether they genuinely cared for him or not!

Teddy finally found a woman who made as much money as he did, and whose family had even more. But that didn't really solve his problem.

Here's the thing: Teddy's money was *dis*empowering to him. It made him feel stalked, like a beast of prey. The more someone might be interested in him for his money, the less she'd care about him and the more likely ending the relationship would be just fine with her. Even with a pre-nup, she'd probably come out way ahead if she bailed.

Sure, Teddy's money was empowering for him when it came to the mating game, but only in a way that was ultimately disempowering! On a very obvious level, because he was young, good looking, and rich, he was a very eligible bachelor and, as they say, he could have any woman he wanted. Which was great as long as things didn't start getting serious. But at that point all the things that made him such a catch made him wonder if he couldn't do better.

A terrible thought! So he would break up with one terrific woman after another just because he'd sniffed out some imperfection, and then off he'd go looking for someone even better.

And this meant that pretty soon he'd run through most of the women in town and had gotten a pretty bad reputation. Plus he was feeling pretty old now to be starting a family.

So when Teddy did find that woman with the right amount of money and decided to settle down with her, mostly because his guy friends were already having kids by now, he was pretty shelf worn. And his new wife, unimpressed by his money, was pretty impressed by the huge favor she was doing him by rescuing him from an endless blighted bachelorhood. And she made him feel it in a most disempowering way.

Back down to earth. Teddy's story is extreme, but the issues it brings up are universal. Suppose two everyday people fall in love and a financial difference arises between them. What then? How does that play out?

Yes, generally speaking, if you make all the money to pay all the bills, that gives you a lot of power:

- "I just don't think we can afford that house." "Look, I earn the money, and I say we can afford it."

- "Oh, come on—I really, really, really want to go to Paris. I've always wanted to go there." "I don't know . . . I just don't feel like paying for a trip to see a bunch of museums and eat a lot of French food."

- "You won't pay for our dog's chemotherapy!?" "I know we both love her, but she's eleven years old and I just don't think it's worth it."

Now you know as well as I do the different directions these conflicts can go in. Most of them not good. A person might guilt her partner who has the money into paying for cancer treatment for an older dog, but then that could lead to a lot of bitterness. Not to mention the ton of resentment there'd be if the partner with money refused to pay.

But having money always gives that partner an edge. It's demoralizing to always have to ask for money. It's humiliating to feel as if you're begging.

The thing is, though, that the dynamic can work in another direction. Suppose dermatologist Emily has a lot more income than struggling artist Mark. But suppose also that Mark has a fragile ego. And when he gets depressed it affects his art. The disempowerment dynamic switches. Now Mark is disempowered by Emily having all the money, for sure—which one of them pays for dinner when they eat out is a nightmare for him—but Emily is even *more* disempowered by his fragility. First of all, she's a genuinely kind, sensitive person who cares about him. Second, his hat-in-hand status really does get him all shook up. It's a huge gender thing in our culture. Men who are supported by their wives are too often seen as weak, creepy, despicable users.

So in his fragility, and in Emily's unwillingness to hurt Mark's feelings, Mark gets a lot of power. Perhaps not the spending power he'd have if he were the one with the big bucks, but the tone in their relationship—the very culture of their relationship—is one where Emily is generally solicitous of poor old Mark. And Mark? Well, Emily's loaded, so it sort of works out that he doesn't seem to have to be so solicitous toward her.

Weakness is power

So we see that disempowerment dynamics are a funny thing. For sure, power is power. A loud voice. A well-known tendency to fly into a near-psychotic rage. A history of punching holes in walls. Being a notorious gangster chieftain (that'll do it for sure!). Of course.

But as we saw with Mark and Emily, sometimes, perhaps just as often, *weakness can be power too.*

Let's go back to Jamie and Blake. Suppose that whenever Jamie lays out some need or takes some position in a conflict, and the two of them go back and forth over it, before you know it Blake is in tears. Really crying. "*Boo hoo.* This is so overwhelming. I never know what to say. *Gulp gulp sob sob.* You're always right and I'm always wrong. *Sniffle sniffle.* Fine. Whatever you want. *Boo hoo.* I can't stand up to you."

Now what effect do you think this would have on Jamie? What effect would it have on you?

If Jamie were a psychopath, or just a jerk, there'd be nothing more to do than gloat over her imminent victory, standing there with Blake on the floor in a state of abject surrender. But most people will be powerfully swayed. "Well, if it means *that* much to you . . ."

In Michael Korda's book *Power*, he talks about *bosses* who use weakness to get what they want at the office. Threats of nervous breakdowns, anguished cries of how "I'm surrounded by enemies," pleas for help: all these get the staff so worked up that they do anything to make Mr. Topguy happy. According to Michael Korda, the corporate world is full of men and women like this. I know relationships certainly are.

Suffering and limping your way to total victory.

Are those real crocodiles I see?

Okay, you've caught me. I've sort of said, and I'll say it *explicitly* now, that tears are a way to gain power. So am I *actually* saying that if your partner cries during a power struggle, or if you cry, these are fake tears? Real or fake terror? Real or fake suffering?

Well, it's not so simple.

Let's start with a baby. I think we can all agree that babies don't fake tears. Babies are hallmarks of integrity. On the other hand, crying itself in babies evolved to help babies survive. Perhaps babies themselves didn't realize it, but good old Mother Nature—or evolution if you'd prefer—figured out that just the way the squeaky wheel gets the grease, the crying baby gets the breast. So as the baby becomes a toddler and develops a bit of savvy, if only unconsciously, it realizes that crying—to say nothing of total meltdowns in the cereal aisle of the supermarket—are really good at getting what you want. The toddler learns the power of crying.

Well, the same thing happens over time in a relationship.

You may be someone who cries when you're frustrated. That's very common. Are your tears authentic? Sure.

But the story of the *use* of your tears in your relationship is not just, "Hey, that's the way I feel so there's nothing I can do about it. My tears are my truth." That's sometimes true, but more often the rule applies that behavior is shaped by context. Sometimes we do what we do because of who we are. But sometimes we do what we do because of what we've learned works.

If you're a crier and you are in a relationship with someone who's putty in the hands of another person's tears, then you'll continue to cry when you feel disempowered as a way to re-empower yourself. That's just you.

But I'm telling you, whether you like hearing it or not, that if you happened to be in a relationship with someone who was immune to the effects of sobs and tears—and there are people like that—you'd eventually move on to some other tactic that worked better. Your tears are you, but if they don't work to help you get your needs met, they'll *tend* to drop out. Not always. Not for everyone. But in general.

And suppose you're not normally a crier, but on this one particular occasion the two of you were having a conflict and you started crying and—*surprise!*—your partner totally caved. Don't you think it would be at least a bit more likely that you'd turn to tears more often in the future? If only unconsciously? Sure.

When it comes to gaining power, whatever works at the level of authenticity is at risk of being used at the level of inauthenticity.

This does *not* mean that the feelings that come up for us and that we put on display in the midst of conflict are mere sham, mere acting. Not at all. It just means that the need to not feel disempowered—as a tiny baby or as a big strong adult—is so intense that we will always turn toward what works the way a flower turns toward the light.

And you know, this might be a really good time, while we're at it, to look at what is at the very heart of the disempowerment spiral. There are lots of reasons—as you've seen—why we get caught up in it so easily and find it so hard to pull out of it, but there is one that's perhaps the most important.

The disempowerment spiral

We have to start with love. We all know that part of love is that gaga feeling that you just have to be with the other person. You just have to *have* them. You feel you'll do almost anything to get this person because you feel you can't live without them.

But of course you can have—and many of us have had—the same feelings toward a house. You fall in love with a house and you'll do anything to get that house.

These feelings are totally understandable. It's good to have the whole head-over-heels thing at the beginning of a relationship. It's a kind of certificate that this is something "bigger than both of us." And let's just call that the *Wow!* part of love.

But it's just the beginning of real love. Let's say I love my little dog Fluffy. (I don't have an actual dog Fluffy. My last actual dog's name was Davy.) And let's say I put ribbons in

Fluffy's fur, and spray Fluffy with expensive perfume, and give Fluffy big hugs, and carry Fluffy with me when I go shopping for shoes. Because I just love her soooooo much.

I think you might be right to question my love for Fluffy. Maybe my feelings are genuine, but something huge is missing. I don't treat Fluffy as if she matters to me. Not Fluffy *as she really is*. If someone matters to you—including a dog—then they matter to you as they really are. And dogs find ribbons annoying. They don't like perfume. Hugs aren't in their vocabulary of affection. And being carried around from store to store is stressful for them.

So whatever I *think* I'm doing, Fluffy is thinking she doesn't matter to me. Well, if Fluffy could think. Fluffy is certainly unhappy.

Ground zero of love, the absolute heart of love, is the feeling, "Wow, I really matter to my partner." Not because of your partner's words or because your partner thinks you're pleased with their efforts, but because your partner has taken the time and trouble to know you and, based on that knowledge, to treat you as if you really matter at least as much as your partner matters to himself.

Love means showing your partner that they matter to you. How do you do that? By finding out what actually matters to them and then by treating them based on your knowing that. And then by showing them that they matter to you at least as much as you matter to yourself.

There's something you can do to *nail* this. You and your partner each get a piece of paper and draw a line down the middle so you have two columns. On the top of one side write *Things that you do that make me feel I matter to you.* On the top of the other column write *Things you could do that would make me feel I matter to you.* Now separately write ten things in each column. The more specific the better. Here are some things people have put on their lists:

- "When I come home, ask me how my day was."
- "If you agree to do something, remember to do it."
- "Stop calling me 'honey.'"
- "Don't bring home big bags of potato chips from the supermarket."
- "Initiate lovemaking sometimes."
- "Rub my shoulders whenever you think of it, and not just when I ask."

Then you exchange lists. Now you know what makes your partner feel they matter to you. And . . . do them. Now you have no excuse. You can't plead ignorance.

And the thing is, this is what we expect and hope for in a relationship, this feeling that we matter. That I matter to my partner—the real me as I really am, not his fantasy of who he'd like me to be.

When I don't feel I matter, then emotionally all hell breaks loose.

And it breaks loose in a particular way. If I pull back a bit on my showing you that you matter to me, the usual response is that you'll pull back in your showing me I matter to you. So if we're going through a period where we're frustrated with each other and I don't give you as enthusiastic a birthday celebration as I have in the past, you might well give me a still less enthusiastic birthday celebration when it's my turn. Kisses turn into pecks on the cheek, which turn into nothing. Mutual disempowerment has caused us to enter a spiral in which we mirror each other's lack of positive energy with still less positive energy. It's a race to the bottom.

And every time we have a conflict that is haunted by power moves, the race gets faster.

It's all about humiliation

One of the big mistakes people make in thinking about the disempowerment dynamics in a relationship comes from having the impression that the use of power waltzes into people's lives twirling an evil mustache. Well, maybe in the movies evil and power go together—good guys are always much more relaxed about power than the bad guys—but it's not like that in relationships.

Most of the time power dynamics are set off quite innocently. As I'm writing these words, tomorrow happens to be Valentine's Day. Well, on one Valentine's Day a number of years ago, one hapless schmo obviously forgot all about it and had to scramble to get a gift for his bride. He gave his secretary a hundred-dollar bill and asked her to pick up something for his wife during her lunch break. She returned with a beautifully wrapped box and the fellow felt like he was winning.

That evening they took the bullet train to conflict city very fast.

What was so devastating to her? Well, when she opened the gift she found a bottle of perfume. Nice, right? Except she had a severe fragrance sensitivity; perfume gave her intense migraines. They had been married two years and together for two years before that. How could he not know she didn't wear any fragrance? His gift was the act of a man who didn't know her or care about her enough to know her.

When he tried to explain that he wasn't the one to pick out the gift, he dug himself deeper in a hole. She was *humiliated*. She was made to feel like she was nothing, and for anyone, particularly for everyone with a history of being made to feel like nothing (which includes a huge proportion of women*), the emotional pain is intense.

Anything someone does or says that's disempowering will also be humiliating.

And that makes power struggles take on a life of their own.

Re-empowerment fueled by feelings. So Jamie comes home from work after a rough day and starts to complain

---

* Even women who grow up being petted and doted on and spoiled will recognize how much of this was based on their parents' fantasy about who they were, and that when they failed to live up to that fantasy the touch of affection grew very cold indeed. The message was clear: we love you to pieces, but mostly for the dreams we have about who you are and who you'll grow up to be. Not who you really are.

about it, but Blake says, "Oh, so you just launch into your monologue without asking about my day."

"You can't possibly have had a worse day than me," Jamie says.

"I didn't say that!" Blake says. "It's just that you didn't even ask about my day. You just take the stage as if I don't exist."

"Do I have to ask *permission* to share my feelings when I'm in *pain*!?" Jamie asks.

"Well, you never think about anyone but yourself anyway, so why would you start now?" Blake asks with blazing sarcasm, and walks out of the room, slamming the door behind him.

You can probably analyze this as well as anyone by this point.

First of all, this is clearly not the first time these two have struggled over this. They've done this dance before.

Second, this is a conflict. A tug-of-war. A battle for turf.

Third, it's a fight over a scarce resource. And that's really important.

**All relationship conflicts are struggles
over scarce resources.**

In this case, the obvious scarce resource is *time*. Jamie and Blake have just come home and only one of them can be the first to recount the horrors of their day. If Jamie goes first, then Blake must wait.

It makes sense that we fight over scarce resources in our relationships. No one is going to scream in anguish, "Did you eat up the rest of the ice cream!?" if the freezer is filled with ice cream. What's shocking, though, as the years roll by, is the growing awareness of how many resources in our domestic lives are scarce. Money, time, space. Energy for each other. Respect. Even love and attention.*

But what's really going on in this struggle for who gets to tell their tale of woe first is the issue of "Don't I matter to you?"

When Blake complains about Jamie launching into an account of a terrible day, the real issue is, "If I mattered to you, you'd at least check in to see what my day was like."

When Jamie says, "Do I have to ask *permission* to share my feelings when I'm in *pain*!?" the issue is also, "If I mattered to you, you'd listen to what's clearly a cry of distress."

Remember, if I treat you as if you don't matter, you feel humiliated. Humiliation is kind of like being ground into the dirt. Being turned into a thing.

Now for some people, the word *humiliation* feels too strong. "I never feel humiliated," they say. "If you put me down, hey, that's on you. You're the jerk."

But it really depends on the power dynamic. A *lot* of women talk about walking past a bunch of men yelling out catcalls and remarks about their body as humiliating. Yes, the guys are jerks. Yes, you can stick your nose in the air or tell them they're jerks. But they have undressed you with their eyes and talked about your body parts and treated you

---

* My book, *The Weekend Marriage: Abundant Love in a Time-Starved World* talks about this in depth.

like a thing, and there was nothing you could do to stop them. That feels like humiliation to many women.

And many men have the experience of getting into an argument with a woman and she said something so cutting and hurtful that he couldn't help experiencing it as anything but humiliating. She said those words both intending to wound him but also as if there were no one inside to feel those wounds, and there was nothing he could do about it. At that moment her power was overwhelming.

And with help-seeking couples, the issue of humiliation almost always comes up. It's always recognized as a real force in the struggle between the two people.

Now the thing about humiliation is that it triggers an intense need for a strong response. Suppose your boss chews you out. That sucks. It's humiliating in itself. But suppose she chews you out in front of a bunch of your co-workers. *Now* what's your reaction? It's way harder to take. And that's because you're way more humiliated. What's more, you can measure your humiliation by your increased rage against your boss. You might be mad at her for chewing you out one-on-one, but if she does so in front of the whole office who knows what you might do in your rage? Quit on the spot? Plot some act of sabotage?

How power fits into this. Power *is* the humiliating part of all of this. If your four-year-old kid calls you a poo-poo head in front of the rest of the family, well, *he's a four-year-old!* He has no power and no one takes him seriously. Only another four-year-old would be humiliated by this.

But when Jamie launches into her my-awful-day soliloquy, she's grabbing, from Blake's point of view, what should be talked about first. It's like grabbing the last cookie on the plate without asking if anyone else wants it. But way worse. It's more like, "You, Blake, don't matter enough to me for me to ask you if it's okay if I unload about my day before I ask you about your day." That's certainly how Blake hears it.

On some deep emotional level, everything we do to get our needs met, *if it's not respectful of the other person's needs,* will feel like a power move, will feel deeply humiliating, will be experienced therefore as disempowering. And the disempowerment plus the emotional fuel supplied by the humiliation makes it inevitable that the other person will do or say something to re-empower themselves.

The humiliation almost guarantees that the attempt at re-empowerment will go beyond a simple re-balancing: it will seem like a power move all by itself.

No wonder Blake ends by saying, "Well, you never think about anyone but yourself anyway, so why would you start now?" and walks out and slams the door.

And there you have it, the power struggle in almost all relationships, what I call the disempowerment dynamic. Someone needs something, wants something, does something, says something. Usually all quite innocently. No thought of *asserting power*. Just "me being me" in the moment. But somehow it strikes the other person very differently. It feels like a use of power, whatever the intention, and that use of power feels humiliating as well as disempowering, and the other person has to do the same, which has a similar effect on the first person.

We all feel helpless in the face of this dynamic. It really does seem to have a life of its own. We've all had the experience of trying to stop the snowball from rolling downhill, but it rolls downhill anyway. How many times have you and your partner started a discussion about some difficult issue and you vowed to yourself that this time you're going to hold it together and have a productive discussion, but nevertheless before you know it the two of you are tangled in a mess of hurt and angry feelings.

Now you know why.

The solution is the problem

Perhaps the worst part of this dynamic is the way we get into this mess not just on a wave of emotion, but also as a solution to our problems! It's very important to understand this, because, look, we're not stupid! Why in the world would we keep doing something that's painful unless it made sense to us?

And in the moment, using what power we have to get our needs met makes sense. "Let's see . . . There's a conflict I'm a-havin' with jerk-face over here and I'm getting really frustrated. If I just busted a move, maybe I could win the pot!"

It seems to make so much sense! And we all have had the experience of times when it *has* worked. We put forward a threat, an emotional storm, something like that, and the other person caved, we won, and it confirmed our sense that power tactics make sense. We might never have used the word *power*, of course. We might just have said, see, when you're assertive, when you stick up for yourself, when you refuse to be bullied, you can get your needs met.

High-five!

But that works best, when it works at all, with people you'll never see again or with people over whom you have real power, such as store employees you could complain about to their boss. In a relationship, what you think might work in the moment is likely not to work as things play out.

Here's how things actually work most of the time:

We try to get our needs met. → Our partners do something to block our attempts. → We feel frustrated, helpless, and disempowered. → We try to re-empower ourselves. (This is when we bust a move!) → The thing we do to re-empower ourselves blocks our partner's attempts to get their needs met. (They now feel just the way we did a moment ago!) → Our partners try to re-empower themselves. (Just the way we did.) → That makes us feel blocked. → So we're back to feeling frustrated, helpless, and disempowered again. → So again we try to re-empower ourselves . . .

And round and round the merry-go-round goes until it blows up or until everyone is disgusted and exhausted.

The solution really *is* the problem.

But we believe we have no choice. And our hurt feelings keep us hanging in there punching if only to maintain our self-respect.

So, yes, it seems as if it has to be this way. But it doesn't. I'll show you.

Here's something that's happened to all of us, many times. We're walking down a corridor and we meet someone coming toward us. We move over a bit to the right, but at the same moment they move to our right also. So we move to our left, and they do too. This can go on a few times.

You and this other person are, for a moment, trapped in a silly dynamic neither of you wants to be in.

So what happens? Usually one of you smiles or laughs, acknowledging the silly situation you're both in and dramatically steps aside. The other passes. The two of you chuckle, and that's the end of that.

There are lessons to be learned from this familiar situation.

First, it's easy to get caught up in a dynamic that's in fact no one's fault. It takes two people to keep this power struggle going.

Second, for a while anyway—a few moments in this example, a lifetime perhaps with the disempowerment dynamic—it seems self-sustaining, as if it could go on forever.

Third, if neither wants to be in this dynamic, all it takes to end it is for one person to make that gesture to end it. To step aside, in this example. Or, when it comes to our relationships, to say, "Look at us. Look at what we've been doing, the two of us. I'm pretty sure neither of us wants to stay stuck in this dynamic. So let's both step away from it and do something new."

That's all it takes. *"What the hell are we doing, honey? Let's stop it!"* That's all. Stopping it is huge. Agreeing that you've both been maintaining this dynamic is huge. If you can do that, you're already halfway there.

7

So Close and Yet So Far

"When is it safe to be naked?"

Two people have just made love. Now they're lying in each other's arms. For a while there's silence. Then one says, trying to hold on to the intense closeness they've just had, "What are you thinking?"

And the other thinks, *Oh, crap! I don't know what to say. I sure can't say what I really was thinking. Or what I'm thinking now . . .*

They're so close, yet they're so far apart. And out of just this issue— our hunger for closeness, our sense of the burden of closeness, our need for distance, our fear of distance— come a hundred power struggles that give us distance most of us don't want and that few of us know how to reduce.

The issue of distance and closeness is the last but all-important missing piece when it comes to understanding the power dynamics in our relationships. You can't understand a relationship unless you understand what's going on with both partners' longings and terrors when it comes to getting close and being far apart.

The paradox of distance

This is one of the most wonderful, and yet weirdest, things I can think of: you have two people—and at one point (many points probably) you were one of those two people—who are complete strangers to each other. You're utterly uninterested in each other. The thought of having anything to do with the other's saliva, or any other bodily fluid, would be completely disgusting. And intimate touching? No! Not with a stranger!

And yet . . .

Weeks, or maybe just days later, maybe just *hours* later, the largest distance known to humankind has been traveled. Somehow—maybe one of you just said, "Excuse me, did you drop this?"—you get to talking, time passes, and the next thing you know you are swapping spit and so much more with a former total stranger who now perhaps knows one or more of your deepest secrets.

And before you know it, the two of you are sharing a bed and then a *life* together. Perhaps even creating new life together.

But are you really all that close?

And do you really want to be all that close? Or, perhaps, do you want to be much closer still?

And what if you don't agree about how close is just right for the two of you?

I've often done this demonstration at workshops. I'll have two random people come up to the front of the room. They don't know one another. I tell them they're just going to chat, to get to know one another.

But before they start, I tell them I'm going to whisper something in each of their ears. In Erik's I whisper, "As you talk, keep in mind that your preferred distance from Linda is about three feet. Try to maintain that distance." In Linda's ear I whisper, "As you talk, keep in mind that your preferred distance from Erik is about six feet. Try to maintain that distance."

What follows next is generally both hilarious and disturbing. Slowly and shyly at first, Erik will try to get a bit closer to the three-foot distance and Linda will backpedal to try to maintain the six-foot distance.

Now play this out in your mind's eye. What do you think happens? The three-foot-distance-preferring person, Erik, moves toward Linda, who moves away. And the more Linda moves away, the more Erik moves closer. Soon they move faster. Then faster. And faster. Often one ends up almost literally chasing the other around the room.

So what did we just see? Something very important. We saw how a small difference in preference—"Jeepers, honey, I just want us to be a little closer than you'd like"—turns into a full-on chase. Except that in real life, as opposed to this demonstration, the "chasing" takes the form of pressure, evasion, demands, secrecy, making fights just for the sake of creating distance, and frustration all around. Power struggles!

The need to feel close

I just talked to a guy yesterday who was shocked, *shocked!* at the idea that his wife could or would or should be his best friend. "What? No! Marie . . . I *love* Marie. I'd give my life for her. But she's not my best friend. She's my wife," he said, looking at me as if I'd just arrived from outer space.

According to Larry, love is one thing, getting close is something else. He loves Marie to pieces, but there's a world of things that are important to him that he has no desire to talk about with her.

Now I don't know Marie, but I know a woman Jakki who really believed in close relationships. What did she mean by that? Well . . .

- You do as many things together as possible

- You have no secrets from each other

- You share your money

- You share interests

- You talk about each other's work

- You know what's going on with the other's body

- You're comfortable being naked with each other

- You never close the bathroom door

- You are in important ways closer to each other than to anyone else

So you have a very wide spectrum, with Larry on one side and Jakki on the other. All kinds of variations are possible. And healthy! There's no one right way to be. Who cares whether one or both of you close the door when you go to the bathroom or not! Still, most people would agree that you should want to be closer to your life partner than you are to the average person in your life. At a minimum! The problem comes when you can't agree on a satisfactory level of closeness. And that can be a big problem.

Is it safe to be naked?

The process of going from distance to some kind of closeness, from being strangers to being intimates, is one of progressively and mutually asking and getting answers to the question, *Is it safe to get naked?* Not just literally naked, of course. Taking your clothes off can be the easiest part for a lot of people these days. I'm talking about "If I tell you my secrets and show you my faults and flaws, weaknesses and vulnerabilities, will that be safe for me or will I live to regret it?"

And it turns out (as I'm sure you know), that this is really hard.

First of all, we come into any new relationship with a history of being hurt in previous relationships, particularly given that we are getting married later and later. This has created a very dangerous dynamic in contemporary relationships. Because of all the relationships that haven't worked out for one reason or another, and because of all the stories our friends have told us about their relationships not working out, we're wary.

Being wary as a solution is sensible but dangerous. We try to learn as much as we can about the other person, and to share as little as we can about ourselves. I know what you might be saying now: "I don't lie and I don't hide." I believe you. I understand. You're not a liar or a sneak. But we *can't help* but be careful about what we reveal about ourselves.

And the more we like the other person, the more we've been hurt in the past, the more careful we are.

What's more, often the deepest darkest secret isn't some fact—"My dad once did fifteen years in prison for armed robbery"—but a trait of yours. Your temper, maybe. Or your laziness. And maybe you're not even feeling you're hiding it. Maybe you're just not feeling as committed to reforming as you might have claimed.

But however it happens, the danger lies in an inevitable disclosure of something your partner is going to feel they would have wished they'd known about sooner. "If only I'd known what a bad-tempered slug you are!"

Postponed conflict is only far more serious conflict.

But if we really like the other person, we're almost overwhelmingly tempted to play chicken with disaster. We keep our secrets—secrets are just distance in the realm of knowledge—in the hope that it'll all, someday, somehow, be all right. "Oh gee, honey, I just could never find the right time to tell you . . ."

And that's why so many power struggles are essentially over the question of "Why didn't you tell me that . . . ?"

Second, even if we didn't have a history of being hurt, the stuff we have to share is really hard to tell another person. How do you tell someone—and when!—that your mother and two of your sisters are seriously mentally ill? How and when do you mention that you have a heart condition that could shorten your life? How and when do you mention that although you have a really good career now you were very much hoping you could stop working—permanently—once your kids came along?

The "when" is often the bigger question. It's so easy to say, "When? Well, not now" in the early stage in your relationship. But as we all know, the longer you go without saying it, the harder it is to say it. Soon it feels almost impossible to say anything. And so we lock ourselves into a lie.

And third, there's the other person. The more we're with someone, the more opportunity they have to show how generous, open minded, open hearted they are. If only! The problem is that even if you're with a really nice person they may not be as open as you'd like to what you want to share.

If a year into your relationship you reveal that your mom has Alzheimer's and that you've known about it for a year before you two met, even though back then it was in the very early stages, your revelation might not get the whole-hearted acceptance you'd hoped for. After all, as generous as we might like to be, as much as I might *want* to be there for you, it's extremely hard for my first thought not to be, *What does this mean for me?*

We've already said all the easy things to say. Who's ever forgotten to say, "Oh, by the way, did I ever mention that Tom Hanks is my uncle?" There are no *good* buried secrets.

So our disclosures are almost always going to involve shoving our partners into a ditch of thinking about *what this means for me*. As a result we will not be, or not feel ourselves to be, rewarded for our attempts at getting closer by being more honest.

Bottom line:

While we want so much to feel it's safe to share everything with our partner, in the real world it usually isn't as safe as we like. This enforces a greater distance in relationships than some of us, though not all of us, would like.

Just imagine the conflicts that can come out of this. I lay my disclosure at your feet like a cat proudly bringing home a dead bird. How much I want to be petted and praised for that! Look at my honesty and courage, the risks I take for us to maintain closeness and trust! What a heroine I am!

But to you, I'm just bringing home a dead bird, and who wants that? Unless I've told you my secret right away—in which case it's never really been a secret—I've shown myself to be hiding something from you. Plus, now I'm bringing you bad news, probably bad news about *me*. Because if it were bad news about the plumber it wouldn't have been so hard to tell or so hard to take.

It's like when you give a loved one a gift, one that cost you a lot and meant a lot to you to give, except that the recipient recoiled in horror at your gift.

"How could I not have made you happy? It's just what you've always wanted!"

"How could you not have known how unhappy this would make me?"

"But couldn't you read into this my extremely good intentions?"

"What good are intentions when you drop a bomb like this on me?"

Thousands of couples a day have fights like this, and the hurts can last for years. And it's impossible not to translate the other's actions as being some form of terrible power move, some blow, some bomb.

Closeness = intimacy = love. Or does it?

It can come as a huge shock for two people who've been falling passionately in love to discover that they have completely misunderstood the kind of relationship the other person wants. The beginning of a relationship distorts a lot of things because even when people prefer a lot of distance, at the very beginning they can still act as though they can't get enough of the other person.

But the time when things have calmed down may also be the time when they've started to make commitments to each other, and a commitment can look and feel a lot like a preference for closeness. Sam and Pam might agree to move in together for all kinds of reasons, but that doesn't mean that Sam actually wants to be as close to Pam as Pam wants.

Think of it like the difference between cats and dogs. To be clear, I've lived with both much of my adult life and I like both. I don't pull one way or the other. But they're very different kinds of creatures. Dog love is not cat love.

My dogs wanted to be as close to me as they could. Intense intimacy was not a problem for them. The more the better. For my dogs, I was their life. People who like dogs understand and accept this.

It was different with my cats. They were like wild creatures with whom I'd managed to achieve an amazing level of trust, and our relationship was based on their expressing their trust in me. But they had no need to be close to me, not dog-close anyway. People who like cats understand and accept this.

But with people, if a cat-type person marries a dog-type person, there's gonna be trouble. And that's because they're going to have very different visions of what love is. It's not even a case of "Yeah, close is better, I guess—I just wish I felt more comfortable being close." At least there you share a frame of reference.

But different types of people can look at love and intimacy in completely different ways. Imagine how stunned Darlene would be if she assumed that love means intimacy, which means getting close, and suddenly her partner Dora said, "I don't understand what love has to do with getting close to someone."

"What!?" would be Darlene's reaction.

"Well," Dora said, "do you want to hear about how my day at work went?"

"I do!"

"Darlene, I love you to pieces, but I *don't* want to know about how your day at work went, because it's always the same, and I don't like telling you about how my day at work went because I'm always ashamed at how boring my job is. And by the way, just so you know, I do not like it when we're sitting in the living room reading and you interrupt me every five minutes to tell me something about what you're reading. Why can't we love each other and still have some space?"

And Darlene's heart would sink, because for her "space"

was the enemy of love. While for Dora it was space that made love bearable.

And here again the groundwork is laid for what can be a lifelong conflict. By that I mean, a chronic conflict where there is no perfect solution for both partners, like a decision about whether to have a third child or not. But that doesn't mean it can't be handled much better.

Most couples handle a conflict over wanting more closeness versus wanting more distance with, of course, power moves.

The first thing to be said about this is that

The person who wants more distance always wins, in the short run, because power moves always lead to hurt feelings, which make people need to move away from each other.

In the long run? You know, it's just sad. Two people love each other. They really do. They really want to be together. It's just that, so to speak, one wants them to be three feet apart and the other wants them to be six feet apart. And they spend the rest of their lives tearing each other to pieces over that.

It happens all the time.

Here's what it looks like in practice: Miguel is uncomfortable with how close Tricia wants to be most of the time. He doesn't talk about himself. He doesn't check in with her. He doesn't tell her about his plans or share his thoughts. So Tricia's miserable, and they fight about that. Miguel gets the distance he wants, but Tricia is stuck with a lousy marriage and Miguel is stuck with an unhappy wife and Tricia is stuck with a man who's unhappy with having an unhappy wife.

Eventually, deprived of the closeness she craves, Tricia has an affair.

Miguel implodes in misery.

Now Tricia can't reach him at all.

They get divorced.

There are dozens of different scenarios, but they're really all the same: they end in a broken marriage.

But not because of the conflict over preferred distance! The marriage ends because of the power dynamics the couple uses to deal with the conflict.

If Tricia and Miguel have a fundamental conflict over how close each prefers to be, okay, that's a problem. But if they use a conflict-free, power-free, struggle-free method for dealing with this issue whenever it comes up—which this book offers, of course—then every time an issue comes up (they're on a long drive and instead of wanting to talk, Miguel just wants to listen to music on the radio, for example), they can come up with a "best possible" solution. Not a perfect one, but the best possible under the circumstances. And guess what? Ninety percent of the time, the "best possible" solution is plenty good enough for both people.

Beware of the distance trap

Here's how the issue of distance and the issue of power collide. Let's say you and your partner have a conflict about something, but you work it out. Fine, no problem. But if you don't work it out, you're in a state of anger, resentment, and an unresolved problem. Now that state itself is a problem, as we all know, because we've all been there. So what do we do with those negative feelings plus the still-lingering problem?

We almost always deal with it by making distance. We talk less. Interact less. Go off and do things on our own more often.

And typically we just deal with the problem each in our own way. We can't agree on how to parent little Caitlyn with all her issues? Fine. I just do things my way, and you do things your way. Which—duh!—pretty soon leads to more conflict and, before long, to more distance.

Making distance in all its forms is the Swiss Army knife of relationships. There's never a problem for which distance isn't a solution. If you twist my arm and make me go to some event that I really don't want to go to by using some power tactic, as they say, "You can make me show up but you can't make me show up happy." We're there but our emotional distance can be measured in astronomical units.

So I'll just lay it right out:

In most marriages, what *can* be dealt with by making more distance *will* be dealt with by making more distance, because that's always the easiest solution.

This is really just basic human psychology. If you're trying to solve a crossword puzzle and you conclude it's just too tough, you'll abandon it. We abandon things that are too tough for us all the time. And that makes sense. When you're not getting output for all your input, move on!

People in a relationship do the same thing when they can't resolve their conflicts. Take sex.

Poor Lucy. She likes sex. She likes sex with her partner Darrin. But she feels Darrin is unimaginative and doesn't want to take the time with her that she craves. He's willing but seems bored and doesn't seem to know what to do, and she can sense that he just wants to get his penis in her vagina.

Darrin doesn't really disagree with most of this.

So where's the conflict? Well, he denies he's bored, and he sort of feels that Lucy is making a mountain out of a mole hill.

In any case, what in fact happens is that the whole making love thing moves along too quickly for Lucy and she doesn't really know how to slow it down. But she does know how to let Darrin know she's disappointed, and then of course Darrin's let down by her being let down.

And every time they try to talk about it, their sense of helplessness and frustration leads them to make power moves:

- "Don't you care about me?" said in a peevish, judgmental way

- "You want me to spend forty-five minutes kissing the inside of your elbow." (Making Lucy's needs seem ridiculous)

- "Okay, fine, you're just not a good lover. I guess that's it, then."

- "Well, maybe there's something wrong with you. Have you ever thought of that?"

At one point Darrin asked Lucy to "just write down what you want me to do and I'll do it." She was furious. She felt it put her in the position of being a sexual dictator. It made a mockery of her having legitimate needs. It nullified the idea that their having sex was something they did together. It made Lucy look like a demanding person when she wasn't.

Not that Lucy was much better. Her core strategy, if you can call it that, was to shame Darrin into shaping up. The problem being that shame is a bad strategy in any case, but particularly when it comes to sex.

So of course, predictably, the power dynamics Darrin and Lucy fell into short-circuited any possibility of actually making progress with their problem.

Instead, again of course, distance was the solution. Which meant, in this case, less sex. That is, they made distance from each other in the sexual arena. They did less of what was not working well for them.

Now imagine that process spread out over many, many parts of a couple's relationship. They don't deal with child-rearing issues because of the painful power dynamics they fall into when they do. And that's why they don't deal with their financial issues either. And why they don't deal with what to do about their sick dog, who just gets sicker and sicker.

The relationship—and as relationships age they too often fall into this pattern—more and more becomes about less and less. It becomes narrowly based on the few areas that are conflict free. It becomes a relationship consisting mostly of small talk and routines. Conflict? Yes, terrible conflict that's dealt with by silence and distance. And a loving committed relationship has drifted into two roommates making do.

And why? Not because there is conflict. But because the folks use painful, unproductive ways of solving their conflicts.

And this means that as people stay together longer, it's worth asking why. If the couple says their satisfaction with their relationship is "good," what is that based on?

In too many cases, it's based on the fact that the couple is in a very distant, narrowly based relationship, where they do in fact get along quite well in the areas where they're conflict free. So "good" may just mean "we don't fight and struggle the way we used to. We have an amicable but very low-temperature, narrowly based relationship."

But they may also be yearning for more closeness, even the partner who prefers a little more distance than the other. Because neither of them wants this much distance.

In case you've wondered why people have affairs, well, actually, there are many reasons. But a huge proportion of affairs grow out of the witch's brew I've just described: two people, hungering for some sort of closeness, yet driven apart from one another by the power dynamics in their relationship.

What's keeping them from that closeness, and the warmth that comes with it? The fact that when they try to get close they fall into conflict and don't know how to resolve it without making power moves.

It doesn't have to be this way, and it's never too late.

So if you've been wondering why, in spite of your best intentions, it has been so hard for you to solve your problems, work through your conflicts, and get your needs met, *now* you know. And in just a moment, you'll see how to get unstuck. How to find your way back to the love you know is there between you.

PART II

Your Solution

8

Do You Really *Want* to Solve
Your Problem?

"What is the whole person you are?"

I knew a woman who wanted a horse. I mean, Allie really wanted a horse. And she could afford it, though only if she made some compromises. Her wife was willing to go along with her getting a horse too. So, yes, she wanted a horse and she could get one.

So why not? Allie was a huge animal lover, and this would just complete the picture, bringing more bliss to her life.

She and I talked about it, a lot. More horse talk than I ever thought I'd have in my city-girl life. And once we ran through all the issues that come up when you have any pet from a hamster to a horse—feeding them, making sure they have exercise and companionship, and dealing with their poop and pee—it became clear, as Allie put it with a sigh, "Well ... I guess I don't want a horse as much as I thought I did."

And just maybe, in the same way, a long-lasting happy relationship is your horse.

It's something you want, for sure. But how much work

will it take and are you willing to do that work? With that partner of yours? *Should* you even be willing to do that work?

No work at all, really . . . maybe

I guess the first thing to say is that getting rid of the power dynamics in your relationship might not take much work at all. Not for some people, that is.

For some people, just eliminating power moves will do the trick. We've talked about that already.

For other people, just reading the rest of the how-to chapters without making a big deal about putting them into practice will still make a big difference in how things go in your relationship. It's not like learning to play the violin, where you have to be really good at it before it doesn't sound like crap. It's like cooking hamburgers, where if you're even just a little good at it you can make people a lot happier than if you weren't good at it at all.

I'm just saying it's way easier than caring for a horse. Or maybe even a gerbil.

"I gotta be *me*!"

This is the part that's hard. Choosing between "me" and "us." It's not that it takes work. But it does take a decision.

Remember: you *are* free. You don't have to be in this relationship. It may be hard for you to leave, and it may be much better for you to stay, but you're still free to leave.

A while back we talked about the question of whether there is room for two whole people in your relationship—all of you with your needs and all of your partner with their needs. What I know is that there is almost always more room for more of both of you than you ever imagined. Stay tuned: you'll see.

But there are ways you can make things harder. You can prioritize your needs way over the health of the relationship. And you can insist on the freedom to be yourself, whatever the impact of that on your partner.

Let's look at what it means if someone insists on this absolute freedom.

Angela had grown up with controlling parents. She'd felt as a kid that her very self was under attack much of the time. It was not only about how she dressed and wore her hair, but how she expressed herself and what she expressed herself about. According to her parents, her opinions were selfish or crazy. There was something wrong with her for not being the way her parents wanted her to be.

Well, she managed to outgrow her parents' control, but she also outgrew her tolerance for any form of control at all. So when she got married to Steve, she was oversensitive to his expressing a difference of opinion, or a different need if that need affected her, like when he pushed back on how utterly un-health-conscious the food in the house was. She'd easily feel attacked, as if Steve were trying to control her. And she'd get very upset, saying all kinds of things to Steve, as if he were a monster for merely having his own opinion. The kinds of things that people later say they didn't mean, but they sure sound like they mean them when they're saying them.

And when Steve talked to Angela about this, she, of course, got upset. "These are my feelings. What are you asking me to do? Lie? Pretend? Be all fake? Hold it in? This is how

I feel! I can't be in a relationship if I can't express how I feel. Do you want me to be a robot, or like someone numbed out on drugs? I'm a real person. If you can't handle that, go marry a fake person. I'm sure there are a lot of fake people around you can find and go have a nice calm fake marriage with, you phony son of a bitch."

Whew!

You see the problem. Angela's freedom to be herself, to live out her uninhibited authenticity, is Steve's nervous breakdown. That's bad for Steve. What may be bad for Angela is the possibility that once she'd burned through Steve's patience, she would never be able to find anyone willing to put up with what she called her full authenticity.

Who do you instinctively side with here, Angela or Steve? Angela who just wants to be free to let out her feelings, whatever they are and whenever she wants to let them out? Or Steve who just wants to be free from being under assault when he screws up?

And would it make a difference to you if I changed the genders? What if Steve was the one who lets loose, yelling, swearing, maybe pounding a door? And maybe telling Angela in his full authenticity that he was sick of how she'd been "letting herself go"? And Angela was crying that Steve was being mean to her?

The deep, deep question is, *What* is *the whole person you are?* Is that whole person someone who puts "I gotta be me" over everything and is willing to die alone if that's the price it takes? Well, if you're being honest with yourself and that's what you really want, who am I to argue?

Or is that whole person, that whole *you,* someone who

of course, as we all do, would like to be yourself as much as possible in your relationship but would also like to *have* a relationship to be yourself *in*?

And of course being yourself is just one of your many needs. Just one of my many needs too!

Oh, and by the way, if for you "free to be me" means "free to have my feelings," well sure, feel free to feel! Let 'em out! Where power moves make trouble is specifically when the two of you are working through a conflict. But let's say your partner has just come home from work at nine p.m. for the umpteenth time and this has pushed you over the edge. So you let loose. "You know what?" you say at full volume, slamming shut your laptop. "I've had it with your always coming home late, your never being around, never being *here*! You might as well just move a cot into your office. It's like I don't even *exist* in your life."

So, okay. You're only human. You're a person. You're having your feelings. You're sharing—loudly and passionately—what's going on with you. Now it's true that this might very well feel like a power move to your partner, like a sudden assault, particularly if, from their point of view, they're doing the best they can under the circumstances. Plus, they're exhausted!

But your saying what you said, the way you said it, was not an attempt to work out conflict. It was the sharing of a need. It was letting your partner know that there was a problem to be solved, and if the two of you differed about how to solve it, then, yes, there'd be a conflict. And if, in trying to solve that problem and work out that conflict the two of you blew up and used power moves of any other sort, that *would* lead to things working out badly.

**Letting loose with your feelings doesn't have to be
a problem in your relationship. It's only a problem—
because it serves as a power move—when you're
in the middle of trying to resolve a conflict.**

But merely providing the information that there *is* a problem to be solved? That's what feelings are for. Feelings are information, and a relationship needs as much information as possible. Other than power moves, the second most destructive force in relationships is two people not knowing what's going on with each other.

Turning the dial to a better life

So imagine a dial that's all about what's most important to you, and the question is where you'd set the dial:

$$\Downarrow$$

My relationship   *Getting my needs met*

"Hmmm … Do I really want to work on my relationship? And how hard do I want to work? Or should I just keep struggling to get my needs met and hope that things don't get worse in our relationship?"

Right now, you're not doing great either way. A lot of your needs are going unmet, and at the same time your relationship isn't in great shape either. But imagine if you could move the arrow more to whichever part of the dial you wanted.

You could focus on getting your needs met. Probably by doing a lot of the things you're doing now. And you're free to do that.

But I can tell you that unless you're a genius and your partner is a crème puff you'll be setting off on a trip right out of your relationship. Which might be okay with you. You might think: *These are the things I need to be happy. I'm gonna go for it. If I get them, fine. If not, I'm outta here.*

If that's what you want, *do it*. If this seems like a good deal to you, go for it. And so here's where you'd set the dial:

My relationship   _Getting my needs met_

Another choice is doing nothing. You can say, well, Kirshenbaum probably knows what she's talking about but I think it's going to be too hard to change anything. Hey, we're not divorced yet! So we'll just plod along, dealing with relationship issues as they come up and struggling—yes, not very productively—to get our needs met, but at least, well, it's what we do.

Which means you'd be sort of here, in the mushy middle:

My relationship   _Getting my needs met_

Okay, fine. But I just want to say this. Doing nothing *is* easiest in the short run, but what you're really doing is betting that doing nothing is easiest because the risk of divorce isn't that high, or even if it is high, it's not that big a deal. So you get divorced! You'll just be trading up when you meet your next partner. Onward and upward! That's your bet.

Now I've always said that divorce is a good option when

you have an unsatisfying and unfixable relationship. If it's not good and you can't make it better, of course move on. It's worth it *even though* breaking up is hard and expensive.

But you have to ask yourself this: Are you betting that doing nothing is best because the risk of divorce really *is* low in your case and, if you do get divorced, the financial and emotional cost really *isn't* that high? Or is that bet actually based on laziness?

I mean, come on! You're talking to *me*! I'm the laziest woman alive, and I will rationalize anything out of sheer laziness. I remember once seriously thinking that the years getting in shape added to your life were the last years of your life, while the years spent getting into shape were the best years of your life, so what's the point? Save the time now by not working out, die a couple of years earlier, and you still come out way ahead! Now that's the kind of thinking laziness can drive us to.

What my laziness blinded me to was that, first, working out didn't have to take much time out of my week. Second, I could see the benefits right away. Third, I was way underestimating the risk of damage later on. Lack of exercise could shorten my life by a little or a lot. Just as bad, I could stay alive with a seriously diminished quality of life as a result of growing older in bad shape.

So, if you want to make choices, make them. If you're lazy, well, welcome to the club. But the two things none of us can afford are ignorance and stupidity.

And that's the thing. In our laziness and fear of change we always underestimate the risk of things getting worse and the difficulties we'll face if they do get worse. Such as getting older in a worsening relationship. By the time you realize you can't stand it anymore, you're also at a time in your life when it might be hard to find a new partner. Then what? Change may be hard, but it's worth it.

When hope makes sense. What if changing the way you deal with conflict as a couple is easier than you thought? (It probably is!) What if the two of you can discover ways for more of both of you to find room in your relationship? (You probably can!) What if not doing the best you can to root out the power struggles in your relationship will have far more negative consequences than you imagined? (Sorry, but it probably will.) And what if taking the disempowerment dynamics *out* of your relationship really does allow love and passion to flow back *in*? (It does!)

Which brings us to the third option, which is the one I wholeheartedly recommend because you have everything to gain and nothing to lose:

⇓
_____

My relationship   *Getting my needs met*

It's not that you give up on getting your needs met. *No!* That would be terrible and make your relationship unsustainable. A relationship has to be a place where both people get their needs met. But the third option is one where you prioritize getting your needs met in a way that strengthens your relationship. The only thing you have to give up is the illusion that because power moves sometimes work in the short run, they are a good idea in the long run. No, power moves are never a good idea. They usually just create power struggles in the short run. And in the long run everyone's exhausted and really pissed off with each other, to say nothing of the fact that they've very likely got a dead relationship on their hands.

So where does the part come in where I assert my needs?

It comes, trust me! The part where you are working to get your needs met is tightly woven into every step of the process! Here's the thing, though. It may all feel a bit unfamiliar to you because you'll be asserting your needs outside the usual mode of a power struggle, and so it may not feel like an "assertion" at all.

I worked with a couple just this morning . . . Anthony had a huge need for his wife Crystal to make fewer demands on him as they were about to go through a very difficult period—he'd be recovering from back surgery. Anthony would be there as much as he could for her and their son, but Anthony also needed to be left alone sometimes to recharge his batteries. Of course Crystal was overburdened too.

Add to that the fact that they were—as they themselves characterized it—a couple of battling Italians—and you can imagine the power dynamics that could erupt as each "asserted" their needs in no uncertain terms.

But within twenty minutes of talking about both of their situations, the conversation got to a point where Crystal turned to Anthony and asked, "Okay, Tony . . . Tell me what you need this summer."

He said what he needed. A very sweet and polite version of "leave me the fuck alone," *after*, of course, he'd agreed to a couple of easy and reasonable things she'd asked for. And she immediately said yes, unreservedly.

It's not magic any more than baking a cake is magic. Baking a cake is easy! You just have to follow a few steps and in a funny way, the cake bakes itself. And it's the same here when it comes to pulling off the seeming magic of getting your needs met and saving your relationship at the same time.

If you want to give it a try, let's get going.

9

The Anger Chapter

"Nothing has quite the power to declare itself
as 'mine' as a passionate emotion does."

I suspect there might be some eye rolling now about . . . well, about many things maybe, but certainly about the issue of anger. Maybe I glossed over the free-to-be-me issue too quickly.

All of us—me too—see anger as a natural and healthy emotion. We want to be able to share our anger with our partners in the safety of the loving intimacy of our relationship. We see our anger as part of who we are. This was expressed rather well recently by Agnes Callard in a piece called "The Emotion Police," which you can find online at www.thepointmag.com:

> *My body, my mind, my job, my interests, my talents—these are all "mine"—but nothing has quite the power to declare itself as "mine" as a passionate emotion does. . . . Consider, for example, anger.*

For sure, this is how a lot of people feel, including me. And here I come along—what was Callard's phrase? . . . the emotion police!—and maybe you think I'm saying you shouldn't get angry with each other, at least when you're trying to resolve your conflicts.

Am I saying that? If I were, I'd be the biggest hypocrite on the planet. I wish I could drag my husband in here right now, my husband to whom I've been married since college, and ask him if I ever acted in my own life as though anger were a sin, a faux pas, a relationship crime?

He'd probably laugh himself sick. When he challenged me at many points in our marriage—and there were many— I probably said something very much like "Hey! This is my anger! Back off, buddy. Don't you dare tell me to 'chill.'"

You can't get rid of someone else's anger, you shouldn't, and you have no right to try.

And yet I'm sure this talk of power moves sounds to many of you like anti-anger propaganda. Clearly there's something about anger I'm not thrilled with. So let me fully explain my stance.

First of all, I'm *not* telling you what to do. I hate the idea of anyone policing or judging anyone. If you want to be in a relationship where the partners run around expressing their anger with each other when it comes up, go for it! And if it works for you, keep it up!

In part, it's a cultural thing. There are ethnic groups where flare-ups of anger are so normal that folks would be shocked if they didn't occur. This doesn't mean that anger is never toxic in these cultures, just that *all* anger isn't *always* toxic. In some cultures, expressions of anger don't have the impact they do in other cultures.

But my entire professional life has involved clinical and research issues like the psychological and interpersonal dynamics involving anger. So while I can't tell you what to do, I can tell you the truth.

Anger is to relationships what fire is to forests. Campfires are great, and if you are aware of their dangers you can have campfires all over the place and toasted marshmallows galore. What you can't do is kid yourself about the dangers of a campfire in the forest. Or about the dangers of anger in a relationship.

What dangers? Oh, so many. Well, actually only four, but they're really important.

First of all, and skating over some really important cultural differences for the moment, people in general delude themselves as to the impact of their anger on their partner. If I yell at you, I am aware of my anger's boundedness. But you aren't. So it's scarier for you than it is for me. I may know I don't mean the things I say. You *don't* know that I don't mean them. So it's hurtful for you. I may feel I am just expressing myself. You may very well feel attacked.

So it's likely that what's anger when it comes out of me is bullying by the time it reaches you.

Second, anger can often swing open the gate for a free-for-all. Fuck you. No, fuck *you*! No, *fuck you*! And awaaaaay we go . . . Some couples do well with this. They feel they've blown off some steam, cleared the air, gone on to have make-up sex, and all is well. And if that's true, great! But for many, many, couples—most, actually—it's not like that at all. These free-for-alls, these blowups, leave hurt feelings and shattered nerves. All you want afterward—for a long time—is to stay the hell away from one another.

Third, there's a toxic accumulation from all this anger. It builds up like soap scum in the shower, except that it's harder to get rid of. Worst of all, as the habits of anger harden into hostility, this toxic accumulation becomes invisible, then becomes a wall, then may be impossible to get rid of.

Fourth, anger can be a particularly unfortunate interruption of the process of working out differences. You're already wary and uptight with each other! The forest around the campfire is tinder dry. A flare-up of anger can turn into a huge and discouraging deflection. It can turn the power balance into a direction that leads to a suboptimal solution, to put it mildly!

So what do we do with our anger? Well, then, do you just throw anger out the window because it can be dangerous?

Of course not. So let's take our anger really seriously and ask ourselves what it actually is.

It's a feeling, of course, but more importantly it's a pointer. And this pointer gives you and your partner four crucial bits of information. It tells you:

1. *that* something is threatening your well-being

2. *what's* threatening your well-being

3. *how big a deal* that threat is to *you*

4. how important it is to you that *your partner* understand all this and respond appropriately to it

---

And these are the four reasons we get angry.

If you're the I'm-afraid-of-spiders person in your relationship and your partner is the I-kill-spiders person, then all you have to do is yell, "Aaarrrggghhh! There's a spider in the bathtub," and if your partner jumps up and gets rid of it, then you are a lean, mean relationship team, and you've covered all four of the points above in a New York minute.

But if you've asked your partner a hundred times to put a gate at the top of the stairs so your toddler won't fall down and your partner just pooh-poohs the whole thing or promises to do it and then doesn't, and then when you get angry your partner makes out like you're a crazy person, then there's something seriously wrong in your relationship.

But note: anger wasn't what made things work in the first case. And it didn't help in the second case. Yes, sometimes anger works, every once in a while, perhaps just often enough to convince you that it's a useful if not totally reliable tool. But the cost of always having to use this tool mounts up and mounts up into a burden of rage that's hard to get rid of.

So many, many times instead of getting to the point of blowing up when the two of you are walking around in molten lava for several days, you can take the Four Steps *Out* of Anger:

1. Just say *that* something is threatening your well-being

2. Explain *what's* threatening your well-being

3. Say *how big a deal* that threat is to you and why

4. Show *how important it is to you* that your partner understand all this and respond appropriately to it

If you do this, you can accomplish everything you want, but without building up the obstacle of anger. It's so efficient. Good for getting your needs met. Good for your relationship.

Understanding how to work your way out of anger is really important information for the life of the relationship!

In fact, relationships die when consistently, over time, with one issue after another, what's important to you is ignored by your partner and you experience that loss as a threat. So the question isn't whether your anger is natural. It is. It isn't whether your anger is justified. It is. The question is:

Is a display of anger worth the cost?
Generally, it isn't.

Can you get your needs met and satisfy the four
reasons we get angry without a costly display
of anger? Usually, you can.

Basically, anger is a mutually stressful way of our getting our needs met because we haven't found a better way. Let me ask you a simple question: Let's say you were at a restaurant and you were served your food and there was a problem with it. Which scenario would you prefer?

1. You call the server over, explain the problem, and the server immediately offers to take care of it.

2. You get furious, call the server over, yell at the person, and the server immediately offers to take care of it.

Who wants to resolve an issue *with* anger if you could resolve it *without* anger? If I could get my needs met without anger, why wouldn't I—or anyone—opt for that? It's faster, less stressful, and there's less collateral damage!

And the good news is that that's just what you're in the process of seeing how to do here.

**Anger is the natural response to helplessness
in the face of feeling disempowered.**

No disempowerment = no anger. There is never a reason for anyone to feel disempowered if you follow the Four Steps Out of Anger.

But what if I still feel angry? Look, we're all just people, and so I have no illusions that this book or a ton of books like it can eliminate anger from our lives. But that's not really the goal. The goal is to minimize unproductive anger, anger that makes things worse not better, and to avoid deceiving ourselves about the costs and benefits of anger.

In the meantime, anger will be with us and we need to know how to deal with it healthfully and productively. You can do that if you ask yourself these questions:

Do I want to discharge my anger or share it with my partner? The fact is that you have three good choices.

You can vent to a friend. We do that all the time, and if we don't do it so often that we burn our friends out, it's a great solution.

Or you can release some anger by having a really good workout or yoga session or yelling your head off in the car or something like that. This can take a huge edge off your anger.

Or you can discharge your anger in the presence of your partner—really let him or her know how mad you are. Now if you're not concerned about riskiness or messiness, then just do it! But if you want to avoid what is honestly a lot of risk and mess and fallout from your blowing up at your partner here are two big tips.

Here's how to safely let your partner know how mad you are:

- Please don't let loose in the middle of trying to work out a conflict, even though—I know!—this can be just the time when you're likely to be set off. It'll set things back, or worse.

- Do this instead: It's called the Blow-Up Session, and if you love your freedom it'll feel artificial as hell. But it works! Just say to your partner something like, "Look, I'm really mad at you now and it's getting in the way. When would be a good time for you to listen to me, and how long can you listen to me for?" "I could do it right after dinner, but if you're gonna really let loose I don't know if I could take it for more than, I guess, two minutes." Now you've made an agreement. You are essentially empowering your partner with respect to something—your blowing up—that would otherwise be very disempowering. You get your feelings out; your partner feels able to put some parameters around it; and you both come out ahead.

- At the end of your dramatic monologue, your partner says back to you what he understands is the nub of what your anger is all about. Let's say you two were talking about where to go on vacation, and your partner felt the options you mentioned were too expensive in light of your other goals. You ask for a Blow-Up Session to let loose the anger that has surged up. You say all kinds of things—as we do at a time like that—and your partner says, after running it over in his slow-working mind, "You know, what I heard—and I'm kinda shocked by this—is that you're still really, really mad about how I wasn't there for you when you were pregnant with Madison." Bingo. He heard you.

I'm telling you this works. But here's another question to ask yourself.

Which is more important to you, freedom or effectiveness? Yesterday I was picking up my grandson from school, and the usual traffic jam in the pickup zone was worse than usual. I was, like, seventeen cars back, and clearly we were just going to be stuck until we all got unstuck. The lady in the Mercedes right next to me—I won't call her Ms. White Privilege, although she could have been cast for the part—at some point jumps out of her car, with her daughter in the backseat, and starts shrieking and gesturing toward the bottleneck.

If I've ever seen an exercise in futility, that was it. No one could hear her, and even if they could no one could do anything about what she was saying, and even if they *could*, her rants would certainly take away *my* motivation to do anything about it. A few minutes later, we'd moved up a bit and the crossing guard had stopped us. I had my last glimpse of the crazy lady, in her silent bubble, windows rolled up, pounding, pounding, pounding on the steering wheel, yelling like a total nut, her kid sitting in the backseat thinking God knows what.

But she was free. No one had told her to calm down, and I pity the fool who might have tried.

I don't know that woman but I know countless people I've worked with over the years, and they've told me what I can easily imagine this woman saying: "Look, I know that what I did was stupid and useless, but I don't care. I was mad. That's the way I felt, and what was I going to do? Keep it bottled up and get ulcers or cancer or something? I'm so tired of people—men, my mother, my teachers—trying to control me, telling me to be quiet, always telling me to shut up, to shut up, to shut up. Like if I'm not the good girl they want me to be, then I'm good for nothing. Well, the hell with them, and the hell with anyone who tries to tell me I'm not free to express my feelings."

And you know what? I did understand her. That's what people told me! And if you're a woman—and for many men too—that's what you've been told. For many of us, the freedom to express our feelings is both the greatest luxury and the most fundamental freedom.

So, yet again, one more time, I'm not telling you what to do. Do what you want! I certainly know how you feel because I've been there. To me marriage *meant* finding someone with whom it would be safe to bust loose with my feelings.

But I've found that operating like this just isn't *effective*.

First of all, it's not good for you. Let's say someone or something makes you mad. Okay, there may be a situation that needs to be dealt with. Or there may be—like in that middle-school pickup-zone traffic jam—no situation that needs to be dealt with.

Fine. So you deal with what can be dealt with. And let go of what can't be dealt with. This isn't advanced calculus, folks.

And what about those unexpressed feelings? Won't they turn toxic? Well, we all feel as though they will, but the research says the opposite. The research says that episodes of expressed rage are very stressful, and we all know that stress takes its toll. The woman in that car next to me—if she was always blowing up like that—was exacerbating a stress-related disease waiting to happen.

On the other hand, if the angry feelings aren't expressed, what happens? Do they turn into ulcers? No, they turn into nothing. They just evaporate, not even leaving a residue. There's a whole junkyard of exploded hypotheses about unexpressed anger causing health problems. It just doesn't.*

So there we are. Freedom versus effectiveness.

What you choose is up to you. Feeling you have the perfect freedom to do and say what you want is going to lead to a lot of friction and to your either being stuck in that friction (not freedom!) or to your bouncing from one relationship to another. Merely accommodating the other person will lead to a nightmare of oppression. Don't do that!

So try what I call the effectiveness option, which means simply that you take your needs seriously. The needs *about which* you're getting upset. That you take your partner taking *their* needs seriously—their needs being as important to you

---

* What *does* cause health problems is stress, which can come from humiliation, which can cause anger, and that's where the confusion comes in. It's ongoing situations that we experience as humiliating—at work, at home, in our neighborhoods—that put us at health risk from stress. Whether we get mad or not, or express it or not, has nothing to do with it. And of course that humiliation is always the result of someone using their power against us. If it's constant (say, on a job) or, even worse, systemic (say, due to racism), the health effects will be worse. Now anger does have a use here. Not as an occasion for a blowup but as crucial information about what is going on and how important it is to you. And if what's going on is serious, then you have to take action.

as your own. That you take keeping your relationship healthy seriously. And that you work through the process we're going through here, which I promise will maximize the chances of both of you getting your needs met.

Yeah, you won't be expressing your anger as often, but you won't be having anger to express as often either.

So, anger is always an option. And then there's the effectiveness option. Here's where we too often get into trouble.

We think of anger as our default option. We think that anger costs us nothing in terms of our getting our needs met and in terms of the health of the relationship. And we neglect the effectiveness option, which is simply to ask ourselves, "How would I deal with this if I were to focus on being effective in getting my needs met and protecting our relationship?"

And you know, even a mediocre answer to that question is healthier for both of you and your relationship than the anger option. But wait! I have a really *good* answer!

10

One, Two, Three, *Go*

"A best solution just appears and it sells itself."

Most of us feel more confident when tasks are broken down into three steps. Easy as one, two, three. Lather, rinse, repeat. If it only takes three steps it couldn't be that hard, so we have less trepidation when it comes to trying something new.

Well, you're in luck. I'm going to teach you the **1, 2, 3 Method** to help you resolve conflicts that in the past have led to angry breakdowns in your ability to work things out with one another. There are only three things you have to do, and you can sometimes do them incredibly quickly. You've probably done them already, many times, without even realizing it.

Let's look at this common example: Logan and Lucy get home from work at about the same time. Logan collapses in his chair, Lucy collapses on the couch.

"I'm exhausted. The last thing I want is to make dinner," Logan says.

"Oh, me too," Lucy says. "So what do you want to do: go out or order in?"

"I don't know." Logan sighs. "If we order in, we have to

wait forever for them to deliver. But I'm almost too tired to move. But I'm also hungry."

"Well, what about Devlins?" Lucy says. "It's just down the street and, yeah, all they have is bar food but it's always good and they make it fast."

Logan sits up. "Love it. I always forget about Devlins. We can be there in less time than it takes to talk about it."

Now that's a pretty basic conversation, but it's also quite an accomplishment for two exhausted, hungry, probably stressed-out people. And what's even more striking, in a mere thirty seconds they accomplished all three steps that I'll outline for you for resolving conflict without power moves.

The first thing that happened was that Logan said he was too exhausted to make dinner and Lucy said she was too. Well, that's step 1: *mutual understanding.* I know it's not always that easy to accomplish, but that's all it *is*: two people coming to a shared understanding.

The second thing that happened was that they *explored options*: going out or ordering in. It just took a moment.

And the third thing they did was *brainstorm possible solutions*. Lucy mentioned the bar food at Devlins. Good food close at hand. Now fortunately this was right up Logan's alley, but if he was sick of Devlins, he could have brought up Hong Fat, only a few more minutes farther away, and the food was really good and came really fast there too.

Now look, I know choosing what to have for dinner is not on par with some of the major conflicts that come up in relationships. And I know very well that if conflict resolution was always this easy none of us would ever have needed to resort to power moves, none of us would have ever felt disempowered, and none of us would ever have been in the angry, hurt place so many of us are in in our relationships. I couldn't possibly minimize the difficulties couples face, because I so often see those difficulties in the lives of my patients, my friends, and myself.

But what I am saying is that the underlying process that Logan and Lucy used for their little problem is the same process that'll get you safely through the most difficult conflict you've ever faced.

The point is that the solution I'm offering here is natural and organic. It doesn't come from the lab. It comes from the same success-based research that's guided me and my partner through all fifteen books we have written together. We analyze the process used by people who are already successful with a problem and then present it in a way that everyone can use it. It's a bit like finding a cure for cancer based on the ways the human body eliminates cancer through its own immune response, which is exactly what many scientists today are trying to do.

So let me lay out the **1, 2, 3 Method** for resolving conflict in a bit more detail.

The 1, 2, 3 Method for Resolving Conflict

1. Before you begin to discuss solutions, make sure each of you understands what the other thinks and feels about the issue you're facing.

2. Come up with plenty of options. Be sure you've put as many options as you can on the table.

3. As a way to arrive at a final agreement, take different options and together explore how they would play out and discover what their pros and cons are.

Truly, even if you were negotiating a peaceful resolution to World War III, you wouldn't do anything different. And yet it's what Logan and Lucy did to figure out how to avoid making dinner.

Conversations

So why should you trust that this **1, 2, 3 Method** for resolving conflict will work for *you*?

The answer is: for the same reason that when I want to lose some weight I don't stock my house with potato chips. It's not that chips are inherently bad and we have to banish them in order to lose weight (I, for one, think total deprivation leads to disaster), but I love potato chips and as the old commercial goes, I can't eat just one.

So what does this have to do with conflict? Let me explain.

You now know all about power moves and you're on the lookout for them, which is great. That's enormously helpful. You also know how in the course of working out a conflict both you and your partner are emotionally vulnerable. Love is all about being there for the other person; everything else is just words. And when there's a conflict suddenly our partners are there for themselves, and at a minimum you feel abandoned.

So the very fact of conflict—the very fact that I discover my partner no longer shares the dream we've talked about of retiring one day to a place in the country, for example—is incredibly disempowering. He's betrayed me! I'm immediately primed to want to re-empower myself. To make a power move.

That's why so many attempts to "resolve" conflicts are just occasions for striking poses in the guise of reasonableness. For example, Helen wants to quit her job as a home-health aide and go to nursing school. Joe, her partner, makes good money as a truck driver but they need her income if they're going to have any extras. But Helen doesn't want to stay stuck in a low-wage, low-status job all her life.

So here's how she approaches Joe.

"Honey, you work really hard and make a good living driving those big rigs. But let's face it, you're never going to earn a hell of a lot more. And of course as we both know what I earn is just piddling. So here's what I want to do, and I want you to hear me out." And she tells him all about her plan. He interrupts her a couple of times with questions, but she shuts him down. "No, Joe! Please! Give me the courtesy of waiting until I'm done." When she finishes, she ends by saying, "Joe, we're gonna get by with me in nursing school, and afterward I'll be making so much more money. Honestly, you'd have to be an idiot not to think this is a super good idea."

Now think about how this hits Joe. This whole idea is dumped on him out of the blue, and then Helen tops it off by saying he has two choices: go along or be an idiot.

Now a forced choice—take it or leave it, my way or the highway, agree or be an idiot—is disempowering big time. Plus, he feels, she's called him an idiot for even thinking there might be things to consider about her idea.

So he says, "Well, I must already be an idiot, because I can think of a lot of problems with that plan of yours." And he proceeds to tick off a list of but-what-abouts, hammering them home, each one resounding in Helen's ears like huge *nos*.

This is why I talked about keeping chips out of the house when I'm dieting. Conflict in and of itself, and in spite of our best intentions, seduces us toward using power moves. Willpower and wisdom can and often do help, but you can't rely on them.

So just the way dieting is much easier in a world without temptation, peaceful, effective conflict resolution is much easier in a world without . . . guess what? Conflict! And that's what the **1, 2, 3 Method** keeps you away from: struggling head to head over *my way, no my way, no my way.*

Each of the three steps in the 1, 2, 3 Method is about staying away from conflict while allowing the best possible solution to emerge from the best possible information.

In step 1, you're just listening to each other talk about how you both feel about the issue you're facing. And let's be honest: in most situations you both have doubts about both sides of the issue.

In step 2, you're just kicking around options. Is in fact nursing school Helen's only or best option? This is worth looking at, not because Joe's her enemy, but because as her true partner he can maybe, just maybe, come up with an even better option, given what he's come to understand in going through step 1. You never know what wonderful possibilities you'll uncover in step 2.

And in step 3, what you do is take these options, one at a time, for a test drive. "Okay, let's look at what it would actually be like if I went to nursing school, what it would be like afterward, and what it would actually be like if we kept on just the way we are." It's nothing more than a full and fair exercise in "what if?"

And what's astounding is how often during this step the conflict just resolves itself. No arm wrestling at all. A best solution just appears and *it sells itself.*

And all these are just *conversations*! Like discussing how you think your favorite TV series is going to end.

Think of the time you'll save. Every power move is likely to lead to a power struggle—a fight. Every fight takes time. And recovering from every fight takes time. Imagine if every time you drove to work you got into a couple of fender benders. Yikes! Each one would take hours to deal with: calls, discussions, repairs, and so on. Who would want that?

Why have these fender benders in your attempts to work out conflict?

Negotiation?

People often ask how this differs from negotiation. Well, honestly sometimes negotiation goes a lot like this. But usually they're quite different.

Negotiation is between people who are fundamental adversaries. Not necessarily as people but in their roles. They are adversaries who have significantly different interests. You may be buddies with your landlord, go out drinking with him all the time, but he's in the business of renting property and so he wants, as is his right, to make as much money as he can. You're just someone trying to survive, so you want to pay as little for your rent as you can. And it's your rental agreement that, in the end, is your main connection.

But things are very different with two people in a committed long-term relationship based on that thing we call love.

In some sense, your relationship is about process, not just outcome. What I mean is that having a relationship is in large part about working together to make decisions and solve problems. For example, before you were together, you were probably quite capable of buying your own clothes. You don't need each other now to buy clothes. But part of many relationships is getting input from each other about the clothes you buy because it's not just about what you like to wear but what your partner enjoys seeing you wear.

What's more, going through the process of making a decision or resolving a conflict—if you can avoid battle scars and actually arrive at something that's best for everyone—is a real triumph for any couple. And that brings up an important topic I haven't talked about so far.

Couple self-esteem

Jeff and Sara loved their summer house right on the beach, but they had to share it with Jeff's two brothers—it had been in the family for years—and it was always a hassle to settle on who would get to stay in it when.

One day Jeff came home from work and Sara told him that one of her sisters-in-law had told her that Jeff's brothers wanted to sell their share in the house to Jeff. Things were rocky for them financially and they needed the money.

Now this was a dream come true for Jeff and Sara. A no-brainer. Suddenly their beloved summer house could be theirs alone. But it would be complicated. Negotiating a price with Jeff's own brothers. Working out the financing. Dealing with the fact that in reality Sara liked the house a lot more than Jeff did.

Plus things had been shaky in their relationship recently. They'd been fighting a lot about less important things than this.

After Sara told Jeff about the sister-in-law's call, Jeff said, "Wow," very quietly, and then went silent.

"So?" Sara asked.

Jeff sighed. "I don't know. We've not been doing well for a long time, you and I. If we open this up, it could get real messy and ugly. I see a lot of fights. I mean, yeah, this is a great opportunity, but I think we'll just mess it up. I mean, we flat out can't pay what they're asking—and you probably disagree with that . . ."

"I do!"

"Okay, so there you are. I'm just saying I don't trust us to open up this whole can of worms. It's just gonna be a bloodbath. We really can't afford it, *we really can't*, so we can't say *yes*, so let's just say *no* and be done with it."

"We *can* say *yes*, and as usual you're too stubborn and stupid to realize what a great opportunity we have here. But . . . so you're saying you won't even discuss it?"

"I mean, why bother?"

"Why bother . . . ," Sara said. "Maybe for once we agree."

This is low couple self-esteem in action. Maybe Sara and Jeff didn't feel like failures as people, but they felt like failures as people in a marriage. They both felt they'd put in time and effort, and yet things had gone from good to bad. And this sets up a harmful dynamic in itself.

When two people feel good about themselves as a couple, they feel good about their ability to tackle the normal things life throws at them: good or bad, simple or complicated. And this actually helps *give* them the ability to tackle these things.

When you were a kid did you ever jump over ditches? I did. Maybe more than my share. Confidence and success went hand in hand. When I felt confident, I'd make a strong run and the closer I got to the edge the faster I'd run, and then right at the edge I'd make my leap . . . and over I'd soar.

But when I didn't have confidence, I'd slow down as I got near the edge, and it was that slowing down out of fear that made it necessary for me to stop.

Now you might say that Jeff and Sara were prudent not to get into a struggle that would turn into a terrible battle, just the way I'd be prudent not to jump over a ditch that was too wide for me.

But here's where the analogy breaks down. If I'd wanted to become a broad jumper I could have worked at getting better and better, and done so safely. It's different with Jeff and Sara. For them and so many other couples caught in cycles of power dynamics, couples who have come to expect blood-baths, not resolutions, low couple self-esteem is causing them to shrink the range of their shared life as a couple.

Hmmm, they seem to say, we can't do this because we're not confident that it'll work for us, and we can't do that for the same reason, or *that* . . . and next thing you know their shared life together is like one of those sad skinny polar bears whose world has shrunk to a small island of ice in a huge polar sea. We can't make love because we can't talk about our sexual issues without getting into a hurtful, unproductive fight. We can't talk about moving for the same reason, so we stay stuck living in this expensive dump. We can't talk about having another child for the same reason, so the time for having another child is at risk of slipping through our fingers.

Now, look: I assume that if you're reading this book your couple self-esteem isn't what it should be. But don't be afraid. One of the main features of the **1, 2, 3 Method** for resolving conflict is that it will restore your couple self-esteem. How?

By breaking down the scary business of resolving a conflict into three steps consisting of things you already can do, do well, and do easily.

Imagine if you came to a brook and you thought of leaping across it but it was so wide you had no confidence you'd be able to do it. But then you looked and a little way downstream, where the brook was just as wide, there was a place with three large stones in the brook. All you had to do was leap from the bank to stone to stone to stone to the other bank, and you could see this was something you really *could* do.

This **1, 2, 3 Method** was designed specifically with your couple self-esteem in mind.

One more issue: How does using the **1, 2, 3 Method** for dealing with conflict apply to the question of giving feedback to your partner?

"Do these pants make me look fat?"

Feedback is too often used as just a fancy word for unwelcome criticism. If you go back—way back!—into the roots of love, we sure as hell don't get together to be told what's wrong with us. We get together to be loved, admired, and cherished. Yes, as adults, we may expect to come in for a bit of criticism— "Honey, if you want me to come by your apartment, you're gonna have to clean your bathroom."—and some folks who aren't the best housekeepers in this case may more or less expect something like this.

But let's face it: We definitely do not want to be on the receiving end of a lot of "feedback." So let's try to sort this out.

On the other hand, a certain kind of feedback is vital to the health of a relationship. If I brush and floss the way a person's supposed to and yet my breath still smells bad, my partner is going to want to stay away from me and I won't know why until he tells me my breath smells bad. Which I won't want to hear, but which we both need me to hear.

Now, once we start talking about feedback, two questions come up. One is: *How do I give feedback to best preserve the health of our relationship?* I'll show you how to do this later in the book.

And two: *What does feedback have to do with conflict?* Feedback is just one person saying they have a problem with something about their partner. And lots of times there's nothing more to be said. "Well, uh, those aren't the most flattering pants in your wardrobe." "Okay, thanks."

Done. Finished.

But sometimes feedback is just a way to open a door to an unmet need.

"I don't like your mother."

"I know. She can be trying."

"Yeah, but that's not what I'm saying. I'm saying I don't want her to come here so often or spend so much time here when she does."

"Now wait a minute, buster. What right do you have . . ."

And the two of you are off and running.

The point I'm making is that if feedback can just stay feedback—"I wish you didn't have to work such long hours."—then it stays in the feedback arena. But . . .

Most of the time, buried within most feedback is a need. And you're much better off going to the need and bypassing the feedback.

In other words, "Would it be a big deal for you if you didn't wear that green hat when we went out together? I really don't like it." That goes right to the ask and is way better than saying, "You know, I think your green hat looks really stupid on you."

And if that need is a problem for your partner, then you're in the land of the **1, 2, 3 Method**.

So . . . let's go through it now.

11

Step 1

I Hear You Hearing Me

"Feeling understood is the orgasm of intimacy."

Kevin, a middle-aged, twice-divorced man with a teenaged child met a middle-aged divorced woman, Amber, with a teenaged child of her own. They fell in love and *before* they got married they agreed: no more children. He didn't want to become a father at his age and although she was still fertile, she said she didn't want to become a mother again either. So by mutual agreement he got a vasectomy. And *then* they got married.

About a year went by, and Amber was a-sittin' and a-thinkin' the whole time and she realized, *Oh, I do want a child!*

Boom! World War III. He was outraged that she would go back on such a well worked out agreement, ratified by a vasectomy. She was outraged that he would say *no* to what she thought of as the deepest need a woman can possibly feel.

His opening remark, when she told him what she wanted, was, "You've got to be fucking kidding me."

Now if you're a woman, or any human being, you've got to think that's a pretty lousy reception to her saying she's changed her mind. And it is.

But if you're a therapist, always on the lookout for how things go wrong, her very request could understandably be seen as a huge betrayal of a basic foundation of their marital contract, because he'd made it quite clear going in that having more kids was a deal breaker. For him, this was the switcheroo of the century.

Let's face it, though, conflict is based on outrage. That's the whole problem!

Now Kevin felt betrayed and outraged by Amber's very proposal. And Amber felt outraged by his sweeping it off the table and stomping on it. But I've learned in all my years of working with couples that context is everything. Power dynamics run deep and they always have a history.

Amber wasn't a fool. She knew Kevin would flip his wig at her proposal. But then, in a quick return to Fool City, she thought she could muscle past him with a super-strong, super-passionate statement of how inarguable her proposal was. You know, like the guy in the bar hoping to take out the bully with a sucker punch.

So her "proposal" itself was a power move. No wonder Kevin was outraged.

But what about their initial pre-marital understanding? Yes, she'd said *yes*, and if this had been a legal contract it might have stood up in court. But in fact Amber had felt pressured by Kevin. She wanted to marry him, she felt they could be really happy, and under his no-more-kids-or-else pressure she denied her real feelings. She betrayed herself.

So as the words were coming out of Amber's mouth, there were two huge power moves already at work. These guys were primed for outrage.

And so we all are. There wouldn't be conflict if we didn't feel outraged or betrayed or humiliated or deprived or scared or hurt. Because all of these are so profoundly disempowering, there's pretty much nothing else we feel we can do but bust a move that we think will re-empower us.

And that's why we need step 1 of the three-step process so badly.

Step 1: Hearing each other out

What do you do if you find yourself in a minefield? Duh! Don't step on any mines! Yeah, but what if you don't know where the mines are? Well then, of course, you're screwed. *But* here you're lucky because, first of all, you *do* know where the mines are and, second, I'll show you how to avoid them. So it should be a piece of cake, unless you succumb to that part of us that sometimes wants to blow things up. But we're not going to do that now, are we?

Look, this step is important. It'll set the mood for the rest of the process. Do it well, and that'll give you a lot of confidence. Fortunately, it can be pretty easy. If you think of this as a kind of game, one with just a few rules, you'll do really well. Let me lay out the rules, and then we'll talk about them and discuss ways to avoid getting into trouble.

Step 1: *Hearing each other out*

1. Don't take positions. Don't say, "I demand, I must have."

2. Just talk about how you feel and about what's important to you and about the meaning things have for you.

3. No disagreeing or challenging or arguing or judging. There's a place for your needs. This isn't it.

4. Your only goal, your only focus, is to fully understand each other, and to make sure the other person feels understood.

5. Asking questions to deepen your understanding is the best move of all.

Here's what this will accomplish:

- You will lay a groundwork of understanding that is essential for a good, mutually acceptable solution to emerge.

- You will avoid power moves. No stepping on landmines. There are no landmines to step on.

Now I've coached countless couples through this process, and I'll coach you through it too.

The importance of trust

In chapter 9 we talked about anger, and in that chapter I gave you tips for how to deal with your anger effectively. Well, it's never been more important to block out anger than in this first step. People who teach first grade know they have two jobs. One is to teach the kiddies the curriculum—to read sentences, write words, add numbers. The other job, on which the first job depends, is to make the classroom feel like a safe, comfortable, this-is-for-me kind of place.

Well, in the same way, when you're trying to rebuild your marriage by resolving your conflicts, one job is to resolve conflicts, but the other job, on which the first job depends, is building trust. Because look: if you get to an agreement, you have to be able to trust that

- your agreement is based on the truth

- you really *are* in agreement and not in a coerced or half-hearted or misunderstood agreement

- you are going to stay in agreement—at least until you mutually agree to change your agreement

- you will carry out your agreement

Without trust you're in trouble. And *that's* why at every step—like sticking to your agreement that this'll be an anger-free zone—maintaining trust has to be a top priority.

Hearing each other out

When Amber got around to telling Kevin she did want to have the baby she'd previously told him she didn't want to have, here's how she did it: It was late at night. They were in bed and Kevin was tired. Without any preliminaries, Amber said, "Kevin, you need to listen to what I'm about to say. Look, I'm a woman and I guess there are just ways we work that maybe men can't understand. So, yes, I know I said I'd go along with our not having a baby [actually she'd said she fully agreed to it, as she later admitted to me], but the desire to have another child has risen up inside me and I can't do anything about it and I can't deny it. I'm sorry to do this to you, but I need to have another child."

And *that's* when Kevin said, "You've got to be fucking kidding me."

So other than the fact that what Amber said is just one big fat power move, what's wrong with it? You got it! It's not an invitation to the experience of two people hearing each other out. Here's how such an invitation might have gone if Amber had had her wits about her.

First, timing is everything! Amber would have picked her time. A time when they were both relaxed, had plenty of time to listen to each other, and were likely to be in at least an okay mood.

Hint: never discuss anything important close to bedtime. You're tired, which means you aren't going to be bringing your A game to the discussion. And if things get complicated, you'll just be getting more tired.

Then she'd have said something like, "Kev, there's

something I've been wanting to talk over with you. Would now be a good time, or maybe another time?"

This "now or later" move helps Kevin feel he's not being ambushed or cornered. It's empowering, not *dis*empowering. And it's always good to empower your partner, because then they won't have to empower themselves!

So let's say Kevin says, "Yeah, let's talk about it. What's going on?"

"Well, I've got a problem I hope you can help me with." This is always a great move. People want to help us with our problems. It gives them the anticipation of feeling good. "Okay, so we've agreed not to have any children, right? I know that was very important to you." Brilliant! Amber sets the stage by making sure Kevin feels heard and understood. This always makes people feel more receptive.

"Yes . . ." Kevin says with maybe a touch of skepticism.

"So here's the thing. And I'm so afraid to talk to you about this because I know how you feel [a good move because our partners usually want to protect us from what we're afraid of], but the fact is I've been having thoughts of wanting a baby. A lot of thoughts. And I can't seem to make them go away."

Kevin pulls back a bit. "Are you telling me you want to have a baby?" This is okay. It's a clarifying question, and they're always okay.

"Well . . . I'm saying I'm having a lot of thoughts about having a baby and that what I'd thought was over and done with is still alive. I don't want it to be alive. But it is."

"So—"

"I'm not saying I demand to have a baby," Amber

interrupted. "But inside me it's a huge thing, and I do want us to be able to talk about it. I just want us to talk about it."

Kevin was silent for a bit. Then he said, "Well, I guess you can't get pregnant from our talking about it."

And that was how Amber would have knocked on the door and Kevin would have opened it.

"I hear you hearing me"

All right, so what do you do next, if you're like Amber and Kevin and the door is open and you're somehow supposed to "talk about it"?

It's not about listening, though of course listening is important. It's not even about hearing the other person, although that's hugely important too. It's about your both being able to walk away from this discussion *feeling* heard *by* the other.

And every need and feeling and hope and concern of yours—from "I want us to stop hanging out with the Coopers. They're fun but they drink so much and . . . you know" to "I'm concerned that we've been eating too many pickles"—is just the wrapping on a package filled with all kinds of information. And "talking about it" means getting at all this information.

We don't feel heard until the other person has shown us they really understand everything we think and feel about something and what it means to us.

And the thing is, we don't feel charitable toward the other person's needs and the position they're taking *until* we feel they've really heard us.

Let me restate that. Your partner won't feel charitable and open toward *your* needs and toward what *you* want until they feel you've really heard and understood *them*. And not just heard and understood. Also taken it on board as important to them because they're important to you and you're important to them.

Amber has to make Kevin feel that she really understands his need to not have any more children and that that need—his need—actually is important to her because he's important to her.

If you're not taking the time to get to that place, you're getting nowhere.

Questions that make all the difference. Here are some questions you can ask that are non-confrontational and that can create a deep feeling of mutual understanding:

- How important is this to you?

- Why is this important to you?

- What does this mean or represent to you? (In other words, what is it really about beyond the thing itself?)

- What would it mean for us if we did what you're talking about?

- Help me understand how this would work?

- How would we be able to afford this?

- What would you need from me?

- Why has this come up now?

- Tell me what it would be like if we did this?

- What would it mean to you if you couldn't have this?

In certain cases you might ask questions like:

- You know, we've tried this in the past and it hasn't worked; why would this work now? (Tone of voice matters a lot when you ask this question. It has to sound sincere, not as though you are rejecting what the other person has to say.)

- What about the fact that, as we know, I've been opposed to this in the past? (Notice this is not saying you're opposed to it now.)

- I know you, and it's really hard to believe you want this [or can do this]?

- Help me understand how this would even be possible.

None of these questions are challenges or statements of opposition. They're just opportunities for one of you to find out more and for the other to feel better understood. Questions like these are, at heart, deeply respectful.

Not reacting

Now let's face it: you're both going to end up hearing things you don't like:

- Partner: "This is something I've always wanted." And you are thinking, *So how come I've never heard about it before?*

- Partner: "We can't afford it." And you're thinking, *You stingy bastard.*

- Partner: "All I'm talking about here is your getting home from work early on Tuesdays." And you're thinking, *Sure, and drop a hand grenade into my chances of a promotion.*

So what do you do? Well, you just have to remember your goal.

Right now, right here, your immediate goal is creating as much mutual understanding as is humanly possible in an atmosphere of caring. And why? Because the near-term goal is to work out a conflict without any bloodshed, and to come up with a resolution that's the best possible one for both of you so it'll be sustainable. And because your long-term goal is to have a relationship that's liberated from resentment and unresolved conflicts.

So if your partner says, "This is something I've always wanted," and this is the first time you've heard about it, go for understanding. Always go for understanding. Say something like, "Wow, that's interesting. I've never known that. Tell me more. How did your desire for that start?" Show curiosity, not judgment.

Or if your partner says, "We can't afford it," you actually could simply say, "Help me understand that. How did you come to that conclusion?"

And if your partner were to say, "All I'm talking about is

your coming home from work early on Tuesdays," you could say, "What do you mean by 'early'?" Or, "Help me understand how you think I could manage that? You know how Roy is."

You get the point. You're not reacting. You're creating understanding. Maybe your partner's smarter than you think. Maybe they've thought of things you haven't. Maybe they have feelings you haven't considered.

And where does your authenticity come in? It comes in big-time in your staying true to what you need as you work through this process with your partner. Your authenticity comes in your not betraying your own needs by blowing a chance at the best possible mutually satisfactory solution.

And of course you'll both get a chance to be understood in this process. At some point, when one of you has started to feel heard and understood, the other can say, "Is this a good time for me to share some of my thoughts?" The other person will be much more able to hear if they've been asked for permission to listen.

How do we know when we're done understanding each other?

This process of hearing each other out can take between a minute and many hours. I know, that's a long range of possibilities! If it's a small issue with a small potential for conflict, it probably won't take more than a couple of sentences back and forth for the two of you to feel heard. But an issue with a huge potential for changing your life can take hours of sharing spread over months. But no matter what, you're done *not* when you've said all you have to say, but when your partner has shown you they've understood everything about where you're coming from about this issue and vice versa. *Then* you're done.

And what have you accomplished? A lot of important things! You have not made a mess! You feel better about each other! You feel good about being heard! And you have a profound understanding of each other that'll make a huge difference when you go on to the next two steps of coming up with options and coming to a resolution.

"It sounds like you're asking me to be very manipulative"

"Isn't there something very manipulative about this approach?"

Before we move on, I should probably deal with this question, because so many people ask it.

I can understand why you're asking this. I'm talking about a process in which you're not necessarily sharing your immediate feelings, you're putting sugar on how you say things to make them go down well, and you're guided by a goal, not the currents of the moment.

Sounds like manipulation to me!

But let's unpack this.

By manipulation, the first thing that comes to mind for most of us is someone saying whatever needs to be said in order to achieve their own goals. Seducers, sleazy salesmen, con artists, movie villains—they're the ones we think of when we think of manipulative people.

So let's be clear: the bad thing we're talking about with that kind of manipulation is tricking someone to do something they don't want to do and that's bad for them. So *boo* to that kind of manipulation.

But I remember when my kids were little and it was time for them to go to bed. There are so many ways I could say it. "Okay, you gotta go to bed now." A chorus of *nos*. Or, "Listen, you've got to go to bed and I don't want any arguments." A chorus of complaints. My kids never wanted to go to bed. They just wanted to stay up until they fell over from exhaustion.

Then Dr. Spock came to the rescue and I used the offer-a-choice technique. I'd go up to my youngest daughter and say, "Hannah, it's eight o'clock. Do you want me to carry you upstairs like a little baby or piggyback?" Evidently this was an enthralling question. "Ooh! How *do* I want to go to bed?" It would focus her attention and she'd make her choice and up we'd go.

So what was that? Manipulation? Sure, in some sense. It was also, to use a much better word, effectiveness. I had a number of wise and healthful goals. For my child to get a good night's sleep. For bedtime to be a nice experience. To minimize stress and rancor. And all of these goals were just as much in my child's interest as they were in mine.

Well, it's the same here. Nothing here is that evil kind of manipulation where you end up taking something away from your partner. In fact, that's much more likely to happen with the use of power moves. In this step, and in the next two steps, all the things you're both doing are in both of your best interests and will allow both of you the best chance of the best resolution and the best relationship.

But an important question remains to be answered. What if the first step turns out to be hard for both of you? What if things go wrong?

How should you think about that? And what do you do about it?

12

"We tried. We failed. We're doomed!"

"I fall down. I get up. I fall down. I get up."

You *did* try. I know you did. You tried to listen without judging or reacting. You tried to ask questions and gain real, deep understanding, and to answer questions and offer real deep understanding. You tried mightily to be patient.

But then someone said something that set the other person off, and that person said something that set the first person off, and maybe you tried to rein things in, but no matter. Things blew up, fell apart, whatever.

So you think you failed.

Well, no, you *didn't* fail. Not at all. All that happened was that you tried something that was hard for you, something you weren't used to, something that went against some ingrained habits, and you couldn't do it perfectly on one of your early attempts.

So what? There are a million things you do well now—as an individual and as a couple—that you didn't do all that well the first time. Having sex, maybe. Having people over for dinner, perhaps. Buying furniture. Having both sets of parents over at the same time. (Okay, maybe that's a bad example. Some things really do never work!)

But the point is that you've already done better than you've done before. It took longer for things to turn to crap this time than in the past. You're making progress!

And if you didn't fail (and you didn't), you're certainly not doomed. You will do better and better. And much sooner than you suspect right now, you'll be doing plenty good enough.

How to un-screw up

Here's a dirty little secret. A major reason you're not doomed is that you don't have to be perfect! You can get into the occasional tangle and just *un*tangle yourselves. It happens to the best of us. So how do you do it?

This solution should be easy, but let's dig a little deeper into why some people find this hard. There are lots of reasons, all of them common to most couples. Let's look at some of the most common reasons.

The burden of the past

I was working with this one particular couple, Riley Ann and Laura, who had a history of getting tangled in the most horrendously painful conflicts. But I learned a lot from them, and we made a lot of progress. In one session, Riley Ann and Laura were working toward resolving a conflict quite nicely—that is, efficiently and with maximum attention to both people's needs—when out of nowhere things blew up and stayed blown up for the next half hour.

There you were, trying so hard, and you thought
you were doing so well, and suddenly you
found yourself in the bitterness and
chaos of a power struggle.

No problem!

All that needs to happen is for one of you
to say something like, "Sweetie, look at us.
We've fallen off the horse. Let's forget what we
were just saying, rewind the tape, and go back
to where we were talking about . . ."

If you screw up, just don't get caught up in
your screwup. Give yourselves a do-over.
Remember: you're allowed unlimited do-overs.
The only crime is not taking a do-over.
Besides, do-overs are free!

I couldn't even detect what started it. But it all had to do with how, at one point fifteen years earlier, Laura had been callous and insensitive about the health issues Riley Ann's beloved dog was having. The dog eventually died and Riley Ann had never been able to forget Laura's attitude. Laura had never been able to forget about Riley Ann's holding on to this.

Every couple has these land mines in their past. The mistakes one partner made. The times one partner wasn't there for the other. The times one partner really hurt the other. The ways one partner was an unfair burden to the other.

"We got to visit your mother before she died, but we

never got to visit my mother before she died, all because of that stupid business trip you insisted I go on with you."

Or, "I supported you all through medical school, but you weren't supportive at all when I wanted to go back and finish college."

Or, "You always find time to work out, but somehow you never have time to help out in the kitchen."

So what do you do when some terrible hurt from the past makes its fiendish way into your attempts to make things better in the present?

First aid for intrusive bad thoughts and memories. I guess the first thing to say is that since you're not alone in this—in fact, almost every couple in the world is dragging these ancient monsters along with them—there's no point in freaking out. Yeah, it's awful, but it's a kind of universal awfulness, like the fact that we're all going to die, or the fact that we all have a loved one who has been or is really sick.

Second, you can deal with the hurts from the past. There are, I say immodestly, really good sections in two of my books on healing hurts from the past.* So at some point, but not right now, get a hold of one of those books and do the work of healing the past. To make a long story short, healing the hurts from the past is mostly a conversation that begins like this:

"Let's talk about what we need so this no longer stands between us. What can I do to help?"

---

* *Our Love Is Too Good to Feel So Bad* and *I Love You but I Don't Trust You.*

And this conversation will for sure have to include making certain that the person who was hurt gets to hear that their partner understands the depth and nature of the pain their partner went through and takes full responsibility for his or her part in it.

But unless you guys are really stuck there's no need to do this now. Right now you have a conflict to resolve.

So, third, you mutually agree that whatever issues you have from the past are real and important *but* right now you're going to work on dealing with *this* conflict. And if there's some way the past lives in the present (let's say your partner broke promises in the past and you wonder if they can keep their promises now) and this is a concern in your current conflict (let's say you're trying to work out an agreement that'll require some follow-through from your partner), then deal with your concerns without references to the past.

So if your partner says, "Oh, don't worry, I'll follow through," you can just say, "I'm wondering how we can guarantee that." You'll pretty soon discover what so many others have discovered: whether or not you've been let down in the past, there's no real way you can guarantee you won't be let down in the future. Part of keeping your sanity while you're working things out is accepting who you're dealing with. If your partner is easily distracted and has a bad memory and tends to be over-scheduled and *you know that*, then extracting mere promises that they'll carry out some routine or other is kind of pointless.

Just keep the past out of your process of working through a conflict. And if it shows up, show it to the door.

"I thought we agreed: no power moves!"

Well, power moves are going to happen, for sure.

In obvious ways: "Over my dead body." Or, "Are you insane?"

In more subtle ways: "Are you still harping on that?" Or, "I thought you were working on that with your therapist . . ."

In deniable ways: "Are you for real?" ("But I was just asking if you were serious!") Or, "Oh my God!" ("I was just letting out a little feeling burp.")

The easiest, fastest way to deal with this is to just drive on by. That is, you do this:

If the other person makes a power move, try acting as if what you heard was a straightforward, non-power-move reaction. Reply to the content, not the power part.

If your partner says, "Over my dead body!" instead of responding to this as an assertion of the huge resistance it surely seems to be, you instead respond by saying, "Tell me what's particularly challenging for you in what I'm saying." In other words, you take their power move, translate it into a non–power move ("I find what you're saying very challenging"), and you respond to *that* ("I understand. I'm sure you do. Tell me what you find challenging about it"). That's how you do it.

This is both easy and hard to do. It's easy if you can just muster a little insight and charity on the fly while you're feeling stressed. That's all! Easy! But it's hard if that sort of thing is about as easy for you as doing a backflip.

So if it's hard for you to make lemonade out of lemons like that, here's something that *will* be easier for you.

It all depends on you and your partner both wanting to remove the power struggles from your relationship. If there's conflict, you'll work things out based on what's fair, what's reasonable, what's important to the two of you, how important different things are to the two of you, what your options are, and all the other things people who aren't crazy idiots factor in when working things out. Power moves aren't on the list.

So you'll agree: no power moves. And you'll agree that a power move is something that feels to the other like a power move. Which means that if the two of you are chugging along and your partner happens to make a power move, you have two good choices:

1. *You could ignore it.* Why not? If it doesn't make you feel disempowered and doesn't make you feel you need to re-empower yourself, then the easiest thing is to ignore it. Lots of times when I've coached couples through this, one person has said something, and I've turned to the other and said, "Does it bother you when Billy uses that tone of voice?" And the person has said, "Oh, Billy talks like that all the time. It doesn't bother me."

2. *Or you could say,* "Honey, that was a power move. I felt disempowered. Could you just rephrase?" And the agreement has to be: no debate about whether that "really" was a power move or not. Just rephrase.

So if your partner says, "I think that's very selfish of you to ask for that," you ask for a rephrase. If your partner is stuck, you can always say, "Look, this is exactly the time—sorting out this issue—for both of us to put our needs on the table and work out what makes sense to do. There are things I need but there are things you need."

This is where therapists come in handy. Too bad we can't all have one hanging in the closet for emergencies. But one of the things a pop-up therapist would be likely to say is that needs are needs and don't require justification. They just require balancing out with the other person's needs. And of course, all needs are selfish. What's not selfish is the attempt to balance your needs with your partner's needs in a loving, patient, fair way.

Uh-oh! What if you or your partner can't do this?

When I was starting out as a therapist, the one thing I wanted to prevent was a relationship dying when it could have been saved. That was good in that it helped me develop a lot of skills as a couples' therapist. But I've learned that there's another thing that's worth preventing. And that's keeping a relationship on life support when it deserves a peaceful end.

About 90 percent of the time, working to eliminate the power dynamics makes a relationship much better and so saves a great many relationships. But in some cases it helps a couple put their finger on what has made their relationship unfixable.

Here are some signs that you might be in one of the minority of couples that needs actual therapy if your relationship is to have a chance.

- You or your partner can't or won't stop making power moves

- You or your partner can't seem to even understand what a power move is

- No matter how hard you try, you can't work toward hearing and understanding each other without fear or rage or stress

- You or your partner sees something about the essence of the other person as a power move. Here are some examples:

  o When you are just listening, your face seems like a "resting bitch face" to your partner and they can't get over the feeling you're rejecting them

  o You seem angry to your partner when you're just being intense or emphatic

  o Your partner is always telling you to talk or act differently or you're doing that to your partner

  o Your very body posture sets your partner off or vice versa

- Some crucial issue between you seems unfixable no matter how hard you try to work through it

- You realize in the course of working things out that you just don't like one another

Kitchen sink-ing

That's what a teacher of mine, Virginia Satir, one of the pioneers of family therapy, called it. It's when you throw everything but the kitchen sink into your discussion/conflict/

fight. I sometimes call it the "but what abouts." "But what about the time when you . . . ?" "But what about my getting the racing bike I've been wanting?" "But what about your sister's nose job?"

This is a tough one. It can be hard sometimes to tell the difference between an irrelevant distraction and a pertinent issue. "I brought up my sister's nose job because we're not going to be able to go away that weekend. I have to be available to look after her kids."

"Oh. Good point."

But here's the main thing, if you ever want to have any hope of resolving your conflicts. In particular, try to follow these two guidelines:

1. **Keep your focus narrow, and stay focused.**
2. **Never, ever, ever, ever talk about the past.**

Yes, I know! The past is a wonderful place whereby merely making a factual historical statement—"You couldn't break away from work in time to be with me when Isabella was born!"—you can also score a free power move. It's almost irresistible. Well, resist it. I've lived through tens of thousands of these mini-experiments in restorative justice on the fly, and they *never* accomplish anything but generating bad feelings.

Look, right now you two are in the delivery room of the birth of a new phase in the history of your relationship! This is the time and place where you will create a whole new way of resolving your difficulties, to say nothing of getting one big-ass difficulty out of the way right now. This is sacred ground! So why in the world would you pollute this beautiful place of hope with the rotting corpses of your past misdeeds and failures, regardless of whose they are?

Besides, you're not going to agree on who did what. Or on how terrible the crime was. On which one of you was most responsible. On whether the bad-deed doer has already been punished sufficiently. And so on and so on.

So don't even think of it. Stay in the present. And to help with that:

Make sure you're both clear on what it is that you're talking about!

Here are some examples of what I think of as great questions. I'm sure you'll get the point:

- "Wait a minute. Are we talking about where to go this summer for vacation or about how we need to save more for our retirement?"

- "Help me—I'm confused. Is the issue that I need to take on more responsibilities around the house or that I need to get evaluated for adult attention deficit hyperactivity disorder?"

- "Listen, I really want to help and to be here for this. But I'm not sure if we're talking about whether to build an art studio for you in the backyard or whether I know how to show you I love you."

I know you're not robots and this isn't a formal business meeting. But you're not seeking my help for how to be more loosie-goosie. That's gonna be my *next* book. (Just kidding.) Right now you're trying to figure out how to stop kicking the crap out of your relationship while at the same time working through difficult issues. Which, yeah, can feel sort of like learning how to ride a unicycle and play the accordion at the same time.

So if you want to do this, clarity about what the hell you're talking about is really important. I'm not telling you *what* to talk about. I'm just saying, whatever it is, *know* what it is and *stick* to it.

And finally . . .

Be patient. Be forgiving.

Suppose you'd both decided, as complete beginners, to start taking music lessons. One of you on piano, one on guitar, so you could play duets.

How lovely!

But a problem that might come up is that one of you may be making progress faster than the other. Who knew that dorky Dave would have magic fingers for the guitar? Who knew that music-loving Martha had so many thumbs?

Then disappointment leads to frustration, which leads to impatience, which leads to recriminations, which leads to seeming hard-hearted and unforgiving.

And it's easy to fall into feeling this way when working the three-step process.

Be kind to each other. Be patient. This is a new method of conflict resolution that you're learning. But if you help each other along with patience and forgiveness for each other's screwups, then when you fall down you won't stay down.

You'll be able to get right up.

13

Step 2
Creating Options

"It'll mean the world to me and I think it'll heal
everything between us."

I love this story. You'll see why in a moment . . .

A couple came to me because an affair had blown apart their marriage. Erin, almost forty at the time, had just discovered that her husband, Richard, almost thirty years older than she was, had been cheating on her once a week for many months. Erin, as is often the case, found out by complete accident. She'd had no suspicion anything was going on.

By the way, they each had a child from a former marriage.

Don't worry: we haven't gotten to the part I love yet. We're still in the awful part.

Now if you're ready to label Richard a cheating, lying, no good son of a bitch . . . well, that's how Erin felt, for sure. But she could also see, however dimly, that in this particular case the guy, her guy, was truly sorry for the pain he'd caused.

But still. How could Erin go forward? In spite of what she hoped was Richard's genuine contrition, her trust in him was pretty low. And she felt he somehow had to make it up to her for the damage he'd caused. Still, how *do* you make it up to someone for that kind of hurt and humiliation?

So we spent a number of sessions working through the issues of remorse and forgiveness and trust and, of course, options for creating significant reconciliation. But the options were all either empty-sounding promises ("I'll never ever hurt you again") or else very inadequate-feeling commitments ("I'll clean up the kitchen every night for the rest of our lives").

And here's the thing that they faced and that all couples face when there's a conflict. It truly felt to them as though there were no options that would get the job done. Not that they couldn't find such an option, but they felt that such an option didn't exist.

But then one day Erin said quietly, "You know, there is one thing that would make all the difference. I've always wanted another child. It's very important to me. And you've always said, 'No, I'm too old, I've put in my time with child-rearing and now I'm done.' I get that. Well, I love babies, I can afford help, and I can structure my work around my being there for the baby. You won't have to lift a finger. Guilt free! But it'll mean the world to me and I think it'll heal everything between us."

Boom!

And *that's* the part of the story I love. A crazy option flying in out of nowhere, out of the land of things long since ruled impossible.

At first it still seemed impossible. Richard was as reluctant as before. But now there was one big difference. While he was reluctant—understandably—to father a child at his age, he was willing to go through the process of mutual understanding with Erin. And so for a few weeks they sorted through all his concerns, and hers too, because she too had some. But they did so with patience and without judgment.

There were a lot of "what ifs?" and "supposes" on Richard's part. "What if the baby wakes up in the middle of the night crying and you're really tired from work? Will it really be all right with you for me to just lie in bed while you get up and take care of the baby?"

"Absolutely!" Erin said. "That's the deal."

One of Richard's major concerns was his dying before his child grew up. Understandable! They worked this through. But surprisingly an even bigger concern of his was *Erin's* dying first. Who'd've guessed he'd be worried about this? She was only thirty-nine. But they worked this through too.

Erin was an environmental lawyer, and she said, "I'll put it in writing. All of our understandings and solutions. I really get your position and accept it. I have no expectations or hidden agenda beyond the certainty that, knowing you, you'll love your child."

You know, sometimes things in life work out just beautifully. They did so here. Erin got pregnant pretty quickly and delivered a healthy baby boy. She kept her promise to Richard to the word. He didn't have to lift a finger and never faced the slightest recrimination or sense of disappointment for his taking her up on her offer.

But of course Richard was a good guy and it was impossible for him to keep his hands off the child. No one could say he "pitched in"—it wasn't expected—but both Erin and

Richard himself were surprised at how involved he was. And the icing on the cake was that his involvement was purely voluntary. Nothing Richard did was because he was pressured or guilted into doing it. And Erin got exactly what she wanted.

So what just happened?

On being as happy as kings

It's maybe the greatest super-short poem of all time, Robert Louis Stevenson's "Happy Thought." Here's the whole thing:

> *The world is so full of a number of things*
> *I'm sure we should all be as happy as kings.*

Well, the world *is* full of a number of things, so . . .

But let's catch up with ourselves. There you are—understanding each other really well when it comes to all the dimensions of whatever it is you've been struggling over.

- No, you don't hate his mother. It turns out you *like* her. It's just that when she's around you need some space from her. You just need to get away for bits of time.

- No, you're not stingy. No, you don't hate to spend money. It's just that you're worried about the future. Your position is that as long as you have a plan and you're funding it, then beyond that the two of you can go crazy.

So right now you're two steps ahead of where you've been in the past. You have the real and solid understanding you need to move forward. And you are *not* burdened by the hurts and resentments by which power struggles poison attempts to resolve conflict.

So now it's time to deal with a reality I've seen come into play all too many times. The technical term is *premature foreclosure*. It means you're struggling over an impoverished set of options. One of you has glommed onto one thing, the other's glommed onto something else, and biff, pow, bam, you go at it. You've prematurely foreclosed on all the other things in the world that could make you happy as kings.

Look, I don't want to be too pie-in-the-sky. Sometimes choices are really limited. Sometimes tragically so. I get that.

But here's what I have seen over and over in my work. I have all kinds of patients—everyday folks, professionals, business and scientific geniuses, the whole gamut. And I'm telling you that when they come to me with conflicts in their relationships, it doesn't matter if their brains are like a pebble rattling around in a tin can or if they have brains coming out of their ears.

Their set of options is seriously impoverished.

There's something about power dynamics that actually locks people into a narrow set of options. Stubbornness, my mother would have said. And she's partly right. But another big part of it is that what conflict is good at accomplishing is polarization and the wasting of time. It destroys the ability of two people to use their shared intelligence, experience, and creativity to expand the field of options.

Expanding your options is just super practical. A lot of problems with conflict come from people making power moves. But some of it really does come from a too-limited set of options. It easily becomes a vicious circle. Power dynamics limit people's options, and limited options intensify the power dynamics.

So how do you expand your set of options?

"How's this for an idea?"

First, do you notice how I might seem to be putting off the part where you actually come to an agreement? There's a method to my madness. See, if you go through the three steps without getting too fouled up, you'll never have to actually "hammer out" an agreement at all.

With your shared understanding and your expanded set of options plus, in step 3, taking these options for a test drive, you'll find that the best solution for both of you often just appears and you both recognize it. Not always, of course, but even when it doesn't, you're so much closer than you'd been before.

So relax. Breathe. The resolution to your conflict will come. Without your having to force it.

Now in fact there are lots of things you can do to create more options.

You gotta believe. When people are stuck, their very stuckness, their *feeling* of stuckness, carries with it the conviction that there are no alternatives. It's how the mind works. We initially find a limited set of options, we feel stuck, and then the stuck feelings reinforce the sense that we have few options. We're caught in a cycle.

Most couples in an ongoing conflict are caught in that cycle.

But don't believe the propaganda your emotions are putting

out. All the geniuses and masterminds I've worked with who tried to convince me that they'd run out of options . . . it turned out they had more options, and much better ones, than the paltry ones they'd started with.

So start by saying to one another, even if you don't quite believe it, there are plenty of good options out there, better than the ones we have now. There's a 95 percent chance you'll be right, and it'll make all the difference. Just believing there are options will help you find options.

Talk + play = ideas. I don't like the word *brainstorming* because like a lot of people, I find it intimidating. I don't usually have brainstorms. Have you ever seen a newborn kangaroo? Me neither, but I'm guessing it isn't very impressive. Well, neither are most of my ideas when they first come out. More like a brain burp than a brainstorm.

But I know what works, and let me give it to you in the words of one of the only four people to have two Nobel prizes, Linus Pauling:

**"If you want to have good ideas,
you must have many ideas."**

And the way you get to have a lot of ideas is to sort of talk and play at the same time. By play, I mean the two of you are just kicking things around. Going on tangents. Talking about seemingly irrelevant things. I don't really know how to describe it better than this. It's different for every couple. It's the talk of two people who assume there are a lot of options but they just haven't found them yet.

One thing it's *not* is a business meeting where you're

being judged on what you say. That's work. *This* is play. I know something very serious is at stake, but now's the time to get loose. No ideas are off the table. No paths to an idea are off the table. You're just exploring the possibilities in an open-ended conversation in the hopes of shaking loose an idea.

Here's the genius in having many ideas as the road to having good ideas, which leads to the great idea you were looking for:

First, sometimes what happens is like what happens when you're looking for a name for your baby or your dog or cat. You just try out a lot of names—what does it cost you?—and it's *no, no, no,* until suddenly up comes a name out of nowhere and you think, OMG, that's *it*! You get to a point where you think, "We'll never find a name," but you always do.

It's the same here. Yes, you can get a book of baby names that does all the legwork for you, but you can also go online and find sites specifically for folks in a conflict or dilemma and who are looking for better options.

Sure, many of them may be bad ideas, but it doesn't matter. Remember, you're playing. So just get as many ideas as you can from wherever you can—friends, the Web, social media, the crazy parts of your brain, and give each one its due. If you're stuck because one of you says we can't afford to retire to Carmel and the other says I don't want to retire to Akron, Ohio, then if one of you comes up with, "Hey, what about Albania!"—well, check it out. Who knows? Ten minutes looking into it might reveal that it's a startlingly good alternative for you!

Second, tweak the non-good ideas to see if you can *make* them good. Okay, maybe retiring to Albania turns out to be a ridiculous idea, but maybe this is just a *clue*. Maybe Albania is a horrible idea but retiring abroad—which you had never taken seriously as a possibility—seems like something worth considering. Then you start hearing about Uruguay. And the more you check that out, the more there is to like about it. Turns out, it has everything you like, and it's affordable.

When you explore and expand your options—with an exploratory and expanded mind—you often find that discarded ideas turn out to be great. The house we lived in in Boston for thirty-nine years (!) was one we'd rejected but then reconsidered on the advice of a friend.

The point is that you don't just throw out an idea that turns out to be not good. It may be a major clue. Remember: a lobster is a terrible idea: it's just an ugly giant underwater bug. But baked and stuffed and with melted butter on the side, it's one of the best ideas in the world.

And there's a good way to turn not-good ideas into great ideas . . .

Third, use sentences that start with opening-up phrases like these:

- "You might think this is crazy but . . ."
- "Hey, what if . . . ?"
- "You know, hear me out before you say *no*, but . . ."
- "This just came into my head and I don't know what to make of it, but . . ."
- "This is way out there, but . . ."

- "You know what I just read? It may not apply to us, but . . ."
- And especially, "What if . . . ?"

If there were an option generator, it would be phrases like these that can be openers for what has seemed like a closed world.

Erin did this with what, for Richard, was the bad idea of their having a baby. What she proposed was, in a way, crazy. She was saying, *Yeah, we're married, but we won't have a baby. I'll have a baby, and you'll just be involved with it as much or as little as you want.*

This is not your typical scenario! And that's the whole point! You're stuck in a small box of options, so you have to break out. Almost anything you come up with will, at first, seem strange and unfamiliar if not stupid. For example, although women around the world have used tampons for thousands of years, in the United States tampons were introduced a generation after the mass manufacture of sanitary napkins around 1900. Initially for millions of women tampons seemed like a terrible idea. Until, for a huge proportion of them, it started looking like a great idea.

Great ideas are often just ideas that seem bad because they are unfamiliar. You have to work to find the life in the possibilities around you.

Fourth, question assumptions. This happens often: I'm working with a couple. They're sure they're stuck between a rock and a hard place. And although they bitterly disagree with each other, they work their asses off to convince me that they've ransacked heaven and earth looking for further options and there just aren't any. So I ask a few questions and discover that there are assumptions they're making that are blinding them to a world of possibilities.

Here's an example from my own life where I was stuck for quite a while. I was just starting out as a clinician and was seeing patients in our apartment. There was no separate room for seeing patients, however. Just the living room, our bedroom, the children's bedroom, and a tiny utility room. The living room was nice, but my husband and kids would be imprisoned in their rooms while I was seeing patients. The bedrooms had . . . beds. We were stuck.

Now in those days our bed was right on the floor. Just a four-inch-thick latex foam mattress on a frame without legs. Perfect if your greatest fear in life was falling out of bed.

Then one day, my wonderful husband, not usually the most practical man in the world, was looking at the bed and said, "You know, we don't need that frame under the mattress. We could just put the mattress right on the floor."

"And . . . ?" I asked.

"And . . . well, then if you just flipped the mattress in half you have a kind of sofa . . ."

If it'd been a snake it would've bitten me! I'd been making the assumption that mattress and frame went together like a scoop of ice cream and a cone. I mean, you don't just dump a scoop of ice cream into someone's hand!

But my husband saw that while mattress + frame = bed, mattress = bed too, at least if you were a very young couple with very young children.

And then we'd get up in the morning, flip the mattress in half, toss a coverlet and a few throw pillows on it, and voila!

In a matter of seconds a bedroom was transformed into an office! All because we got rid of an assumption.

Here's another example of how tossing out assumptions broke the logjam when it came to creating options:

Martin and Elly really struggled over where to go on vacation. They both had three weeks' vacation a year, but it wasn't always easy to make it the same three weeks and far worse they were worlds apart on where to go. A vacation that was joy for one was misery for another.

I suggested separate vacations.

"No! Impossible!" they said. They were pretty sure that would either kill their marriage or be a sign it was dead already.

"Really? Why?" I said.

They repeated what they'd said about killing and dying. "How do you know that?" I asked.

"Well," they sputtered, "that's what people do who are on the outs with each other."

"How do you know?" I asked again. "How do you know there aren't couples who are very close but who help keep their relationship vital by going on separate vacations? That way, *both* people get a really good vacation, both people get a chance to start missing each other, plus a huge bone of contention is taken out of the relationship. How is that bad?"

Well, this was still too big a pill for them to swallow. But they talked and we talked and pretty soon it seemed worth trying for one set of vacations at least. I asked them, "Do you think your relationship is so fragile it won't survive your taking separate vacations just once? Because if it's a bad idea for you, you never have to do it again. But if it's a good idea, it'll be transformative."

They took a shot. It did feel weird, they both said. But they also liked it. How wonderful to finally have a vacation where both came back happy and refreshed!

So what did I do that you can do? I took them through a process:

Me: *What's the problem?*

M&E: The problem is we want different kinds of vacations.

Me: *What's the* real *problem?*

M&E: We can't both take the vacation we want.

Me: *How do you know that's true? What if it's not? How could the opposite be true?*

M&E: Well, to do that, we'd have to take separate vacations. A couple just can't do that!

Me: *Again, how do you know that's true? What if it's not? How could the opposite be true?*

M&E: Well . . . if we did that, people would think . . .

Me: *But what would you think? What would your experience be?*

M&E: I . . . I guess we'd each have a really good vacation.

That's it. There's no magic formula for blowing up your assumptions, particularly the ones that are holding you back. It's all just about finding the assumption and challenging the assumption.

Here's another example: Maura and Carina were afraid

they were drifting apart. They certainly didn't think they had much they both liked to do together, besides grocery shopping. In fact, they had, they thought, *no* options. Another source of conflict was that Maura was often gone for a few hours on Saturdays or Sundays playing golf, which Carina said she hated. Almost as much as they both hated my seemingly-obvious idea that they play golf together.

"Really? What's wrong with that idea?" I asked.

Because Carina was a klutz, and she hated golf, and Maura would hate playing with a wretched beginner with a 40 handicap. Assumptions, assumptions, assumptions. Remember (and this is important): assumptions seduce us by seeming to be based on evidence (though it's evidence that's never been examined) or common sense (though it's common sense that's never been challenged). It's interesting how people sometimes know their own lives least well.

Turns out that Carina didn't really hate golf; she just hated the way the game took Maura away from her. Nor was she a klutz out on the course the way she was in the kitchen. Nor did Maura turn out to hate playing with a beginner. They liked hanging out on the course with playing golf as a kind of fun distraction.

Problem solved.

Push back boundaries

Here's another way to think about how to create new options. We all live—all of us—in worlds where we think this *is* possible and that is *not* possible. At least for us. "Oh, I could never do that."

Look, I'm not saying that all things are possible. I could never have played right tackle for the New York Giants. I'm just saying that without any kind of woo-woo optimism it's perfectly reasonable to say that vastly *more* things are possible for most of us than any of us imagine.

So when you're playing around with coming up with new options, don't rule anything out because you think it's outside the bounds of possibility. Yes, there is such a thing as common sense, and it's right a lot of the time. But there are no rules.

Take Luke and Minnie. Luke made a ton of money, but his wife, Minnie, didn't have any money of her own. Luke would pay for whatever Minnie needed or wanted, but it still left her feeling in the position of begging for everything.

"But you're not begging!" he'd say. "Whenever you need money I transfer some over to your account or you just use our credit card. And I never complain . . ."

"You do complain," Minnie'd say. "'Why'd you buy this? Why'd you spend so much on that?' You're always . . . supervising how I spend my money, and I don't . . ."

"I'm not supervising," he'd say. "Look, it's our money, and I just need to know where our money is going. I already know where the money I spend is going—why shouldn't I know about the money you spend?"

"Because you make me feel like a child!" she'd yell.

And Luke would say, "No one can make anyone feel anything." And their attempt to work things out would break down completely.

A brief power-move analysis. Let's digress for just a sec to see who made the first power move. Was it Minnie when she said that her asking him for money made her feel as though she were begging? No. That's just information, pure and simple. X makes me feel Y.* When you just state how something makes you feel, that's really important information you both need to be able to work out a conflict. It's saying that something matters and describing the way in which it matters. And very often when you know the way something matters for yourself or the other person, you're halfway to finding a solution: "Oh! So it's the part of the arrangement that makes you feel like you're begging that bothers you. If we could work out something so you didn't feel like you were begging, then it'd be okay. Yes?"

So was it when Luke said, "But you're not begging"? Yes! You can't tell someone they don't feel the way they feel! Here you have the guy with all the money and a louder, deeper voice calling foul on this woman for saying this is how she feels. No! You can't do that. There is only one reply to someone saying how they feel: "I'm sorry you feel that way. What can I do to help?"

Now did Luke have good intentions? Sure! He genuinely didn't want her to feel as though she were begging.

But he went down a pathway that most of us go down at

---

* What about the often-promulgated idea that no one can make you feel anything? Well! It depends. If my five-year-old grandson calls me a poo-poo head, I certainly do not have to feel deeply wounded. On the other hand, suppose that my fifth-grade teacher, as a punishment, made me stand in front of the class and say, "I'm a stupid poo-poo head." Could anyone legitimately say it was my choice to let myself feel horribly humiliated? And what if my boss told everyone at an important meeting that I was a disgraceful idiot? Can we really choose not to be humiliated when that's what's actually happening?

some point during these conflicts. Our partner's feelings are inconvenient for us. Let's say, to let my imagination run wild, that I cheated on my husband five years ago. He finds out. He's *very* upset. And he starts ranting about his terrible painful feelings.

How inconvenient for me! So I say, "But it was just a fling. He didn't mean anything to me. You're making a big deal about nothing."

My good intentions would be for my words to X out his feelings. And he'd say, "Oh, it's nothing? What a silly goose I've been to have gotten so upset. I'm so sorry! Come here—let me give you a big hug." I don't know—you tell me: Has that ever worked in the entire history of the world?

But you remember: good intentions don't count for anything here. I mean, yes, they're better than bad intentions! But if you've swept my feelings and needs off the table, I'm not going to care what your intentions are.

Okay, back to the issue of pushing back boundaries.

"*I would never do that.*" One problem Luke and Minnie had was that they were caught within a sense of false boundaries. Luke had his money, he felt he was (and he really was) generous with it, but it was, in his mind, his money. Minnie could have all she needed and wanted—which for Luke meant he was meeting the requirements for being a good and generous spouse—but it was his money.

Sometimes I meet with the people I see in couples' therapy separately. One day I met with Luke to brainstorm solutions. "Minnie asks you for money when she needs it—"

"And I give it to her," Luke said, interrupting me.

"Yes, and it makes her feel like she's begging. And that bothers her. So I have a solution. Give her a salary. Figure out what's fair and reasonable to cover all her expenditures— all the things she spends money on, whether for herself or the household. Within the limits of your budget. Arrange to have it deposited in her checking account on a monthly basis. You'll never have to talk about money again."

He leaped at the idea . . . in order to tear its throat out. "No. No! Minnie's my wife, not my employee. She's not on my payroll. Why can't she just be happy with my giving her money she needs when she asks for it?"

And it was clear why this arrangement was important to Luke. Because . . . control. With my salary idea Luke would lose a lot of control. However generous he was, by Minnie having to ask for money, and Luke being in the position of being able to ask what the money was for, he had control. And that meant Minnie was infantilized.

"And besides," Luke said, "Minnie would still think it was begging."

"Wanna bet?" I asked. I had no idea, actually, but I was betting he was wrong.

(Quick digression. Some people have said, "Oooh, I don't like the word *salary*. *Gift* is better. An annual gift. And my response is, of course, fine, whatever. Whatever word makes it work. Whatever word sells the solution to Minnie and Luke. *Gift* may sound more noble and spiritual. But *salary* may sound more respectful and businesslike. Because no matter what the word, the solution is the same. And since we're talking about breaking down barriers, the easiest barrier to break is mere words. A rose by any other name . . .)

The most hopeful thing I know of in life

I've seen it over and over again: People and couples are very stuck and then somehow—*boom!*—they come unstuck. It's the most hopeful thing I know of in life. People change. And then lives change.

Well, there we were, stuck with Luke's feeling threatened by the loss of control implied by not making Minnie ask for the money she needed. So I asked him, "Okay, how much money, approximately, do you give Minnie a year for all the things she spends money on."

"Oh!" he said, as if I'd asked him one of the great math problems of the ages. But he started thinking about it and finally came up with a number.

"And some of that is stuff she spends on herself and some she spends on the house, right?" I asked.

"Yeah. It includes food shopping and everything for the house."

"So what bothers you: the amount she spends, or the way she spends it?" I asked.

And there's the answer to your mystery. A simple question broke the back of his resistance. Who knows why that particular question did the trick, but Luke certainly had a revelation. The total amount Minnie spent didn't bother him. And so what did he care how she spent that amount? Framing it this way enabled Luke to understand what was causing the logjam, and all it took was the right question.

But I have a solution to the mystery.

It's true you will never know why and how this or that question or suggestion broke—or will break—the logjam.

Any more than you can know in advance which one of your mighty efforts will allow you to finally unscrew the spaghetti-sauce jar—the fifth? The seventeenth? Who can ever say?

But with all that uncertainty there's something we *can* know for sure. Look at what I did with Luke. We had a conversation. I made sure Luke felt heard. I didn't use any power moves. I asked questions. I did everything a human being can do to promote openness rather than to provoke resistance. *That's* how people become unstuck and open themselves up to new options. And that's all you have to do.

Do everything you can to promote openness rather than to provoke resistance. And you'll unlock everything you need to break the impasse and end the conflict.

That's really what everything in this book is about.

So . . . how do I actually generate new options?

If you're thinking I'm trying to slide one by you, well, no, of course not. I'll come right out and say it. There's no actual *formula* for producing new and better options. No option-o-matic. No app like the ones that will tell you the perfect breed of dog for you. That is, you can't make it happen the way you can make a cake happen if you get all the right ingredients together and combine them in the right way. If you do that, a cake is *inevitable*. But if you do what I've been talking about here in this chapter, all I can claim is that new and better options are likely to emerge, and they're more likely to emerge this way than any other way.

And this is how people actually come up with options. It's what people who come up with options do. So how do you come up with options? Do these things:

- **Know that there are great options out there, even if you've felt stuck for a long time.**

- **Fool around with all kinds of possibilities.**

- **Generate as many options, good and bad, as you can.**

- **Find ways to make poor-seeming options better.**

- **Use the opening-up phrases I listed earlier.**

- **Question all your assumptions.**

- **Push back boundaries.**

- **Promote openness.**

The only thing I'd add is please be patient. Finding new options is like finding anything. And finding has its own special characteristic, whether you're trying to find your car keys or a cure for cancer. Finding is this weird thing where you can spend what feels like forever making no progress at all—getting more and more discouraged by the day—and then suddenly *boom!* You've found it. No car keys, no car keys, no car keys . . . and then suddenly, in the last place you'd have thought to look, there they are.

So finding is the opposite of building or growing something. Building is slow and gradual—whether it's a novel, a business, a skill . . . you name it. When you build you can see progress, however slow it might feel. When it comes to finding something, it will feel like no progress at all until the moment of final victory. Imagine trying to write a novel, and for a whole year you can't write a single word. Then suddenly in one brief moment on day 379, *blurp* out comes your entire novel!

Couldn't happen. But it happens all the time in the realm of finding stuff.

Including finding options that'll change your life.

14

Step 3

Coming Together at Last

*"It's the two of us against the world,
and a cold hard world it is."*

Guess what? *You're at the last step!*

Think about what you've accomplished! You've gone through some tough rounds of talking about difficult stuff without . . . Well, okay, *not* without falling back into your old power dynamics, but I'm betting that you've done much better than you've done before and gotten much further. And so the progress you've made toward eliminating the power moves from your relationship is a very big deal.

And you've gone through the first two steps of the **1, 2, 3 Method**. How far has that taken you in your ability to harmoniously and productively work through your conflicts?

Well, instead of banging heads, you understand each other about the issue you've been struggling over.

You know what's important to each other and why it's important.

You have the hope that comes with having new and better options.

And you feel better about each other. You're less beloved enemies and more beloved friends. You now know that your partner can listen to you and hear what you have to say and understand it and empathize with you.

One more thing. You may also have found—to your great surprise—that you've *already* resolved your conflict. I'm not surprised. Happens all the time. Why?

Because resolving conflict is way easier than most of us think. And now you may be in a position to appreciate that. It can seem pretty unbelievable. Some mutual understanding, some better options at your disposal, and suddenly an obviously good choice for both of you just . . . appears.

And if not, no problem. You're still in a much better place when it comes to conflict in your relationship, and you haven't even gotten to the "So what are we actually going to do?" point yet.

So let's get there.

"Okay, so what if . . . ?"

Here you are, understanding each other better than ever, and, just as important, feeling understood by each other. So how then do you get to the point where you can agree on the option that's best for both of you?

Well, you imagine you're not adversaries. Not on opposite sides. That it's not the case that your partner is working to oppose you, nor are you working to oppose your partner. At least you're going to act as if he isn't.

What's more, somewhere out there—in fact sitting right

in front of you—is an option that's plenty good enough for both of you. And that phrase "good enough" is key. It may not be best for you, or best for your partner either, but it is something you could both totally live with quite contentedly.

And that's what you have to explore together: not "Do I love this?" not "Is this what I've been dreaming of?" but . . .

Explore the possibility that each of you will be okay with this option.

What we're talking about is *livability*.

So you need to think about *exploring* the options as if you were buying a house and you had a few good candidates to choose from, perhaps none of them ideal. You go through each option with a "what if?" approach:

- What if we were going to go ahead with this option?

- What would it feel like?

- Would we each be able to get used to it?

- Would our basic needs be met?

- Is there any important unmet need that we could address in some other way?

- What is our worst fear about this option, and how likely is it that this fear will come to pass?

- Are the main problems with the option transitional (stuff that we'll get over soon) or are they likely to be long term?

- Are the problems either of us find with this option easily or cheaply fixable?

I just saw a piece online about people's dads who'd said they never wanted a cat. "Over my dead body!" they said. Well, they got a cat, in some cases more than one, and now these dads love the cats. I'm not saying you should get a cat! But I am saying that it's really important to explore what it would be like to live with an option before you say *no*.

And to look at it from the point of view of livability, not lovability.

Then what you do is take the time to sit with each option and talk about it as if it were a house or apartment you were seriously considering. Imagine spending an hour or two wandering through that house, standing for a while in this room or that, sitting on the stairs leading to the bedrooms, lying on the grass in the backyard.

Actively checking it out too. You're both going into the master bath or the kitchen to see what it would be like for you both to maneuver there.

And problem solving. Suppose the layout were different from what you were used to. Suppose the kids' bedrooms would now be right next to yours—how would that feel?

Of course you could actually do this with a house if your conflict were about which house to buy. But you could do this with any set of options, from what to do with your mother if she were old and ill to what kind of schooling to give your soon-to-be six-year-old.

The important thing is what it feels like.

The key thing is that you are exploring this option together as partners, not as people trying to sell the other toward or away from any particular option.

And it feels like you are exploring something *together*. You're not trying to prove anything to each other. You're not trying to score debating points. You're just trying to really get a good sense of what it would be like to live out that option. To live in it. To take it for a test drive. To try it on.

It's okay if you point out concerns: "What do we do if your mother keeps calling us up any time of the day or night to help her with stuff?" It's not okay to talk as if you've found a fatal flaw: "If we go with this your mother's just going to be calling us all day and all night."

It's a subtle distinction, maybe, in real life. But in principle the distinction is huge and clear. "I'm your ally in figuring this out" versus "I'm right and you're wrong." Exploring an option with an open mind commits you to nothing.

What if we mess up playing "what if"?

The goal of all this isn't to make you into brand-new perfect people. If one of you tends to interrupt, that'll probably still go on, though hopefully not as much. If one of you gets over-dramatic, that'll happen too, but maybe not as often and not with as much negativity.

The goal is to be able to do this.

That's it! Not to do it perfectly or even very well. Just to do it. To get through it. To explore options without *getting stuck* in the old patterns of pushing and pulling on one another and *with being able to make use* of the new patterns of using your ability to understand each other and putting that first.

And in that spirit, what if you mess up? So you or your partner say something negative or judgmental! So what? Since your goal is just to be able to do this, that means all you have to do is not get stuck. So . . .

Just don't get stuck.

How do you accomplish this? The difference between the two of you now and the two of you before is that before you didn't know you were stuck. You thought your partner was impossible. Now you know that you were both victims of a terrible method. And so now you just stop, pause, one of you says, "Well, *that* wasn't how we were wanting to do this," and the other agrees, and you pick up where you left off.

Magic!

So how does this help us end our conflict?

The question everyone wants the answer to is how this process ends the conflict when you've started out with two people radically polarized and using a lot of "over my dead body" kind of language.

Just think about the ingredients you've added into the mixture. Besides mutual understanding and better options and the blessed absence of power moves, you now have experienced and explored your options. You tried them on and sized them up.

So how does this work? Most of the time there simply is a better option and once you clear away all the crap and confusion and conflict and misunderstanding, there it is staring you in the face. And then the only obstacle—if it was an option that the other person had wanted from the beginning—is being able to say, "I was wrong. You are right. This is our best choice."

It's funny how often pride is the final obstacle.

In fact, that *is* how this process works. Find the obstacle and overcome it. Except that now you are working together as a team to deal with the obstacles.

Pride. So let's say that pride is indeed the obstacle. Here you have Doug and Jessie who've struggled mightily over the best course of action for dealing with their six-year-old son's ADHD. Now it's easy for an outsider to say to either of them, hey, take one for the team, swallow your pride: the docs seem to be in agreement, so go along with it.

But you can't be glib with deep feelings. Doug had long felt that some form of drug therapy, in spite of the possible side effects, could work miracles. And that was connected to his wanting to feel like the hero to his family, the guy who found hope for their kid and made it happen. Jessie wanted to be the good mom and just couldn't bring herself to go along with what she saw as the risks of giving psychiatric drugs to a six-year-old.

For each of them, saying "You were right" meant conceding "I was trying to take our son down a bad path."

So here's how to deal with pride. Let's say that as they consult experts, the evidence starts pointing in one direction. Both Doug and Jessie have to admit that. Well, you deal with pride by separating out two completely different issues. One issue is what we're going to do. The other issue is who was right.

And so you say, "Look, we said we'd see what the specialists had to say, and there seems to be a consensus, though there are a couple of dissenters. And we agreed, I think, that we'd go with the consensus. I mean, these are real experts. We have every reason to trust them. Besides, as they themselves said, we can monitor things and change what we're doing as we go along. *So that's what we'll do.* As for who's right, well, who knows? Years from now research might prove the experts of today were wrong. Who knows? Maybe we'll both turn out to be wrong. And, hey, maybe it'll turn out we're both right—both methods work equally well. *But we're not in this to be declared right.* We're in this to come up with a good course of action, and the good thing about this plan is that we'll have feedback and we can make changes as we go along."

It's not about who's right.

It's about what you are going to do.

It's not all or nothing. If you've expanded your range of options, then you've probably added in the possibility of taking smaller steps. Whatever choice you're facing, you can make a smaller choice to learn more about making the bigger choice. That's really what Doug and Jessie did. They chose an option that enabled them to get information over a three-month period, after which they could take another look at where things stood. Was their boy doing better? Were there significant negative side effects?

We do this all the time. This is why people move in together before getting married, and have sex before getting married, and that's why these are great ideas. You can foster a dog before adopting a dog. My husband and I got a temporary rental in Los Angeles before making a long-term commitment to move here.

There is actually a way you can do this with any issue you're having conflict over. Suppose the conflict that's tearing you apart is where the two of you are going to be buried. You'd like to spend the rest of eternity lying next to each other. You agree on that. But because of religious issues, one of you can't be buried in the cemetery of the other's religion, and your partner says, "Okay, so we won't be buried next to one another." You could kill him!

But you can, in a way, take these alternatives for a test drive. You can agree that for July you'll both live with the idea that you're going to have burial plots next to one another in a non-denominational cemetery. You'll live with the thought that that's what's going to be. Then for August you'll live with the thought that you'll each be buried in the cemetery you most prefer to be buried in. You'll live with the thought that *that's* what's going to be.

Usually, at the end of two months like this, things have changed. And the kind of change you'll see is important, because we see it happening regardless of the situation. And what is this change? Believe it or not, what you get from really living with an open mind and heart with your options is a new level of wisdom.

Wisdom. It's a fact that we can get used to anything. Not only that, but we can come to embrace what we previously thought was the worst catastrophe in the world. Take a couple who've just found out they're going to have a baby. Hooray! Suddenly, as is the case with all expectant parents, they go berserk about any possible threat to the health and well-being of the developing baby. If the mother looks cross-eyed at a cocktail, she feels guilty for a week. They say, "As long as he or she is healthy . . . ," and can't imagine anything worse than having a child who is developmentally disabled.

But guess what? Some kids *are* born developmentally disabled. But that's not the biggest surprise. The biggest surprise is what happens to the parents. The parents who thought this would be a horrible disaster discover that they love this child, that she brings the family together, and that she feels irreplaceable.

And this kind of thing happens across the board.

So in the same way, what feels now like the catastrophe of not being able to lie in the ground next to one another, or to not lie in a cemetery of your faith, or—to extend the list—to never have a child, or to never visit Greece, or to never have a cabin in the mountains, or to *have* a cabin in the mountains, or whatever it is you're struggling over, *over time it just won't seem like a such a big deal.*

That's wisdom: bringing the perspective you will have someday into the present.

And that usually means taking a chill pill when it comes

to the pressure you feel to have this conflict come out exactly the way you want.

Attitudes, attitudes. Let me tell you about one of the most gripping moments in my lifetime as a therapist. I was working with a woman we'll call Julia and her adult son. I was seeing them separately.

Julia'd had a lot of sad and bad things happen to her. She was an alcoholic. She'd had a kitchen accident in which a turkey had dropped into a pot of super-hot grease, which splashed onto her face, disfiguring her. She'd been divorced. One night when she'd gotten drunk she brought a stranger home and had sex with him in front of her son.

But none of these was the very worst thing that happened to her, according to Julia herself. The very worst thing, she said, was the week when she came to realize that all her beliefs were just attitudes. What she meant was that all the things she thought were true—all her social, political, economic beliefs—were little more than fashion statements. That for her whole life she'd been saying things she meant and believed passionately, as if they were founded on the most solid rock, when in fact they were based on how she felt to be saying those things. She "believed" that it was important to care for the environment, but she realized that just amounted to a cultural fashion, a verbal scarf tossed elegantly over her shoulder. Something to say. But without any depth of meaning for her.

What in the world does this have to do with resolving conflict after you've explored all your options?

It's about the question of how solid the things are that we hold on to so tightly. Or, on the other hand, how easily they could vanish into nothing. And how sad it would be to fight for something, engage in a bitter, costly struggle with your partner over something that you could all too easily cease to care about.

Now at this point in the process, your tight hold on what you originally wanted may have loosened already. That happens as we go through the process of understanding each other better and feeling better understood ourselves, as well as developing better options.

But there's something else you should know. The idea that "communication is the answer" when it comes to couples in trouble is so misleading. You've been communicating the whole time you've been in a relationship! And it's gotten you into a lot of trouble! But you're about to learn something cool.

When people who disagree about something discuss their issue—whatever the issue, whoever the people—would you guess that generally brings about harmony, reconciliation, and something closer to agreement?

Nope, talking things out (so to speak) too often leaves people feeling more dug in, more committed to their original position, and with the two people (or two groups) more polarized. I wish it weren't this way, but it is.

Now of course lots of times people talk and quickly come to an agreement. But that's when they weren't far apart to begin with or—in the early stages of a relationship—when they didn't feel safe enough to let out what they really wanted and how much they really wanted it. When there's a significant distance and people just "talk," power moves take hold and polarization prevails.

Now here's the thing. One result of this is that as a conflict proceeds—hour after hour or year after year—we come to feel more and more deeply and authentically that we really, truly, more than anything want whatever it is that we're struggling over. Usually we struggle for something because we want it. But pretty soon *we find we're wanting something because we're struggling for it.*

What I'm saying is that this passion of wanting is so often as illusory as all those beliefs of Julia's that turned out, she realized, to be mere attitudes. This passion of wanting and certitude of need is just something that grows out of the process of being opposed. Of feeling so strongly that the survival of the self requires us to say *yes* when someone else says *no* to us.

What we think we care about so much—that ache of caring itself!—is just a spinoff from someone denying our desire. And that's understandable, because the things we desire: they *are* the self. But if you can question whether—and how deeply—you want something, whether it's a real need or merely a need artificially inflated by the endless conflict the two of you have gone through, then you might be amazed at the needs you can let go of, at the flexibility you can find.

And let me ask you: why are you here? *Here?* At this place, in this moment, reading this book? It's because you want to rescue your relationship from the terrible meat grinder that's been chewing it to bits in power struggles.

And let's say, worst-case scenario, that with all the goodwill and patience and understanding in the world, in spite of having done everything right, at this point the two of you are still far apart when it comes to what you each want.

Uh-oh. Now what?

Conflict for grown-ups

So then here you are, but you are *not* back at the beginning. Now, instead you feel very differently toward one another. It's just that nonetheless one of you wants another child and the other doesn't. One of you thinks it's a good idea for you to quit your job and start that business and the other doesn't. One of you wants to buy that really expensive dream house you both love, and the other says, *No, we just can't afford it*. One of you thinks it's okay to joke about your flabby belly and the other doesn't.

There are certain key questions that can help you move to a resolution quicker than you might think.

Does it really matter which decision you make? Let me be clear what this question is asking. Justin and Lois both work. The youngest of their two sons will be going into pre-K in a couple of months. Lois has been iffy about having another child, but she's always wanted a daughter and now she strongly feels she wants to have one more child—son or daughter—and that'll be that, signed in blood. Justin thinks of having another child as a big burden on both of them in time, money, and emotional energy.

Each of them feels strongly about what they want, as they're entitled to do. But when I asked them *if there was a cost to making the wrong decision*, they both said something interesting. No, they each said, actually we can't make a wrong decision, just a decision one of us wouldn't prefer.

"So," says me, "since you've been at loggerheads for quite a while, and you've suffered a lot in the past from how you've dealt with conflict, and you've been great about how you've worked through this, why not . . . why not just flip a coin? You know, Mother Nature's way?"

They responded like a five-year-old confronting his first Brussels sprout. Making the life of a child rest on the flip of a coin!?

I said, "Look, I'm not being flippant (sorry for the pun!). But just look at where you are. You're not in agreement. There's no path to agreement. You can't split the difference and have half of a child. No expert can advise you. You've already talked this to death. You both say you'll be able to live with the outcome one way or the other."

After a pause, deadly serious Lois turned to Justin and said, "It can't be a coin. But something . . ."

"How about this as a solution?" I said. "I'll write *baby* on two slips of paper and *no baby* on two others. I'll put the slips in my hat and mix them up. You'll each draw one slip. If they're different, you'll put them back, I'll mix them up again, and you'll each draw one out again. And we'll do that until both of your slips match. We'll take that as your being in agreement. Okay?"

We talked a bit more and we all agreed that they'd come back the following week and if they still felt the same way, they'd go along with my solution.

And that's what happened. The following week, Justin and Lois were looking down at two slips of paper marked *baby*. Justin was pale, but he said, "Well, it looks like we're in agreement."

If either way is okay, except for someone not getting what they want, why not just break the logjam by tossing a coin or something like that?

Is there potentially a big cost to making the wrong decision? To be clear, what I mean by "big cost" isn't just a sum of money. It's a possible setback to your finances, your career, your health, your mental health, your relationship that could significantly torpedo your life. I'm talking about losses you can't recoup. Trains you'll miss that you can never get back on.

And my advice here is quite simple.

When a lot's at stake, you must consult two experts.

Not friends! I know. You love your friends. I love your friends too. But I've seen it over and over again, and I'm sorry to have to say this. From my vantage point as a couples' therapist, a friend is too often a person who is overconfident based on his or her limited experience. That's the fact, Jack.

So by all means turn to your friends for support and help. But as far as advice is concerned? That's where you want a real expert. Someone who is familiar with the kind of thing you're struggling over not just on the basis of their personal experience but on the basis of their close knowledge of many people's experiences. We're used to doing this when it comes to medical and legal matters, to some degree anyway, but we too often don't do this in other areas where there's a lot at stake and significant risk.

Chris and Max had been together for ten years and had an adopted ten-year-old son. There'd always been a lot of painful struggle—all kinds of unnerving or humiliating power moves—whenever they got into a serious disagreement, but this was the big one. Chris earned a decent living as a software engineer. Max loved his job teaching third graders in a private school.

But Chris was starting to hate his work more and more. What he really wanted to do was open a restaurant. Everyone said he was a great cook and he'd actually studied cooking in Paris for a couple of summers. So Chris got a lot of encouragement from their friends for his idea of opening a restaurant. They even offered to put money in, although the amounts they talked about never added up to more than a small fraction of what Chris would need. It's just that Chris was filled with notions of positive thinking and visualizing success and the idea that if you want something badly enough and work hard enough your dream will come true.

Max knew, though, and Chris did too, that they'd have to put up all their savings as well as take out a mortgage on their house to get a running start on the restaurant. When Max resisted the idea, Chris produced a business plan! With numbers! Max didn't know enough to argue with the numbers.

He just knew enough to be scared to death. They could lose everything. And this could mean a setback in Chris's career that he might never recover from. And there might well be unhealable bitterness between them.

And sadly the arguments between them had been all about Chris accusing Max of cowardice, of being small minded, of wanting to hold Chris back. And about Max accusing Chris of being crazy, stupid, and selfish. You get the picture!

But even when they went at things more calmly and with more understanding, they still couldn't change each other's minds.

It's crucial, at a time like this, to name the problem. In this case, finally, Chris named it. "Look," he said, "I think the risk is smaller than you do. That's the whole thing. We're arguing about a fact neither of us can prove. But you're right about one thing. If I'm wrong we're screwed. I so, so, so don't think I'm wrong. But yes, if I am wrong, then it'd be really bad."

So they agreed to submit their situation to two restaurant consultants. Guys with a lot of the right kind of experience in the business. This is what they were told. One was gentle. "The best way I can put this is that at best you have a one-in-fifteen shot at making it. At best." The other, not so gentle. "You'd be fucking nuts to go ahead with this. I'd tell my own brother that."

Now here's the cool part. Chris of course was devastated. His dream was gone and he was going to have to find a whole new way to deal with having a job he hated. But because they'd finally stripped out the anger and bitterness from the way they'd dealt with this, Chris could turn to Max for comfort, and Max was eager to offer it. Their way of dealing with their conflict, in the end, hadn't poisoned the well of their love.

Notice what a big deal it is determining whether there's a big cost involved in making the wrong choice. If there is, consult experts. Not a big cost? Then just make sure everyone feels heard and understood and then use any process that'll preserve both people's pride.

But I'm here to tell you, based on my long experience: if you go through the right process, the decision makes itself. If you're patient.

If you should happen to get stuck

The journey you've taken here is precisely the kind of journey that loosens the ties that bind us to this or that choice or outcome. Because, after all, the question always is:

Is the outcome of this conflict more important than the health of our relationship?

And that all depends on whether or not you used the right process. The process you've learned here will, in and of itself, not only contribute to the health of your relationship by eliminating power struggles, making sure more of both of your needs are met, and eliminating painful conflict. It will also make it much more likely that you'll arrive at the best possible solution.

So if you use the right process and you're still stuck, then together you ask the question above: Is the outcome of this conflict more important than the health of our relationship?

Just think. It's the two of you against the world, and a cold, hard world it is. It's like the two of you are in a small boat in the middle of a big ocean. And suppose the two of you got into a fight. Man, that would have to be a pretty meaningful fight to make it worth risking damage to your boat just so one of you can get your point across. No, I think you'd want your guiding principle to be: we're doomed if we don't take care of our boat. Whatever our differences, let's work them out so that the boat stays safe and strong.

15

What Will Happen for You Next

"Honey, this is hard. But that's okay. We'll get it."

Sometimes change is easy. If you've been toasting bread by using a toasting fork and an open fire, you'll probably fall in love with an electric toaster the first time you try one. (Not that there's actually anyone toasting bread over an open fire anymore these days!)

But most of the time change is hard. We are so used to doing things the old way, and old habits are hard to break. So change—learning—also means unlearning. Going to the gym first thing in the morning means not sitting around sipping coffee and catching up on the news first thing in the morning. If you've been typing the hunt-and-peck way, then learning to touch-type is a form of painful unlearning. You have to *undo* something that's habitual and easy and comfortable in order to *do* the thing that's best for you.

Of course you could say, "Oh, but I'm in so much pain from all the horrible conflict we've been going through that anything would be better." True! But still, when you're in the thick of it and your partner, without intending to, says something you find disempowering, it's still almost automatic to fall back on using a power move of your own. It *feels* deeply logical and it *acts* as if you're on automatic.

But this change is *do-able* if you understand how change actually works.

Slow then fast

Here's the psychology of the thing: we are eager for the change to occur. To quickly learn to play that piano, speak that French, sail that boat. And master the **1, 2, 3 Method** of conflict resolution. But whenever we have to learn something—from a foreign language to just the names of a bunch of people we've met at a new job—it usually feels as though at first we are making very slow progress, or even no progress at all. Even worse, we feel we're bad at what it is that we have to do, or that it's just too hard. Or we blame someone else. And how convenient that here in our relationship there is that perfect someone else to blame lying right next to you in bed every night!

So you have to start out with the right set of expectations.

It might feel as though you're making progress very slowly at first, or maybe even not at all, but *that's not true*. Slow, uncertain progress is what real progress feels like when you're learning something new.

So you have to support each other and yourselves. The feeling you may have that it's oh-so-difficult or that you're going nowhere is false and misleading. You are suffering only because your expectations are out of whack with how learning really works. The golden words are, "Honey, this is hard. But that's okay. We'll get it."

Now if you want to have an experience of making progress fast, or of seeing how far you've come, try the five-minute no-power drill: talk through some conflict for five minutes with as few power moves as you can. And if one of you makes a power move, again, the rule is that the other just says, "Try that again." Or, "Oops, power move." But no arguing back about whether it really was a power move or not. If you say that my saying peevishly, "Oh, please," feels like a dismissive power move, then I just have to give it another go. "Do you really mean that?" Or, "I'd feel very uncomfortable with that."

Do that every day for a week. Compare day one to day five. You'll see what real progress looks like.

Mistakes aren't the problem, they're the way forward

People say everyone makes mistakes, as if mistakes were something bad you just have to forgive, accept, and get past. But that's giving mistakes a bad name!

Mistakes are your best learning tool!

That's right. Mistakes aren't glitches in your way forward. They're the way you *find* your way forward.

If you and I are working out some little conflict and I say, "Oh, *please*," and you feel patronized and dismissed, that's not an oops; that's a way we've learned something about one another. Sure, I may think you're an oversensitive nut for getting bent out of shape just because I said *oh, please*, but, hey, we're all nuts about all kinds of things. I hate for there to be anything at all on the island in my kitchen. See! I'm a nut too.

Being successful with this comes from bumping into each other's vulnerable spaces and learning what they are. And certainly not in judging them. Every mistake is a victory for understanding and compassion.

And *that's* because, perhaps for the first time in your relationship, you're making a map of each other so you know how to navigate without running aground. That's all conflict really is: the two of you have run aground on each other's sensitive spots. Successfully resolving conflict just means not doing that.

Think of it like this. Suppose you had to learn to find your way around a house blindfolded. You'd probably bump into a lot of things. But are all those things you bump into mistakes? No. They're your way of learning where everything is.

So please: whenever one of you points out that you've messed up, give thanks, correct course, and move forward.

How to get to Carnegie Hall

The old joke is that a guy walks up to a man in midtown New York and asks, "How do I get to Carnegie Hall?"

The man answers, "Practice, practice, practice."

Which, of course, is the last thing any of us wants to do. But I have good news.

First of all, don't think of it as practice. Think of it as you have about a whole bunch of mistakes to make and the sooner you get through them, the sooner you'll be doing great. It's not really practice at all. It's more like snow shoveling. Shovel, shovel, shovel . . . and pretty soon the snow is gone. (Or you could just move from Boston to LA the way I did and get rid of the snow that way.)

Second, you'll see the benefits of practice way *before* you get really good. Trust me: even just a 10 percent improvement will be noticeable. I remember learning to play the flute. Actually, I never got very good. But I did practice until being busy with grad school forced me to give up the flute, and I could hear my improvement and it made me so happy.

And third—and this is pretty cool—you will not have to take any time out of your life to practice! You're already "practicing" every time you experience an unproductive conflict. So really now all you're doing is practicing doing it right instead of yet another session of practicing doing it wrong, which you're plenty good at already.

So set your expectations for slow progress at first to prevent unnecessary discouragement, welcome mistakes and think of them as learning victories, and think of practice as a chance to do it right instead of doing it wrong. That's how change will happen for you.

16

Follow the Money

"This is not who we really are."

Meet the Stevens—we could call them the Even Stevens—a rare couple indeed, certainly rare out of the thousands of couples I've seen over the decades. The Even Stevens had the money thing *nailed*. They weren't crazy rich. But here's the thing: they were both professors at MIT, which in Boston meant they each made a pretty good living. More important for what I'm talking about here, they both made almost the same amount of money.

What they did with their dough was interesting. One of them paid for everything. That put a ceiling on their level of expenditure. The other saved everything (in both of their names). That's right: they saved half their earnings. That gave them both a secure future together.

The fact that they lived well within their budget meant that they didn't have money worries, even though they didn't have huge incomes. But the important thing here was that because money was so equal between them, there were no power struggles when it came to finances. Having more income or more wealth wasn't a factor in causing domination or resentment.

It's important to keep the Even Stevens in mind when we think of the rest of us. It's different, *way* different, for most of us. For us the rule is, when it comes to understanding the dynamics in a relationship, follow the money. I'll state it baldly:

The greater the imbalance in wealth or income between the partners in a relationship, the greater the chance of a power imbalance and the more power issues there will be. And the more financial stress there is, the more destructive those power issues will be.

Money inequalities tend to create power problems on their own and exacerbate existing power problems.

Let's take a stereotypical but fairly common situation. Wade owns a few car dealerships (so he takes in a lot of money but, in fact, is under a lot of financial pressure) and Della stays home taking care of the house and their three kids. It's a big house and they do a lot of entertaining, so it's clear to everyone that Della has her hands full. But every penny she has she gets from Wade.

I won't make this unnecessarily dramatic. Every month Wade shovels a bunch of cash into their "joint" checking account, which is really Della's for all her personal and household spending. How does this amount get determined?

Well, pretty much through warfare. Della complains that she has to go to Clippety Do Dah, the cheapest beauty parlor in town to get her hair done, and Wade roars back that she's sending him to the poor house and working him into a heart attack.

Sure, sometimes there are periods where things are fine in their relationship. But before you know it something always comes up and the deal is always the same. Della needs more money, and King Solomon himself would have a tough time saying whether she was justified or not. In any case, Wade has the absolute power to say *no*, and Della has the absolute power to use every power move in the book to get him to say *yes*, and Wade uses every power move he can to avoid saying *yes*. It's warfare until one or the other drops from exhaustion.

Meanwhile, unbeknownst to Wade, Della is part of that huge sisterhood of women who squirrel away what they can from their household money to have money of their own, something infinitely precious to them.

Now here's the thing I want to underline, the big, big point here. I know Wade and Della really well. And they do not want to live like this. This is not even who they are. In a way, that's one of the main points of this whole damned book:

We don't get caught up in power dynamics because we're power hungry. It's the circumstances of our lives—sometimes actual power imbalances—that set us up for conflicts that result in our making power moves, that get us caught up in power dynamics, and that make us look at ourselves and say, "This is not who we really are."

So what do you do about financial imbalances in a relationship?

First of all, for the love of Mike, acknowledge the fact that any imbalances of income or wealth have an effect on the power dynamics in your relationship, whether or not this is your intention. Hey, it's not as though the earth wants to enslave the moon in its narrow orbit. But even if the moon has complained about wanting to go off on its own it just can't. Whatever the earth's intentions, its gravity is just too great for the moon to break free.

That's the way it is with the effects of financial imbalances.

So acknowledging means that as part of Step 1—Mutual Understanding—you fold in the sense of entitlement and empowerment one of you feels the money person has, and the sense of frustration and disempowerment the non-money person has. *And be aware of how both of these lead to both of you making power moves.* This is not about blame. It's about understanding.

For example: "Wade, you give all kinds of reasons why we shouldn't have the bedroom redone, even though it would make me so happy. And they all make me sound like a silly spendthrift. But behind it all, there's always you—in my mind—saying, baby, this is my dough and it's easier for me to browbeat you into going along with me than to just say *no* and provoke an all-out rebellion." Yeah, I know, that's a pretty self-aware and savvy Della, but the Dellas I know all feel this.

As for Wade: "Pumpkin, you got me coming and going on this money thing. You think I'm made of the stuff, and I'm just not. Certainly not after all the bills get paid.* And honest to God, honey, at this point I never know the difference between what you want and what you need and what you're asking for just so you'll give me a bunch of things to say *no* to so I'll get tired of saying *no* and eventually say *yes*. I'm not saying it is what you're doing, but it feels like you are sure as hell just trying to exhaust me." And yes, that's Wade, and all the other Wades out there.

Now just think what this conversation is really about. It's about putting into practice the first principle of communication, which is that *the meaning of a communication is the response it elicits.* In other words, it doesn't matter what you think you're communicating; all that matters is what the other person takes away. The takeaway *is* the communication.

It's like picking out an outfit. You may think, *Oh, I look cool and casual.* But if everyone says, *Uh ... no, you look sloppy*, well, then, you just didn't hit what you were aiming for.

So talking about this isn't about winning your point but about finding out what your point actually is, at least in the ears of your partner. That's what a huge power imbalance can do: it can make us unable to be aware, whether we're on top or on the bottom, of how we come across.

---

* I've had a number of men and women in Wade's position claim they don't have the disposable income their spouses think. Then they've shown me their books. And guess what? In most cases these folks had a big nut—high fixed expenses—and a lot of debt that really did leave very little wiggle room for extra spending. I'm not suggesting we feel sorry for them! I'm just saying that a lot of the Wades of the world aren't just pretending to be out of pocket. They really are skating on thin ice financially.

Second, see that you can somehow work this out as financial equals. Suppose you had equal resources and responsibilities: Then what would you do? How would you handle things? What decisions would you make?

This gets at the heart of things. Is Wade setting limits because there really are financial limits or because he just doesn't like being Della's personal ATM? Is Della testing the depth of Wade's love or the depth of his pocketbook? Is Della wanting to buy things because they're really important to her or because she feels there may be unlimited funds available to her, if Wade weren't such a cheap bastard?

Okay, I know: that's a lot of questions. But these are the kinds of things that need to come out. Not as accusations, but so you can figure out what's going on. It's the therapist question, isn't it? "Why is this couple getting so wound up about this stuff?" So *you* try to answer the question. In the answer lies your solution.

And of course this means being open and honest about your financial realities. My experience is that people supposedly "with money" either have a lot more or a lot less than you might think. Maybe Wade doesn't want Della to know the degree to which his business is operating on a shoestring. Or maybe he's afraid she'd really go nuts if she found out how really, really rich he was. (And then he'd have to face feeling that she really, really *was* with him just for the lifestyle and toys.)

And so the point of this exercise is to understand the real role money plays in your conflicts.

If you don't talk about it—with a sincere desire to understand—you will fight about it.

And *third*, what can you do to level the playing field? I can just hear Wade: "Why I give my little honey all the money any woman could possibly want. What *is* her problem?"

Sigh.

Old Jewish joke: A man goes to the rabbi to complain about his wife. After he gets everything off his chest, the rabbi says, "You know, you're right."

The next day the man's wife storms in to tell the rabbi her side of the story. The rabbi listens and finally says, "You know, you're right."

That night the rabbi's own wife says to him, "You know, I overheard you talking to that husband and wife. You told both of them they were right. How can that be?"

The rabbi thought a moment and replied, "You know, you're right!"

So let's look at this from a couples' therapist's point of view. People come to me feeling in the depth of their being that they know the truth and that justice is on their side. They long, with every fiber of their being, for me to say, as Wade wanted me to say to Della, "Della, all the years of my professional life, plus a consultation with seven thousand of my most esteemed colleagues, have told me that Wade is right and you are wrong." This would be the high point of Wade's life, or Della's if things came out her way.

Now if there are obvious lies or some blatant injustice, I say so and make the couple deal with it. But in the real world I work in, the truth can be impossible to determine, and justice impossible to discern. What's more, that's not what people want most. What people want is a way of living together that minimizes pain and fear and humiliation, and that maximizes their sense of closeness and safety and mutual appreciation. And love.

So I beg most people I work with not to get stuck on issues of truth and justice. I know! That's what you're *burning* to deal with. But there's little hope that struggling over it will be productive. It so rarely is, if it hasn't been productive already.

What is productive is working out solutions that make sense to both of you and that have a good chance of being effective.

Let's suppose I saw my husband kissing a woman at a Christmas party, and to me it looked like a far-from-innocent kiss. But was it? We'll never really know. There's what I saw, there's what he said happened, there's bad lighting, bad timing. The truth, like a well-greased pig, has slipped out of our grasp.

And my husband and I will never ever be able to resolve a just distribution of our assets between us: whose contribution was greater, who did more, who suffered more, who gave up more. Solomon could threaten to chop a hundred babies in half and still we wouldn't find ultimate and mutually satisfying justice. To say nothing of when he's going to pay me back for the pain of giving birth to our two daughters!

But what you can get are good deals starting now and going into the future. At least better deals than you have now.

So Della and Wade can talk about an arrangement that'll deal with both of their greatest needs. And that's how you should structure the conversation: around each of your greatest needs. Wade's need was for there to be an end of Della and him fighting over money. There wasn't all the money in the world, but there was enough for Della to hold her head up among the people she hung out with. And Della's greatest need wasn't to spend, spend, spend. Nor was it to bleed poor Wade dry. Her need, surprisingly, was actually just to know what the deal was with his money so she could feel assured that Wade wasn't being stingy and making her beg for everything she wanted. She didn't want to be a supplicant.

They sat down with an accountant and a financial planner. You can sit down over the kitchen table with your checkbook and piggy bank. The point is that there are arrangements that even things out to the extent that bitterness and struggle cease.

If one of you has more wealth than the other, that person can make a lump-sum transfer to the other.

If one of you has much more income, that person can arrange for an automatic payment to be made in the other person's checking account.

But the point is not to be clever about solutions but to be thoughtful about the most important needs each of you has. If you focus your solutions on those needs, even an imperfect solution will take you very far.

"Our financial worries are tearing us apart"

Now suppose things are pretty equal between you financially. Sweet! But also let's suppose you're under a lot of financial pressure. For one thing you're in good company. So are most Americans. Welcome to the club. But the glib comment that people always fight over money misses the mark. The truth is that when people are under financial pressure, the fear and stress lead to their fighting over *everything* and to their doing so by using the very worst of power moves. Many marriages come apart as a result of this.

Now there's a very simple solution to this: get more money.

Okay, that was a bad joke. I've been there. I remember when my husband and I (with our two toddlers) had no money and a ton of financial fear, and it felt as though we were always walking on the edge of a precipice. One tiny slip and over we'd go. The jeopardy couldn't have felt worse and the cudgels of blame were always at hand. "Get more money" was one of those cudgels.

Anyway, people almost always do what they can to get more money. But too often they can't.

From the point of view of your marriage, though, here's what you can do.

First of all, understand what you've been doing. From your point of view, there's something really wrong with your partner! They're lazy, or stupid, or crazy, or ignorant, or alarmingly unconcerned, or just plain evil, or God knows what! Otherwise they'd agree with your ultra-sensible solutions. "Think of how much we could save if we just moved in with my parents. They've got tons of room. You'll never know they're there!"

So you go back and forth between trying to convince Barney what a mental defective he is and plain old trying to verbally bludgeon him into submission.

I mean, come on! I have transcriptions of these "conversations"! That's what goes on.

And one way or another Barney is doing the same thing. Money fights when you're going through financial stress are always about blame.

Plus this is happening is an atmosphere of tremendous fear.

So how should we understand this when we're doing it? Well, it's pretty much a two-person panic in which both people get trampled.

It doesn't work. It just adds relationship stress to financial stress. And it prevents you from finding a good solution.

And let me ask you this: Is this the way you would design the process of working out a solution to something as important as figuring what to do about your tight finances?

So what do you do instead?

Well, what do you think I'm going to say? At a minimum, no power moves. Then hit the old **1, 2, 3 Method**.

Look, I get it. Maybe one of you thinks going in that it's insane to move in with your partner's parents and the other thinks it's insane not to. Maybe one of you thinks that only an idiot would sell their house in this current market, and the other thinks, given the way things are with you, that you'd be idiots not to.

But you will never, ever, ever make any progress until you understand where the other is coming from and until the other feels understood.

Here's an example of how this can work: I say I wouldn't move in with my husband's parents if you paid me a million dollars (though secretly I do understand that in the short run it is a good idea). But we sit down and without put-downs and bullying we try to understand each other.

At some point I'm going to feel, wow, he really understands why this is a big deal for me. Not that I'm spoiled. Not that I just want my own way. Not that I'm snobbish about his parents. But the truth about what living with his parents will mean to me: humiliation and loss of autonomy. And it's not, for me, a "just suck it up" kind of thing. Not when I have no idea how long we'll be living there.

And as we generate options and get off the *yes, no, yes, no* about living with his parents, we find that there are other options. Then, as we explore those options, we find one that works for us, plus we still have the parents option if things get truly desperate.

Just think: If you've ever taken a tough exam like the SATs or something, however much you struggled to get through it, how much worse would you have done if you'd been fighting off a flock of enraged geese the whole time?

I'm telling you—you have no idea how stupid power struggles make you. But that makes sense. After all, you're putting all your energy into the power struggle, with little left over for problem solving.

It might not take more than saying, "Honey, do we want to fight over this or come up with a good solution to this?"

Well, that was money. Now comes sex.

17

The Sexual Battlefield

"Whenever sex comes up, power comes up."

My husband, who like me has worked with couples and families for decades, was once working with a certain lesbian couple. They were struggling with the issues and power dynamics all couples deal with, plus some usually unique to lesbian couples. They fought about money and child-rearing, for example. The last was particularly difficult, since in their case the two women became a couple after one of them had had her children. The children never had a chance to legally become "their" children.

But as I heard about how things were going from my husband (we often consult with each other), I saw that two big issues underlying all this were insecurity and lack of respect. A lot of the insecurity came from the simple reality that it was all too easy for the woman who was not the mother and who did not have much of a bond with the other woman's kids to just walk away from the relationship. The lack of respect came from many places, mostly from the reckless way both women used power moves, but also from the fact that the non-mother genuinely didn't respect the way her partner brought up her kids.

That's a lot to deal with! But it's all regular couple stuff, and my husband helped them a lot with it.

When he thought their work was done and their goals had been met, they had a big surprise for him though. "Dr. Foster, you've helped us so much with all this stuff. There's another area where we'd like you to work with us, if you'd be willing."

"Sure . . . ," he said.

"It's our sexual relationship. We need help there."

"Well!" he said warily. He later told me he was taken quite by surprise. "This is an area I work in," he told them, "but I think it's clear to all of us that I'm a guy and you're two women. Are you really sure you want me to help you and do you really think I *can* help you?"

What they said was most interesting.

"Look," the other woman said, "we know all about what goes where and what to do and how to do it. We don't need lesbian lessons. What this is all about is the same stuff as before. How we talk to each other. How we struggle for power when it comes to sex. Why it's so hard for us to get our needs met. You can help us with that."

"Okay, good," my husband said. "My wife would think it was hysterical if I claimed I could give sex tips to lesbians."

"No, we're good there."

So that's the thing when it comes to sex and power. We all know what goes where. And while it's true that there are plenty of sexual issues that are technical ("*No, see, you do* this *like this*") or physiological, the vast majority of the time the issues couples come for help with have to do with conflicts around their needs. Which means that *whenever sex comes up, power comes up.*

And in a way, I think this always blows our minds. Think about your best sexual experience with another person. I'm pretty sure it was an Eden free from concerns about disempowerment or any of disempowerment's handmaidens like humiliation, shame, fear, discomfort, or pretense.

So how exactly *does* power mooch its sleazy way into our sex lives?

We want what we want

Sex at the beginning of a relationship is a combination of horniness, newness, a roll of the dice, and the extent to which the two people accommodate to one another.

Imagine a couple I'll call Kel and Nic. When they first met the sex was pretty good because . . .

Horniness? Check! It'd been a while, they found each other attractive, and their engines were running.

Newness? By definition!

A roll of the dice? By the luck of things, they were compatible.

Accommodating to one another? Ah, that's a story to be played out a bit later.

And that's the way it is for so many of us. That's how so many of our relationships start in the first place.

But as you well know, over time things change. For everyone. Sometimes a little. Sometimes a lot. But usually enough for there to be some conflict.

The newness is gone. The initial horniness has been slaked. Whatever initial compatibility there was is still there, of course, except that—human nature—for a couple like Nic and Kel they've gotten used to it. It's old news. The *new* news is the areas of incompatibility that have been hidden to some degree or other by accommodation.

Nic didn't want to pressure Kel, but in fact Nic wants to make love more frequently than Kel does. But when they do make love, Kel is bothered because Nic doesn't seem to want to spend enough time making love as Kel does. And yet no one has said anything.

So far that's just a difference. Here's how it exploded into a power struggle. Nic experiences Kel as withholding a resource: it seemed to Nic as though Kel could make love but just didn't want to. A potential lovemaking session went *poof!* every day they didn't do it. Kel, on the other hand, experiences Nic as pushing, even sometimes bullying.

So what do they fight about?

Not about what they need but about what they experience the other doing to meet their need. "You withhold." "You bully." And about some inner thing that makes the other the way they are—selfishness, laziness, need for domination, not caring. "What's wrong with you?" "Why can't you be like a normal person?" And of course, at bottom, there's the blame game. "This is all your fault. Why can't we just make love a little more often? What's so hard about that?" "Well I'd want to make love more often if you wanted to spend more time with me when we did make love."

These are not problem-solving conversations! There is no collaboration. No attempt at understanding each other, at developing options, at exploring options. It's all just a blind struggle in the vain hope of winning the pot.

But in the sexual realm there's an added dimension to the power struggle. People are much more vulnerable to shame. There is something about sexual needs that can make people feel weird or gross, and there's something about sexual problems that can make people feel deeply inadequate. The couple's self-esteem takes a dive and so any power move that uses shame to get a power boost will for sure become pretty powerful.

The problem is that nothing is more disempowering than humiliation, and so no one will try harder to re-empower themselves than someone who's been humiliated.

Even a question like, "Why can't you just try?" can be heard as implying the other person isn't already doing the best they can.

A question like, "What's wrong with you?" can be heard as saying that your partner is less than adequate as a man or woman. And that's usually deeply hurtful.

So in addition to the usual rule of *no power moves*, I'd like to suggest another rule.

Both of you should always assume that the other is doing the best they can.

I can't begin to tell you how powerful this rule is. If you *act* as though you believe your partner is doing the best they can, and let them know you feel that way, and your partner does that too, then the idea that it's just laziness or lack of caring or some moral defect that's to blame will no longer be in play.

And here's the thing. If your partner *is* fundamentally flawed, there's no point in attacking them for it. You might call it laziness, but if your partner doesn't have much energy for sex—for whatever reason—then for right now that's a fact. You can talk about it, and discuss whether something might be done about it, but it's nothing you can "work out" while trying to resolve your conflict.

By both assuming the other is doing the best they can, your attempt to work things out will be on a platform of goodwill. And let's face it. If you have basic goodwill toward each other, you should use it. If you wish each other ill, you probably have no basis for working out your conflicts in the first place.

"All I can see is how we struggle in vain to solve our problems"

This is one of the most amazing things I've learned in all my years of working with couples. When two people have a problem, they very soon become blind to each other as a person. They even become blind to their actual need, as opposed to their partner's obstructing that need. The power struggle, not the unmet need, quickly becomes the real problem.

Let's trace out how this happens. It starts with accommodation. There's poor ol' Nic, wanting to have sex more often, but not saying anything. Not wanting to seem like a pig. Not wanting to rock the boat. Afraid of confrontation. But meanwhile the fires of frustration are building up so when the subject finally comes out it comes out, hotter and meaner than Nic could possibly have intended, and so it feels to Kel like an attack.

"Jeez, Kel, I'm really getting tired of your always pushing

me away when I want to cuddle or anything! What's going *on* with you?"

Now how is Kel supposed to respond to an issue when it really seems as though the issue on the table is an attack?

Power leads to polarization. When two people struggle with each other over some issue, the difference between them gets magnified all out of proportion. Nic comes in saying, "You never want to have sex." Kel says, "You're always more concerned about what you want and never with what I want." Always versus never. That sounds kinda far apart!

And so pretty soon Kel and Nic—and every couple—are living in a world where the face of the issue isn't the problem at all; the problem is the disappointment and resentment and hurt behind which the problem lies hidden.

Sexual problems are almost never about sex. They're about what people call "communication," but which you and I now know are really about getting stuck in power struggles. They're about two people doing a bad job of trying to get their needs met.

But what about the idea of Kel just giving in to Nic?

The power of consent

So, when it comes to sex in a relationship, here's the question: Is everything negotiable or does *no* mean *no*? And another question: What qualifies as a *no*? And finally, what do we mean by "sex in a relationship"?

Fasten your seat belts. Here we go.

We'll start with the last question first. "Sex in a relationship" can have two very different meanings. The first is "sex now: our having a sexual encounter at this upcoming moment."

Is *that* negotiable or does *no* mean *no*? You can immediately see why here of all places it's so important to get power dynamics out of your relationship. I have a horror story for you. Here was one couple's sex life. Whenever Jack felt horny, he'd come up to Velma and say, "Hey, let's fool around."

This wasn't a welcome suggestion. Velma knew from long experience that any resistance on her part would lead to . . . what? Violent rape? No. Threats of violence? No. But what it had led to in the past was a torrent of exhausting and humiliating power moves—threats, putdowns, interminable whining. So Velma figured caving in was easier than fighting back.

And let's be clear about what caving in consisted of. When Jack said, "Hey, let's fool around," he meant for Velma to bend over and he'd just shove himself into her until he was done about forty-five seconds later.

This was not consent. This was not a negotiation, nor was it the product of a negotiation. This was bullied sex.

The key notion—without going all legal on you—is willing consent. Here's an illustration of willing consent on the part of someone we'll call Bonnie who's in a relationship with Eddie.

They're in bed, and Eddie reaches over and starts to kiss Bonnie. Bonnie kisses him back, but when Eddie touches her breast, Bonnie says, "Wait a second. You know, I'm pretty tired."

"Oh," Eddie says. "Well, we can just go to sleep if you want."

"No," Bonnie says. "I just need to think about this for

a moment. I'm not sure what I want." There's a long pause. "Yeah, yeah, let's do it. It's been a while. I know I'm a bit tired, but I've missed it . . ."

Eddie indicated what he wanted, but the door was wide open for Bonnie to give or not give her consent. So when she said, "Let's do it," it was with willing consent. Just saying you want something isn't a power move.

Now what's absolutely crucial is for you and your partner to have a discussion about what, for you, is the point at which pressure begins. For Bonnie, Eddie's initiating sex wasn't pressure; it was just a proposal.

For Becky, things were rather different. With her and Eric, there'd been a long history of him wanting sex much more often than she did. It's not that he pressured her each time—he didn't. But his repeated initiations felt to her like a state of pressure. Over time things got to this point: he'd come up to her in the kitchen, let's say, and hug her, out of genuine affection, not because he was trying to start anything. But having a mind of his own, Mr. Happy would sprout up, and now Becky is dealing with Hubby and with Mr. Happy too. That in itself felt to her like pressure, as did the hugs that she knew would lead to Mr. Happy getting happier.

And if that amounts to pressure for Becky, then that's what that is.* It goes right back to our basic definition of

---

* A man's erection can cause a lot of confusion in heterosexual relationships. Since an erection is involuntary, the guy can legitimately deny responsibility for it. "Hey, it just happened!" Nonetheless, for many women its very existence amounts to a form of pressure—"Here I am! Take care of me!"—even if the man denies he's putting any pressure on her.

power moves: it's a power move if it feels like a power move. Intentions have nothing to do with it.

So let me propose these rules for the sake of keeping your sex life satisfying and for preventing resentment from building up:

1.   When it comes to any particular sexual encounter, don't say, "Yay, let's go for it" if you're feeling pressured and you're not willing. If you *are* willing, then even if the other person's eagerness might have seemed like pressure at another time, if it doesn't feel like pressure now, then go for it.

2.   And if you feel your partner is resisting your pressure or is reluctant to have sex with you at this time, STOP. Never go forward with sex if there's even a chance you'll be thought to have applied pressure to overcome resistance. It's just not to your advantage.

And here's why that's true for you. If you have sex with someone as a result of your pressure, and especially if that becomes a pattern, you will become deeply resented, and you will drive their desire for you deep underground. Don't do it. It's never worth it.

And you can't say, "Okay, I was doing a selling job, but my partner always had the right to say, 'No.'" This is not just about legal right. It's also about keeping your sex life uncontaminated, uncorrupted by power dynamics. If power is the nightmare of love, power is the cancer of sexual intimacy.

But what about the long run? If we're talking about your sexual relationship over time, then things are a bit different. Now the conversation isn't about having sex *now*. It's about what the two of you are going to agree to expect of each other. How the two of you are going to find a way to make room for both of your needs.

And what needs to be said here is that the **1, 2, 3 Method** of mutual understanding, developing options, and exploring options is all the more important. Especially understanding. And it's *especially* crucial that everyone be sensitive to what constitutes pressure. Because, remember: pressure erodes consent, and you never know, even if you're the one giving consent in the face of pressure, whether the consent was actually given willingly under such pressure.

So if, for example, your male partner gives you an argument about blue balls and "men have needs," just remember, we all have needs, but to privilege certain needs on the basis of a kind of masculine fragility—"Honey, I'm just gonna fall completely apart if we don't have sex, like, soon"—that's not an argument, that's blackmail.

And just to make something clear, women have needs, too. Tons of times, women need or want sex more than their male partners do. But we also need or want respect and things like being loved for ourselves and not just our bodies.

And of course, these are not just issues in opposite-sex couples. In relationships with people of whatever gender identity or sexual orientation there are differences in sexual desires that require the utmost care in making sure power moves are out of all discussions of *Hey, what are we going to do about this?*

You'd be amazed at how quickly the **1, 2, 3 Method** can turn things from despair to hope.

Everything is about sex

I just said that sexual problems are rarely just about sex. And that's true. But when it comes to solving those problems that flips: it's usually the case that almost everything in your world is about sex.

Kel wants Nic to spend more time making love. Part of that has to do with what's called foreplay and what I call everyone getting in the game. I was once working with a couple for whom not enough foreplay by the guy was the issue.

"You want me to spend hours," he said accusingly.

"Well, certainly more than running through your seven-minute checklist," she said.

He turned to me and asked, "How long do you think foreplay should last?"

I surprised everyone, including myself, by saying, "Thirty-six hours."

Both of their jaws dropped.

Back to Nic and Kel. I told them about this thirty-six-hour idea. "No, I don't mean thirty-six hours of licking and kissing and stroking. But let's say, Nic, that you'd like to make love with Kel on Friday night. So I'm saying foreplay starts Thursday morning. That's when you start being especially nice and attentive and romantic and thoughtful. That's when you make a point of thinking about how to make Kel's life a bit better. And you carry that through the whole day, and the evening, and the next morning, and the next day. By Friday evening Kel's going to be in a good frame of mind as far as you're concerned, because you've thought about Kel and Kel's whole life."

So *that's* how everything is about sex. And that's how you begin to deal with conflicts around needs. You can bring everything in your life into the deal. Sex is better when everything in your life works to help make it better. Every time you batter each other with power-move-fueled conflict, it's as if you've fallen down a whole flight of stairs and you have to climb all the way back, bruised and sore, for sex to be even remotely possible.

"I see you understanding me"

What you want to do is avoid the polarized craziness of this:

"I want sex more often."

"Stop pressuring me."

"You're so cold. What's wrong with you?"

"I'm so sorry I don't want to have sex a hundred times a day. Maybe you should get a sex doll."

"Maybe I will. There'd be more life in her."

"She'd be a more decent human being than you are."

This is a summary of a real conversation that really did devolve into both people negatively comparing each other to a sex doll. Way to go with the problem-solving skills!

But I get it. People are in shock when their partner isn't instantly and totally understanding, and they panic. They don't realize that understanding is a process, not an instant response like a dog catching a Frisbee.

That, of course, is why step 1 of the **1, 2, 3 Method** is understanding. Kel listening to Nic to understand not just that Nic wants more sex, but why, what that means, how it fits into Nic's life and Nic's sense of who Kel is for Nic. Then Nic listening to Kel means getting the lowdown on what "not tonight, dear" means when Kel says it. Is it a rejection of Nic? Of sex altogether? Of a certain kind of sex? Of sex at a certain time of day?

I know this as well as I know my own name: two people are rarely as far apart as they feel they are or as they seem to someone watching them struggle. We, or the couple themselves, are never seeing the extent of the issue itself, only the cage of frustration they've built for themselves.

Understanding breaks us out of that cage. But there's much more.

There aren't many things better than good sex, but feeling understood may be one of them.

"Wow, you really get me," is one of the greatest things anyone can say to you. It's the ultimate in intimacy. You can see naked bodies anytime. But to see someone naked on the inside is something amazingly special. And the person who feels seen and cherished feels profoundly grateful.

So what do you do with all this understanding?

Beyond understanding

Maybe nothing. Lots of times understanding by itself solves the problem. That's because many of us find it so damned hard to talk openly and honestly about sex. Once we find out what's behind the mystery that's keeping us from getting our needs met—on both sides—the conflict just . . . dissolves.

One couple I worked with got stuck on the issue of anal sex. He wanted it—she thought he was super gung-ho for it—and she thought it was gross. So they never tried. They argued about it, mostly about how he was trying to force her to do something she didn't want to do, and about how she was rejecting something that meant heaven and earth to him.

When they talked it out without power moves a lot came clear. He had said at some point—which had gotten lost in years of fighting—that he just wanted to try it once and if it wasn't good for her they would never do it again. It turned out that anal sex wasn't even the point for him. It was just that he wanted them to "try stuff," and this was the first "stuff" he could think of. She thought it was about anal sex for him, and it really wasn't.

He thought her rejection was about being close-minded and about her just not wanting something because he wanted it.

After hours of struggling over this, a mere forty-five minutes illuminated a lot. She wasn't closed to anal sex, just leery of it. She was afraid it would hurt and certainly didn't want to be pressured into it. In this atmosphere of understanding, he again said all he wanted was for them to try it once, and she believed him. And they talked about what it would mean to give it a fair chance.

Well, they tried it, taking it slow and gentle. She actually liked it a bit more than he did, but neither of them loved it. Bye-bye anal sex. But they now had a platform of understanding on which to go forward with further experiments. And they were glad they tried.

A world built on understanding, not power, is a different world.

Shortcuts. A lot of sexual conflicts are about more of this versus less of that. Here's a shortcut to a solution.

I asked Nic, "In a normal, busy month, how often would you realistically want to make love?" And I asked Kel, "In that same month, how often would you want to make love if you hadn't been bugged about it all the time?" And I asked them to write down their answers. Kel wrote, "3 or 4." Nic wrote "6 to 8."

Suddenly they're only two sexual experiences *a month* apart. That's what all the fighting had been about! The unbridgeable has become bridgeable.

"Kel, you said three or four. Under the right circumstances, could you go to five? Now please wait a sec before you answer that. Nic, you said six to eight. Could you go to five under the right circumstances? And please wait before you answer."

I let them stew in silence for a minute.

"So?" I asked.

"Of course," they both said, practically in unison.

"And what would be the 'right circumstances' that would make this work for each of you?" This is the crucial question because it brings us forward to the solution we're looking for.

It was interesting. For Nic it was just knowing it would happen. Getting off the roller coaster of uncertainty and having to beg. Kel talked about the part of daily life that made it hard to get enough sleep. We spent a long time talking about how to make that happen.

Fatigue is the enemy of sex, for sure.

But let's suppose Nic and Kel were further apart than that. Is their difference still unbridgeable? Well, even if it were, making the other person feel badly for being the way they are isn't going to help. Which is what power moves do.

The dream behind the power move is that somehow sham-ing the other person will get them to change. Dream on! Power creates fear (and rage, of course) and fear makes peo-ple stupid, so when both people use power you end up with two stupid people! But understanding creates openness and openness makes people creative.

So even if Kel and Nic are far apart when it comes to sex frequency, if they can try to understand each other better and explore the solution space more creatively, they might—no, they *will*—come up with a good resolution. It's my deepest belief that there are usually enough options in any situation to make that situation better.

For example, maybe poor old Nic won't be having sex as often as desired, but Kel, knowing what a big deal this is for Nic, will do something else for or with Nic that gives pleasure.

Now just think about what this would mean for *you*. There you and your partner are, facing the fact that when it comes to some sexual issue you're just too far apart to bridge the distance. Maybe one of you wants to bring a third person into your sex life, even if just for an experiment, and the other is closed to the idea, period, end of story.

But imagine getting through this impasse without bit-terness and rancor and hurt. People are allowed to want what they want, even if they're not going to get it. You dis-cuss it. You work at understanding each other, and you *do* understand each other.

The problem is still there, but the distance between you as people has been reduced.

But what are you going to do about the unmet need?

It's important to understand how needs work in a

relationship. We're grown-ups. There are very, very few needs that we absolutely have to get met. People get along without things they thought they could not survive without all the time. I thought I couldn't survive without getting up and sitting quietly reading with a cup of coffee for an hour every morning. Now, I get out of bed, throw some clothes on, and hit the streets first thing for a long, vigorous walk. And don't get me started on the foods I thought I couldn't do without that I do without now.

We deal with unmet needs by balancing things in our lives. I don't have *this*. Crap! Total loss. *Or is it?* I know I have *that*! And I find it adds up to a new and better balance. I don't have the quiet slow beginning to my day. And I miss it! But I feel much better, and I'm much healthier. And I make up the quiet slow time later in the day. The loss is a loss, but the balance is better. It's a good deal. A very good deal.

So if you can't get some sexual need met, okay, that sucks. Maybe your partner couldn't say *yes* to you about a three-way, not ever. But there's a whole world of possibilities in your relationship. Sure, there are no exact equivalents for the things that it turns out we can't get. And it's not about your partner making it up to you. But here's the thing about understanding. Understanding means that even though this is a horrible idea from your partner's point of view, they can accept that you want it and that your wanting it doesn't make you a horrible person. Just the way you might think that oysters are disgusting but my liking oysters doesn't make me disgusting.

And so your partner can sense the weight your desire has for you. That it's something that you really want that's now never going to happen. And so you talk about options and suddenly your partner opens up to your long-talked-about desire to take a cruise to Antarctica. "Too cold," your partner used to say. But now they think it might be fun and interesting and really cool. And really cold too. But there are clothes for that, and a cozy ship.

Bye-bye three way. Hello Antarctic cruise. An even trade? Who knows? But it feels good.

So when it comes to sex, bridges can be built that you never thought possible. And where no bridging is possible, your world is full of ways to make things come out right anyway.

18

Questions People Keep Asking Me

"Marriage can be a most wonderful place."

There are lots of questions people have asked over the years about relationships and the role power plays in them. I've already tried to answer the core questions. But here are some other interesting and important questions that keep coming up.

You've painted a pretty bleak view of marriage—people fighting all the time. Is that really how you see relationships?

Gosh, no. I've been married to the same guy since the two of us were in college and I'm so, so glad we've been together. But I can see why you ask this question. All I talk about in this book are problems, problems, problems. Particularly problems having to do with power struggles and conflict.

But this book is about problems! So let's step back and I'll share my *overall* view of marriage or committed relationships with you.

Marriage is a social tool, the way a spatula is a kitchen tool. It's an institution designed to accomplish certain things:

1. It's a structure designed to protect people by making it hard for them to split up in a moment of frustration. It's a container that holds people together.

2. Therefore it provides stability for people over the course of their lives, or at least for a longish span of their lives. And so it also can provide stability that's helpful for bringing up children.

3. It's a way to be with a person who will know you as you really are, warts and all, and still love you as you really are.

4. It's a way to create a collective memory.

5. It's a way to have a partner through life, someone who'll be there for you.

6. The better matched you are, the more likely it'll also be a place where you can have a consistency of fun and understanding and relaxation and enjoyment over time.

What's more, marriage and its equivalents *do* provide these things most of the time for most people. I didn't write this book—or any of my books—because there are problems in relationships. I wrote it because so many of those problems can be overcome, and when they are, the love and commitment people find in marriage is totally worth it.

So marriage is a great institution, but it's also a fragile one. As I talk about in my book *Is He Mr. Right?* we so incredibly often choose the wrong person to spend our lives with. According to population survey data, almost 30 percent of women up to age forty-four in a first marriage saw their marriage end in divorce, separation, or annulment. Many of those who did not split up by the ten-year mark continued limping on in unhappy relationships.

And it's fragile because it has too few social supports and a lot of social risk factors. As I showed in my book *The Weekend Marriage*, in the typical marriage today, huge stress has been added in, and time to be together has been taken out. Marriage today is too often a harassed, stripped-down affair.

And people—as this book shows—do not have the skills for dealing with the problems that come up in their marriage. This impoverished skill set is *not* reflected in the divorce rate. Two college-educated people who get married have about a 71 percent probability of staying married for two decades, according to the CDC's National Health Care Report in 2012.[*] But as we talked about in the chapter on distance (chapter 7), there is ample clinical evidence that many of these couples accomplish this not because they have great tools for managing conflict, but because they minimize conflict by maximizing distance.

Remember, there is no relationship problem for which distance isn't a solution. And if you don't mind a marriage that grows cooler and cooler and more and more distant, then this isn't a problem.

To sum up:

- Marriage is a very useful institution and it can be a most wonderful place to be.

- A lot of people are doing okay in their marriages or committed relationships.

---

[*] https://www.cdc.gov/nchs/data/nhsr/nhsr049.pdf

- A lot of people could be doing a lot better.

- And perhaps the biggest barrier to more fulfilling marriages is that we try to resolve our conflicts by using power, which turns a relationship based on love into a relationship centered on power struggles.

Aren't you oversimplifying? Power surely can't explain all the problems that come up in relationships.

Oh, my goodness, *of course* I'm oversimplifying. But so is a surgeon who cures a cancer—a very complicated disease—by going in and removing a tumor, which in some cases can be a fairly simple procedure.

Few things in the human world are more complicated than what goes on in the two-person system we call a relationship. But if talking about the power dynamics in a relationship is an oversimplification from the point of view of trying to explain things, it's extremely effective and helpful from the point of view of trying to help people move quickly from a dysfunctional to a satisfying relationship. Change in the real world is almost always based on useful simplifications like this.

You and your partner start out with a lot of stuff you agree about. Vacations? Beach! Saving money? Yes! Kids? Two, starting in exactly two years.

And as far as the stuff you don't agree about is concerned, that's easy too. You can agree to disagree, or quickly hammer out an agreement. Still no problem. Still a blissful, happy relationship.

So really the only problem is when you find yourselves using power moves as a way of resolving differences. It's power moves *and only power moves* that corrode and corrupt the harmony between two people who start out loving each other. And they're what lead to the hot and painful divorces.

On another level, though, it's not so easy. What I've just described is what happens with most couples. And that's because most couples self-select on the basis of not getting together if they're too different in too many areas. Smart. But also dumb, because what they should really do is select each other on the basis of their ability to work through painful and messy conflicts. Think about it. You own a restaurant. You're hiring a chef. Do you check him out on a slow night so you can see how he manages when he has all the time in the world? Or do you check him out on a super-busy night when you're just a bit short staffed to see how he can operate when it really matters? The latter, of course. But we don't do that in our relationships.

In any case, some couples who start out without too many serious differences develop serious differences later on. Now suppose I married a gorilla. A talking gorilla who was perfectly reasonable and never used power moves. Whatever the original attraction—and I can't imagine what the gorilla could have seen in me—I just don't see us working out our differences, no matter how utterly free of power moves our discussions were. Hugo—the gorilla—would want to throw things around and make a huge mess everywhere. I wouldn't. I'd want to go to the opera and see old movies on television. Hugo would opt for the tire hanging from a chain in our backyard. There'd be that unbridgeable human/gorilla gap.

But at least we'd have an amicable divorce.

I guess I'm saying I'd rather be married to a talking gorilla who didn't make power moves than to a power person.

To switch metaphors, let's say you have a polluted lake. Let's say you had a simple, inexpensive technology that would eliminate most of the pollution quickly. That's what I'm offering. And it's a great offer. But to remove all the pollution? That could be hugely complicated, and hugely expensive, and hugely not worth the time and trouble.

Bottom line: huge differences will sink a marriage, which is sad, but power moves will torpedo even a good marriage, which is tragic. By focusing on resolving conflict without resorting to power, you've done the single most important thing to bring love, peace, passion, and joy into your relationship. Once you've done that, then you can worry about the complexities.

Over and over, when we try to work out our differences, my partner will blow his top, and when I call him on it he'll say he can't help it. So, is that not a power move, his saying he can't help it?

There's a name for this! I-can't-help-it behavior. (There's even a technical name for it: counter-intentional behavior.) Someone does something. It's pointed out to them: "Why do you keep forgetting to bring home the things you agreed to bring home?" And they reply: "I'm busy, overloaded, distracted." In other words, "I can't help it."

So how do we think about this? What do we do about it?

First of all, "I can't help it" is a beauty of a power move all by itself. I slap you in the face. Power Move 1. You get outraged, but I respond by saying, "I couldn't help it." Boom! Power Move 2. Because, let's face it, if I truly couldn't help doing something, then it isn't any kind of move at all, power or otherwise. Snoring is not a power move.

But if I *claim* I couldn't help it, then, hah! don't you look stupid. Because if I couldn't help it, then I wasn't responsible. And then you're a meanie for getting mad at me.

If I really couldn't help it.

So, then, is it true that there are things we really can't help? Sometimes we *do* just forget things. Sometimes we *do* just blurt out something hurtful. Sometimes we *do* just totally lose it. Sometimes we *do* make typos when we're writing. It feels an awful *like* we can't help it, doesn't it?

You have to be careful, though, when you ask a therapist about I-can't-help-it behavior. It's our job to convert that into, first, "Oh, I guess I can help it," and then, second, into the ability to actually help it. So I am both by nature and training and experience reeeeeally skeptical about someone claiming they can't help it when it comes to blowing their top or forgetting their partner's birthday.

Too often, *way* too often, it's just an attempt at having a get-out-of-jail-free card. And then acting all wounded and aggrieved if you don't buy into that.

But, you know, we don't have to grapple with the ontological status of any particular I-can't-help-it behavior. There's a middle ground we can all agree on and that's pretty much true. And that is that

a)   It's just not acceptable to me that you blow up at me ever, and certainly not when we're trying to resolve a conflict.

b) You are not helpless when it comes to controlling your blowups. I've seen you control them. It's just that they're still useful to you.

c) But, yes, I know it's hard for you to stop blowing up. It's been a go-to move in your repertoire since forever. It's a habit and habits can be hard to change.

d) Nonetheless, *hard* is not the same as *impossible.* So while it may feel as though you can't help it, you can help whether or not you work hard on this issue.

e) It's okay that it's hard to stop blowing up. It's not okay that you don't work hard at trying to stop.

I'm just saying, based on decades of experience, that when someone is doing something they say they "can't help" and that thing is toxic to the relationship, the future of the relationship usually depends on that person actually working hard to stop it and actually making significant progress. That's just the way it is.

In the real world, it turns out that people find they can help all kinds of things they thought they couldn't help. They do this all the time.

Come on, tell me the truth. When a couple gets caught in power dynamics, it's usually one person's fault much more than the other, right?

You know I could get in big trouble for giving away this secret, but if you won't tell anyone I said this . . .

Here's the deal.

Beginning couples' therapists or those who are poorly

trained will typically zero in on one person in the relationship as being mostly responsible for the problems. Understandably. One person very often *will* seem more difficult, louder, touchier, less friendly, less *therapy* friendly, or as someone with more "issues." The other will seem to be the nice one.

And, sadly, some of these therapists will get stuck at this level. Having decided that one person is the problem, they'll just accumulate evidence to support that view.

But good, experienced couples' therapists will get wise pretty quickly that all is not what it seems. That the nice, friendly, normal-seeming partner in fact has dozens of ways of making life miserable for their partner, and the "difficult" partner is to a surprising degree the way they are because they've been driven to it by the "nice" partner. Plus "nice" people have countless power moves up their sleeves. The phrase *passive-aggressive* was invented for them.

Here's an example: Brandon was, it seemed, a sweetheart. Emily, not so much. She came in to the first session spitting fire. She'd had it with Brandon, who sat there like a big friendly dog who was being yelled at for something the cat did. Unfortunately for Emily, she had so much pent-up frustration that she couldn't stick with one topic, so it seemed as though she were ganging up on poor Brandon.

By the time we were into the third meeting, my rigid policy of never taking sides or seeing good guys or bad guys was paying off. I began to see the truth. Emily was not the monster she seemed. She proved the maxim that *behavior makes sense in context*. In other words, someone may seem like a nut or a jerk, but once you know their context—and good ol' Brandon was Emily's context—you can totally understand why they are the way they are.

This is what's called empathy. It means seeing how maybe you'd be like your partner if you were in his or her situation. That's doesn't mean you have to like or accept the way your partner is behaving. It just means you can't look down on their behavior from a superior position.

And good ol' Brandon was a guy with the follow-through of a gerbil. He never kept his promises. As nice as he seemed, he was totally blind to Emily as a person, proving that you can be very nice and very selfish at the same time. Whatever Emily asked Brandon to do—put his dirty clothes in the hamper, not on the bedroom floor, for example—he'd find a way to turn it into torture. As if diabolically, he'd leave one sock on the floor, too little for Emily to make a big deal of. Then there'd be a pair of underpants. Then an undershirt draped over a chair. And if Emily said something, Brandon would talk about how busy he was, or how stressed out he was.

Then when Brandon's dirty clothes piled up around the bedroom—remember, this is in the context of Brandon's having *agreed* to put them in the hamper—at some point Emily would lose it. She'd start yelling and saying awful things and *totally* lose the moral high ground. And they'd come in to see me and there'd be good ol' Brandon seeming as if butter wouldn't melt in his mouth.

So, okay. What's the point here?

First, do not play the blame game. Sure, maybe one partner is contributing more than 50 percent of their share to the problem. So maybe it's 60 percent. So what? If it seems more than that, it's almost certainly not what it seems.

Second, and most important, what's the real issue here? Imagine you have a two-driver car—two steering wheels, two sets of pedals—that the two of you have been driving together and that somehow y'all have driven it into a ditch. What are you going to do? Talk about who was more at fault?

No. The fact is that it'll take two people to get that car out of the ditch. That's for *sure*. If you don't both get your shoulders to the wheel, you'll stay stuck.

So the question is not who's to blame for the problem. The only question is, *Are you both working as best you can toward the solution?*

You've painted an unrealistic, antiseptic view of what people are like. No one can do what you're suggesting, except saints and robots. People have feelings. What about *feelings*!?

You're singing my song. I know just how you feel. It's the way I felt at first as I was developing this approach. That it maybe was the way folks *should* handle conflict, but that no one could do it in real life. Certainly not *me*!

But here's what I've found is true: Although conflict is an inevitable part of life, it is only *a part*. For most people, only a small part—although it can feel like an elephant sitting on your chest.

All I'm talking about in this hopefully life-changing book is what the two of you do to *resolve your conflicts*. Especially your most difficult, significant conflicts. Let's face it, how much of your couple time do you spend, let's say, figuring out whether to let your mother-in-law move in with you? Or whether or not you "really" respect your partner? Yes, for a while it might be all you talk about, but in the grand scheme of things it's probably an issue that'll come and go. So all you have to do is chalk up this conflict as being one of those things where you have to keep your shit together—no power moves, stick within the three steps—until you've worked it out.

Sure, it's a new way of doing things for you, and you'll be on a learning curve, but *you don't have to be perfect. You just have to get better.*

You don't have to be perfect.
You just have to get better.

Besides, real-life people, just like you, *do* do it! Every day. All the time. In fact, we all already do it all the time. At work and in our social lives, we work out conflicts with people we don't love at all without resorting to power moves. Yes, I understand that no one can press your buttons like your partner. But the process I've outlined here is designed to protect you both from having your buttons pressed.

Honestly, it's not hard. It's just different.

Anyway, who said you had to go around without having your feelings? This is just about protecting your ability to work through *conflict* safely and productively. But sure, in the course of your everyday life together, be as real and emotional and let-it-all-hang-out as you want! Be natural. No eggshells! It's just that you want to be able to keep the conflict-solving space safe.

And by the way, who said you couldn't let it all hang out using the process here? It should be actually easier here to share your real thoughts and feelings. That's because you both should be feeling safe from feeling attacked in any way.

Won't trying to work out our conflicts like this take over our lives?

Jeez, I hope not! But no, it shouldn't take over your life at all. Definitely not.

I get why you're asking though. The bad old way seems faster. Just sort of powering through, you might say. It's almost addicting, and here's why. We all hope that this time, in this conflict, we'll be able to make that one power move that'll enable us to achieve a quick victory instead of a long, drawn-out fight. Most of the time, in most relationships, that fails.

But every once in a while it works! Your partner is tired, or maybe they just aren't as opposed to what you want as usual. So you have your quick cheap victory.

And what that sets up is *the principle of intermittent reinforcement*. Remember? You know how this works. Think of a slot machine. Most of the time you lose. In fact, in the long run, *everyone* always loses and the house always wins. But every once in a while you win. On a random basis. And this, for the human psyche, is wildly addicting. It will keep us persisting at what is in fact a losing enterprise forever, if we just have that once-in-a-while success.

That's why people persist with power moves. It's a loser, but the occasional win keeps them hooked.

Plus we ignore the huge costs of the power dynamics in our relationships. The souring of mutual affection, of course. The time it takes to make up. And what about the joys of make-up sex? Well, that's adorable when you're first starting out. It rarely stays a "thing" over time when over and over there are bitter or exhausting struggles to make up.

And divorce can be pretty costly too.

Then let's not forget the cost of making bad decisions. Non-collaborative decisions are always bad! Really! Here's why. If you get what you want, but your partner loses, then you've bought your win at the price of their resentment. In fact, the battle's not over. The struggle persists.

But the **1, 2, 3 Method** I offer here actually doesn't take longer than a fight. It depends most of all on the size of the issue you're struggling over. If it's huge—like what to do with the rest of your lives!—then the **1, 2, 3 Method** will be much shorter! You'll be able to get right to the issues and options you most need to work with. The alternative—getting caught up in power struggles—will basically mean running around in circles for what seems like forever.

If it's a smaller conflict—what to do with two weeks in August—it's still way faster to invest in understanding where the other is coming from and why and in developing options, rather than to beat your heads against the other's resistance.

And that resistance, by the way, mostly doesn't exist, as you've learned here. It's mostly not about where your partner and you are coming from but about the power-based method you've unwittingly been using that creates the illusion of resistance.

Is it ever wrong or unfair to even put forward a need?

This is such a great question, even if it does open up a big can of worms. On the one hand, you could say that your relationship should be a place where you can always be honest about what you need. If something is important to you, then bring it out into the open as a topic for discussion. The worst that will happen is that it'll be clear that this is one of those needs that just isn't going to be met, not ever in this lifetime.

Like my husband's dream of having a motorcycle. He can bring me a whole PowerPoint presentation about the feasibility and desirability of his having a motorcycle, but it will no more add up than you can build a ten-foot-high house of cards in a windstorm. He's too old to start riding a motorcycle. So...over my dead body! End of story.

But he doesn't lose points for asking.

On the other hand, is it really true that every need can take its legitimate place at the bench of justice? For example, suppose Dolores and Ed are driving home from burying Dolores's sister, whom she loved more than anything, who had died suddenly from an aneurysm—even though she was only in her forties. And so of course Dolores is heartbroken. Devastated. She can't stop crying.

They pull out of the cemetery, go down a few streets, and get onto the freeway just as daylight is waning. That's when Ed says, "Hey, honey, I know this has been a sad day, but I'm really stressed out. I wonder if you could just bend down and give me a blow job." (Yes, this actually happened.)

He's just being honest about what he needs, isn't he?

Yeah, but come on! It's one thing for this need to bizarrely come into his mind. It's totally another thing for him to mention it to his wife at a time like that!

But the interesting question is: Why are certain needs, like Ed's at that moment, clearly out of bounds?

Suppose there's someone I see all the time with whom I'm very friendly, even though we're not exactly friends. One day I have an emergency and ask her if I can borrow five dollars. Out of bounds? Probably not. Suppose I ask if I can borrow five thousand dollars. Out of bounds? Oh, yeah.

Why?

It's all about two key relationship issues:

- Who are we to each other?

- Do we have a duty to acknowledge the other as a person in her own right?

If I put forward a need to someone, it has to be based on who we are to one another and on my understanding of who that person is and how he or she feels.

Let's check this out.

Five bucks is no big deal in a casual friendship with someone you see all the time. Still, it's something you'd only want to do in an emergency, because in general, and maybe for this person, people get weird about lending money.

What about what Ed pulled on Dolores? How is that different? For example, isn't she his wife and if she is, isn't she supposed to want to do anything for Ed? What if Ed said, "I'd do the same for you if the situation were reversed"?

So it really is a "who are we to each other" kind of thing. Are we people who just do whatever the other person asks for? Or does Dolores have a right to expect that who she is to Ed includes being someone who deserves respect and understanding? Wouldn't 9,999 people out of 10,000 in her situation be outraged by what they'd call Ed's insensitivity?

And *insensitivity* is the word we use for not knowing or seeming to have the slightest interest in knowing how we feel. So Ed fell down big time when it came to the issue of who Dolores was to him and of his responsibility to understand her feelings. He treated her as if she were nothing.

And that's where our ability to put forward a need comes up against a barrier.

Come on, realistically, there are times where you can't use the 1, 2, 3 Method, right? Like when you're both rushing to get out of the house in the morning.

Okay, fine, let's say you *are* both rushing to get out of the house in the morning. You both have important meetings to get to. And there are kids to drop off. There's a razor-thin margin for error.

And then it turns out that one of your cars won't start.

Who gets to use the car that works? Who's gonna end up being late? And how are you going to figure this out without your *both* ending up being late?

(My blood pressure's through the roof just thinking about this.)

But things like this happen.

Now you have two really good choices and one really bad choice.

The bad choice is a highly compressed maxi-fight. Huge intensity, short duration. That's what happens for most couples. And it usually ends with the classical fight-ending word,

"Fine!" Hatred and contempt fly through air like confetti in a windstorm and the car keys are flung at the other person.

A version of this bad choice is the short-circuited fight. Someone says, "Fine, you take the car," before anything's been resolved, as if the whole huge fight is just *assumed* with all the accompanying ill will.

But here are the two really good choices. And you tell me: Do you think you could accomplish either of them? (Personally, I really think it's very doable for most couples.)

Really Good Choice number one is a super-compressed version of the **1, 2, 3 Method**. Perhaps using the number tool. You can do this in just a few *sentences*!

"Oh, crap. This sucks. But look, on a scale from one to ten, how important is it to you to make your meeting on time? Think of a number while I think of one too."

"Good. Okay, uh, I have a number. Eight and a half. I'm supposed to be running this meeting, and I'm going to get grief for probably missing it, but Janet can step in for me."

"Okay. I gotta say, I was thinking like, nine and a half for my meeting. I mean, the meeting will happen without me, but all the big shots will be there and this is all about my being in the window for that promotion. But wait, if Janet can step in, can she just pick you up? And I could take Sammi to school and I'd just be a tiny bit late."

Pause. "Fine, with or without Janet. You go. I'll figure it out."

"I love you so much."

"Me too."

Okay, I lied. It's more than a few sentences. But still—forty-five freakin' seconds! I timed it. That's all it took to come up with a good-enough solution that preserved everyone's dignity.

Really Good Choice number two might surprise you.

"Honey, I need the car. I really do."

"I know. But I need it too. I really do too."

"So what are we going to do?"

They stare at each other over an abyss of potential disaster. Then one simply says, "Look, we never trained for this, and I have no idea how to handle it. But anything's better than a fight. You just shut up and take the keys and get the hell out of here. Tonight we can figure out how we should have handled this."

Voice trailing off, "Love you . . ."

So . . . there's no place where you can't do this.

Is it really possible to live in this never-never land of sweetness and reason? I've never been that kind of person or seen that kind of relationship.

Hey, come on, who do you think I am? If I'm anything, I'm a realist. And one thing I know about the real world, yours and mine, is that it'll never be a place of pure sweetness and reason (unless the two of you never deal with anything, in which case what it really is is la-la land).

This is not about making your lives together a fantasy world. Here's what it is about:

The goal here is only to take the power dynamics out of your attempts at conflict resolution as much as you can, even if you only make things 10 or 25 percent better, so you can feel better about each other, better about your relationship, and better about the quality of the solutions you come up with to your life dilemmas. And so your relationship overall functions better.

Now I admit that it's rare for couples to achieve that perfectly. But only because they've never known how. Hey, two hundred years ago no one knew how to ride a bicycle either.

The goal is improvement. The goal is making your attempts at conflict resolution *sufficiently* nontoxic so you don't feel beaten up or beaten down and so you actually come up with agreements that are smart and work for both of you.

And I know from experience that achieving this goal *is* possible for *at least* 80 percent of help-seeking couples.

What do you do about a relationship where one person just has more power than the other?

Well, the first thing you do is not assume that it's true. Even if you're the person in the relationship who feels way down on the power ladder. Just because you feel they have more power doesn't mean they don't feel *you* have more power.

My assumption is that disempowered people work hard to equalize the power balance and that they usually accomplish more than we think when it comes to re-empowerment.* Which is a triumph for the individual and a tragedy for the relationship: if no one wants to be one down, then everyone's trying to get one up, and life together is a constant struggle for more power on both sides.

Still, though, sometimes one person really does have more power than the other. And that can be a real problem. But it's a problem that can be worked through.

There are three kinds of power advantages a person can have, and each involves its own solutions.

First, there's *structural power*. This comes not from who the person is but from the person's situation in life. If I'm president of the United States, then that gives me structural power with respect to my husband. I can always point to the requirements and burdens of office and say, "Gee, honey, I'm so sorry, but I have to cancel our date night because they've moved up the schedule for the G7 meeting and all the other heads of state will be there." And there's not much my husband can say about it.

It's the same if, for example, you have eighty-seven billion dollars and your partner works as a barista. You can do anything, and your partner has to ask you for almost everything. A huge structural imbalance.

The solution is to work out a structural answer to the structural imbalance. Lots of times, of course, you can't completely equalize things. But here's the key: you will feel much less disempowered and much less helpless if your partner

* Check out James Scott's *Domination and the Arts of Resistance: Hidden Transcripts* (Yale 1990) for an amazing and illuminating discussion of this across the world.

shows they really understand your situation and takes the most significant steps they can to balance out the imbalance.

If I'm the president, my husband can be in charge, among other things, of where we go on vacation, within the limits set by the Secret Service. The billionaire, whose money might be largely tied up in family trusts, can arrange for their partner to have enough money of their own so they don't feel dependent.

What you can't do—as a couple or as the more powerful person in this relationship—is ignore this imbalance. It can easily be toxic and the toxins will fester.

Second, there's *bargaining power*. Let's face it. Sometimes one partner is quicker witted, more articulate, has more experience advocating for himself or herself, or is less easily manipulated. Or perhaps they just get more emotional in a way that has a strong effect on the other person.

This is the "you can talk me into anything" phenomenon. It can be really frustrating to be in a relationship with someone like that.

Well, we've actually dealt with this already.

Remember, anything that makes you feel disempowered is a power move. So suppose your super-smart partner, who's a successful trial lawyer, puts on a PowerPoint demonstration for why he's right and you're wrong. You just feel flattened. How do you argue with an entire presentation?

But you can call foul on the PowerPoint presentation as a power move. "Hey, buddy, why not just talk like a person."

And much more important, you can move out of the power move game and instead use the **1, 2, 3 Method**. Your partner's bargaining power will evaporate. There's no bargaining power in trying to gain mutual understanding, or in generating options, or taking those options for a trial run.

And then there's *crazy power*. This is hard to define. If I get upset and you say I'm being crazy, what's really going on?

Am I actually being crazy?

Or am I being "crazy" as a power move?

Or is your saying I'm being crazy a power move, and a pretty ugly one at that?

So you can get caught in a loop in which instead of struggling over how to manage your money, you struggle over which one of you is crazier.

I'll tell you one thing. It's *never* a winning move to say, "Honey, that's just crazy." Or, "Sweetie, you're just being crazy." In the entire history of the world, no one upon hearing this has ever smacked themselves on the forehead and said, "My goodness, you're *right*! I'm gonna sane up immediately."

So don't do that.

But what *do* you do if your partner in any way seems to you like a nut as you two try to deal with a conflict?

And here's what I mean by "seeming like a nut":

- *Expressing an irrational need.* Don't even go there. All needs are irrational. Yes, of course, some needs seem more "normal" or prudent than others. One patient of mine needed to have all jars and bottles on the shelves with their labels facing outward. Her husband thought that was nutty. But he wanted to spend his time writing scholarly articles that would never make any money. She thought *that* was crazy. So unless a need is truly destructive or self-destructive, let it alone. You may be sure you're right, but this is a fight that'll go nowhere fast.

- *Acting as if you don't exist.* Calm, cool, and collected. Not crazy-seeming at all. But sometimes it can hit you that the person you're dealing with isn't so much irrational as they are someone for whom you and your feelings and needs carry no weight. All the conflicts you've been having with them: they're all about their needs and their need not for you to be *happy* but for you to *shut up.* And it's a matter of almost complete indifference to them how they get the outcome they want—anything from appeasing you to terrorizing you. What do you do about this? Hang tight for a minute and I'll tell you.

- *Sabotaging the relationship building you're both committed to.* It's really crazy when someone acts against their own priorities. So suppose your partner tells you they want to work with you on making your relationship better by using some of the ideas in this book—at the very least cutting back on the power moves—and then it turns out that it's just the same old stuff with a lot of excuses about how it's too hard and "I just have to be myself." It's not that, for example, walking out on your partner in midsentence and slamming the door is crazy in itself. But when you know—and your partner knows you know—that this will sabotage the relationship building they were saying was important to them, then that really is nuts. So what do you do about *this*?

When your partner's a Power Person

Now we're getting close to the danger zone, if we're not already there. Sometimes we come to suspect—or maybe it hits us over the head—that our partner is basically all about power. He or she just wants to win. I call this being a Power Person.

What is a Power Person? Well, a Power Person is not just a powerful person. Someone may be good at getting what they want and go a little crazy sometimes (and do all that much better than you), but while all of that may create an imbalance that's a real problem, it doesn't make them a Power Person.

The sign of a Power Person is the desire for control for its own sake. And how do you tell if your partner has that? Ordinary people, even if they're good at the power game, just want what they want, and once they've got it, they stop. They don't want all of the marbles; they just want their marbles. A Power Person wants to control you. The ideal state for a Power Person is for you to have few or no needs and little ability to get your needs met. A normal politician (if there is such a thing) would have wanted to be top guy in Germany in 1932. Hitler wanted total control in all of Europe, at the very least.

To determine if your partner is a Power Person, answer the following questions:

- Is your partner basically fair? That is, if you come up with a good reason for why a certain decision should go your way, would he be able to accept that?

- Do you seriously believe that your partner has been trying to gain more and more control over you in your life by snooping on you, limiting your access to friends and relatives, telling you what to believe, and things like that?

- Do you think your partner just wants to win more than simply wanting to get her specific needs met?

- Do you feel that your needs and your feelings don't really seem to exist for your partner?

If you answered no to question 1 *or* yes to question 2 *or* yes to question 3 *or* yes to question 4, then you're in a relationship with a Power Person. In which case I'd advise you to get out of the relationship. You can't cure a Power Person or learn to live with her. Instead you need to describe your situation to an attorney who can advise you on how to extricate yourself from this relationship safely.

But what if, in general, you detect that there's just "something wrong" with your partner? It happens. Sometimes we realize, sooner or later, that there is something wrong with the person we're sharing our life with.* It could be something with a well-known name. Alcoholism, for instance, though a mere label doesn't make it easy to apply that name to our partner. Labels don't always seem to fit as well as we'd like. Yeah, Joey drinks his way through the weekends but he's cold sober during the week. Nancy's never really drunk, but every single freakin' night she seems to be just one wine cooler too far into fog-land.

---

* If you're undecided about whether to stay in your relationship or to leave it, many people say that the gold standard for books on this topic is my *Too Good to Leave, Too Bad to Stay*. It will lead you through a process where you see for yourself what's best for you to do. No more indecision!

But more often we notice something more nebulous. Our partner, with a good solution for resolving conflict in their very grasp, just won't use it. Or they have a weird lack of interest in understanding how you feel, or they just can't seem to grasp how you feel, or they just don't seem to care. You don't feel as though you're dealing with a normal human being.

Here's where so many people make so many mistakes. A lot of my practice of the past decades has involved seeing the fruit of these mistakes.

Mistake 1. Getting used to living with a problem person

Ah, the wonderful adaptability and resiliency of human beings. It's quite a miracle. But it's one thing to get used to having, for example, a special-needs child or a partner who's lost a leg. But a partner who makes your life miserable, for whatever reason, but certainly because in one way or another he or she routinely makes you feel disempowered no matter how often you talk about the toll this takes on you and your relationship . . . well, that's not something you deserve to spend a lifetime getting used to.

Being used to a bad thing doesn't stop it from being a bad thing.

Mistake 2. Making excuses for a problem person

It's his job. It's all because of her parents. It's because of his time in the Marines. It's because of the way her first husband did a number on her.

All those things may well be true. And if so, that makes it all the more sad that this person, whom you love, has these awful problems that make your life, and their life too, so miserable.

But just because there's a good explanation for the person's problem doesn't stop it from being a problem that is making your life miserable.

Mistake 3. Not dealing with the fact that you are living with a problem person

Yes, you may face the fact that your partner's go-to move is anger, for example, in the sense that you recognize it and even complain about it. But what I'm talking about is facing the fact that your partner has never changed and shows no promise of changing and, based on what they've said and done, has shown no desire to change. Which means dealing with the fact that this is going to be your life for the rest of your existence.

So if you can acknowledge that you've been making these mistakes, how do you fix them? You need to ask yourself four questions:

Can I live with this for the rest of my life? For the sake of all that's good and holy, you have to be honest with yourself here. "Live with this" doesn't mean grimly bearing it. It means living with it the way you might live with the fact that your husband has gone bald. A twinge of sadness. Maybe the occasional regret. But 99 percent of the time you truly don't care; it's fine. *That's* living with it.

But if you can see that in spite of all the super-wonderful

help in this book your partner is still going to give you a hard time and your needs are still going to go unmet and you're still going to most often feel uncomfortably disempowered, then can you live with that? Can you, today and for all your tomorrows?

Now suppose you do not want to live with that. Here's the next question.

Does your partner want to change? And here's how I define *want*: in this case it means working hard in the face of pain and difficulty. Actions, not words or good intentions. We all know what that looks like. We've all seen people work hard for things and we've all seen people not work hard for things. Working hard means doing whatever it takes. Not working hard means doing as little as you can.

But suppose your partner does seem to want to change. They say so, anyway. Then, the next question is this:

Can your partner change? The past is evidence of the future. Roberto was a kind, loving, devoted family man. But he'd grown up in a totally disorganized family and never learned self-control. When he enlisted in the Navy right out of high school, he excelled. The highly structured environment there worked for him. He always knew exactly what he had to do and how to do it . . . and what would happen to him if he didn't do it. Then when he wasn't on duty, he could drink like a fish and everyone would still think he was a great guy. Roberto rose all the way to Master Chief Petty Officer. Quite an accomplishment.

But his wife Viola wasn't the Chief of Naval Operations, and their family wasn't the Navy. So she had enormous difficulty getting him to change. He would say he'd try, he'd say he'd do this or that—like let her know where he was during the day (which was a big deal to her because he'd cheated on her with another woman)—and then nothing would happen.

Still, the past is evidence of the future. With the support, encouragement, structure, and force of the entire United States Navy behind him, alongside of him, all around him, Roberto could do whatever was required of him. At home, that was his *me* zone. And he wasn't going to do anything unless someone made him do it. And the only power Viola had was to cry.

Now here's why this is all maddening and confusing. There sitting right next to you is a human being you love. A human being with skills, talents, and accomplishments. A human being who cares about you and who's shown evidence of that in the past. A person who holds down an actual job that yields an actual paycheck.

So it's hard to believe that this seemingly functional person can't change.

It doesn't matter. If, with respect to the issues with which you need them to change, they haven't changed, in spite of endless promises and seeming attempts, then that's the real past, and that's the real future, in all likelihood.

Of course, it's easy to get caught up in the "but what ifs?" "But what if we tried *this*?" So here's what I say about that. If this is your first—or third—time around the dance floor, try it. Alcoholism? Try AA. Lack of motivation? Try psychotherapy. And yes, if it doesn't work the first time, try again. A different AA meeting or a different psychotherapist can make all the difference.

But the "but what ifs?" are a trap, and trap theory is an entire area of psychology. Investing in possibilities is good up to a point. But the danger is that once you start investing in a series of trying this and trying that, you start feeling you can't give up after all the time and money and emotional energy you've invested in trying to help your partner change. That's the trap. You get suckered into feeling it's stupid to give up after all you put in to hanging in there.

There's a best-practice way to avoid this psychological trap. In advance, set a go/no-go point in your own mind. And write it down. It should go something like this:

"If after three years of our best efforts and our best attempts at finding help Sweetie Pie has made little or no progress, then I'm going to declare that Sweetie Pie just can't change."

You should define what to you qualifies as progress. One hint: trying hard is not progress. Accomplishment is progress. If it were weight loss, then losing fifty pounds and keeping it off for a full two years might be a way to define progress. Progress means a meaningful accomplishment that shows signs of sustainability.

And you should also decide in advance what no progress will mean for you when it comes to what you will actually do. You will have to do something. What's the point of all this self-torture if you're going to end up living with ol' Sweetie Pie the way he's been all along? And if you wait until the end of the three-year period—or however long it is—to decide what to do, then inertia and feeling sorry for Sweetie Pie will paralyze you.

It doesn't mean you have to get a divorce if you determine your partner just can't change. Not at all. But since you've been in real pain, you will need to make some structural change to protect yourself from that continued pain. There are dozens of alternatives. Living under separate roofs. Keeping your money completely separate. You need to talk to someone about the most sensible change you can make to spare you from the pain that won't change because your partner won't change.

Does the change make a difference? You know, to some degree you can answer this question right now, even before there's been much *attempt* at change. Just use your imagination. Suppose your partner has made the changes you want. Conflicts are now a thing of the past. That is to say, you can talk about anything without falling into power struggles.

But is that enough?

Sometimes we get so focused on the stuff that bothers us the most—because it's so right in our face—that other stuff, just as bad, lurks half hidden on the back burner.

So suppose Dottie no longer goes ape shit when you try to present her with needs that are different from hers. She no longer feels the dagger of opposition at her throat. She can accept a process of working things out collaboratively. Wow! So all's well?

Well, kind of, except that if you had to admit it, you'd have to say that Dottie was boring as a bag of ball bearings. For a while this has been off your radar screen when you've been too busy dealing with banshee Dottie to worry about boring Dottie. But with the crazy gone, Dottie droning on about the minutiae of daily activities, well, you love her to pieces, but this was already driving you crazy.

So here's the question, really. Who is this person I'm in a relationship with? Be honest with yourself. No illusions or delusions. No thinking of them as they could be or as they were. Just as they really are and have been.

And you're not judging this person. Not at all. They may be a wonderful person, a paragon of excellence, someone whose true goodness far exceeds yours. Or not. But still. No judgment. You can accept them and love them for who they are.

But a life partner is a companion for the journey. Think of it as the two of you making your way through a trackless and unforgiving wilderness. Life is tough. And we all need the best possible support for that journey. This might sound crude or cruel, but if you were going to buy a car to drive from Cairo to Cape Town, from the top of Africa all the way to the bottom, you wouldn't get a car you felt sorry for or just because you thought it was adorable! You'd get the car most likely to fit your needs and be sturdy and reliable. You're not judging all the other cars. You're just standing up for what you need for a long and difficult journey.

So if Dottie is boring, or Dan makes bad decisions, or Martha is always too busy with her nine pugs, or Manny will never be interested in you and your life . . . well, what I'm asking you to do is to *see* this. See it for what it is. Is it okay with you? Can you live with it?

All I ask is that you don't kid yourself.

All relationships are imperfect people putting up with another imperfect person. But there are only three ways of dealing with an unchangeable imperfection:

1. *Getting used to it.* This can happen. We get used to annoying or disturbing things all the time. But if you haven't gotten used to something about your partner in, say, five years, what's going to make you start getting used to it now?

2. *Deciding that it's worth it.* You know: the good outweighs the bad. My husband is not good with time. Well, after seven hundred years of marriage I know this isn't going to change. And it's as annoying as hell. But it doesn't factor into our lives all that often: we've learned some workarounds (if we have a plane to catch, I decide when we leave the house). So it's worth it to keep him around. But if he liked to dribble a basketball around the house every time he went from one room to another? Sorry, sweetie, but if you're gonna do that, we aren't gonna make it to 701 years.

3. *The D word.* No, not divorce. Distance. Which might mean divorce, but doesn't have to. It just means redefining who you are to each other and how you live so that the thing that's a problem you have with your partner (and let's not forget a big problem your partner might have with you!) can become small enough to make everything, on balance, okay.

Let me say some more about number three. Remember boring Dottie? Well, is she the problem or is the problem the way you structure your lives? Yes, I know you've done a lot already. Whenever you drive somewhere together you listen to a podcast on the car radio. Getting together with other couples as often as possible.

But you can always go further. For example, have you tried honesty? Not cruelty! God forbid! But honesty with kindness? Remember three principles:

1. There is always some distance at which a relationship can work.

2. You never need more distance than the minimum distance that makes the relationship work.

3. You can talk about anything with anybody if you make sure to address their fears and needs. If you want to have a conversation with Dottie about how you find her boring, it'll make all the difference if you begin by making it clear to her *first* that you love her and want to be with her and care about her.

So even if your partner can't change or the change wouldn't make a difference, there is very possibly some distance you can make—short of divorce—where things would then be good enough to keep the relationship going. So what would that distance be? What would the change be that would create that distance?

Examples? They're endless. You live in separate apartments in the same building. You live in houses next door to one another. You live in separate bedrooms. You stop expecting to have sex with each other and instead have an agreement to have sex (or not!) with others as long as you don't talk about (or *do* talk about it) with each other. One of you resigns from the country club or church you've both belonged to for a long time.

The point is that the thing you do to create distance

creates enough distance about the right issue to make your relationship good enough again.

So, what's the big takeaway from all of this material about realizing you're stuck with a power person or a problem person?

Most of all, you need to know that you'll be okay. It sucks being where you are but moving on feels scary, or impossible, or maybe even selfish. But if the other person can't change, then this person is making your life worse not better. Moving on will make things better. Staying with this person is like someone who's shipwrecked jumping into a lifeboat full of holes.

And you need to act sooner rather than later. Things won't get better. At best there's only the illusion of improvement because of your threats. (Of course all this assumes that you've worked for at least six months with a good couples' therapist you both like and trust and who is all about helping you change things, as opposed to your talking things to death.)

My partner and I can agree on things pretty easily. That's not the problem. The problem is that after a while my partner more and more stops following through on what we've agreed. And then I want to kill him! What do you do about that!?

Wait a minute! Are you married to my husband too? (Truthfully, he's much better now than he used to be. He can change!)

But seriously, this is one of the most common complaints about partners throughout the full range of gendered and non-gendered identities. People work out a conflict by agreeing and then not complying.

How do we understand this, and what do we do about it?

In the world of power, tactics fall into two main categories: force and evasion. Usually we think of force either as quite direct ("That's just stupid!") or indirect ("I don't understand how you can say that," said in a patronizing way). But evasion is more often the power move of choice of those who feel disempowered.

And noncompliance is a form of evasion. Consciously or unconsciously, here's what goes on inside the mind of someone who feels they just can't win with their partner. Pat unconsciously says to himself—or it's as if he does—"I just can't deal with Irene. She's always complaining about what she needs me to do. What about what I need? I'm not going to get my needs met here. I'm not even going to be able to articulate my needs. So the easiest thing is to just say *yes* and try to go along and see what happens."

Noncompliance is rarely part of a well-thought-out scheme!

"I'm sick of having to remind you to take out the garbage," Irene says. "Don't wait 'til Thursday morning! Take it out Wednesday night before you settle down for the evening. Okay?"

"Okay, honey, I promise," Pat says. "I'll do that."

And the promise is sincere. Pat really means it and basks in the glow of his good intentions.

And he may remember for a few weeks, but he's tired after work and all he wants to do after dinner is sit in front of the TV for a few hours before he goes to sleep. So a couple of times he forgets to take the garbage out Wednesday night, but he does get the garbage out by Thursday morning, so it's okay because he gets it out. So maybe he can relax at night and still get the garbage out for Thursday morning pickup. Until one day he waits until he hears the garbage truck and then it's too late. And he hears it from Irene! "Do I have to remind you of everything? Do I have to carry the burden of having to think about something I shouldn't need to think about?" The resentment of the prospect of having to take on yet one more chore just because this supposedly well-intentioned jerk has his head comfortably in the clouds makes Irene miserable, and she misses no opportunity to make Pat feel miserable too.

Welcome to the politics of housework, but this applies to all areas that couples struggle over that require any kind of follow-through.

Now the wrong way to think about this is blame and shame. The person who's tending to be noncompliant with agreements either starts out seeing the other person as being more powerful, or else as they get more and more resentful that person will see the other as more and more powerful and they get all mean and angry. So now you have an angry powerful person getting angrier and more powerful and a noncompliant putter-off-er becoming more and more evasive. Who can say who's to blame? Certainly no one will benefit from playing the blame game.

So what do we do about it? You use the **1, 2, 3 Method** you've seen here with the following additions.

At every stage make sure there is a full and wholehearted understanding of how fairness comes into play. *Is* it fair that Pat takes out the garbage? Sure, maybe. But that needs to be fully understood. *Why* is it fair that he do that? If Pat doesn't buy in to the fairness part—or just gives lip service to it—then everything else is built on a foundation of sand.

Also, as a part of taking the agreement for a test drive, talk about how the agreement will possibly fall apart. How *will* Pat remember to take out the garbage without Irene reminding him?

It's understandable that Irene would say, "Hey, you're a grown man. You hold down a responsible job. I shouldn't have to remind you to take out the garbage." True enough! Millions of spouses and partners would say, "You go, girl!" to this.

But what Pat should be and what Pat is are two different things, and the only way Irene can get around this is by creating the story in her head—and millions of partners do create this story—that Pat already is who he should be and is just pretending to be lazy or absentminded to get out of taking out the garbage.

So the hard fact you both have to face is that you can only deal with compliance issues by facing them thoughtfully and patiently.

What would be a foolproof system for these two particular people in their particular situation? That's always the question. Generalities don't work. Accept that the solutions that will work best are the ones both of you come up with and agree on.

One way to go is to look at a system of consequences for noncompliance. "Okay, so we'll agree that if I don't take out the garbage [or pay the bills on time or come up with good ideas for date night half the time or initiate sex at least once a month or set up a 401k at my job] I'll treat you to a girls' [or boys'] night out." Consequences can be consequential!

Another way to go is to figure out how to get the person to do the thing they weren't doing. A system of reminders for the forgetful. Our computers and smartphones are loaded with ways to create timed reminders. The two of you can be creative about this.

And forgive me for saying this, but you may just want to take a second look at your sense that you're sick of reminding your partner to do this or that. Just a quick second look. If you always remember the garbage thing anyway on Wednesday night, why not agree that, okay, you'll remind your partner to do it, and right then and there they'll do it, without delay. Is that really so bad? After all, is it the reminding that was bothering you or the resistance and delay once you did remind them?

Most of the time, couples find that the failure to follow through was really about the failure to think through what the two of you were really agreeing to do.

Bottom line:

Make sure a thoughtful and honest discussion, leading to a smart approach to the issue of noncompliance, is part of your resolution of any issue.

You said you were going to tell me how to give feedback. Okay, so how do you do that?

Yes, back in chapter ten I said I'd answer the question, "How do I give feedback to best preserve the health of our relationship?" To save time, I'm just going to answer this by giving some rules. These rules aren't about "should"; they're more like cooking rules: things go way better when you follow these rules.

Feedback rule 1: Don't give feedback at all if instead you can state your feedback in the form of a need that you're putting up for discussion. For example, don't say, "Your clothes are dated and unflattering." Instead say, as your opening move, "You know, can we please go shopping and get you some new clothes?"

Feedback rule 2: Don't give feedback about things your partner simply can't change, even if they bug you. If you've discovered, for instance, that your partner isn't a brilliant thinker, there's no point in saying anything. If I'm not as smart as you are, what could I possibly do about it?

Feedback rule 3: Feedback works best when it's asked for. Wait for that, if you can. It works least well when it's not asked for. Try to stay away from that. If you feel you have to give unasked for feedback, ask permission to talk about "an issue of concern to both of you." For example, suppose your partner has put on a lot of weight and that's affecting your sexual desire for them. It's a touchy subject for sure, but they've probably noticed something is going on. You could say, picking the best possible moment, "Honey, I'd like to talk with you about something that's kind of delicate that affects both of us. When could we do that?"

Feedback rule 4: Feedback isn't saying something negative. It's creating a path forward in partnership and with hope and respect. So you wouldn't say, "You've gotten fat." You'd want to say something more respectful that connects the two of you, like, "I know you know you've put on weight. And here's the thing: I'm afraid it's affecting our sex life. [This is a joint concern.] I wish that weren't true, but it is. I'm sorry. Is there anything I can do to help with this? [Signaling you're in this together.]"

Feedback rule 5: Use the "Oreo" technique. No matter how kindly you frame it, feedback is undeniably bringing up something negative about your partner. I'm expecting to hear words fall from your lips about how you cherish me, but instead you're telling me my ass is fat! I'm now feeling distinctly less cherished! So do this: Say something positive and loving and supportive to your partner. Then do the feedback thing. Then end with more affirmation and support. The two positive cookies making the rich crème filling of negativity more bearable.

Now here's the thing: Feedback is essential for the health of a relationship. You need to know that your snoring is actually a big deal for me. I need to know that...well, I may think I'm perfect, but if you think, for some unfathomable reason, that the ratty-looking bathrobe I live in is disgusting and off-putting, then I need to know that.

Feedback is when we learn that our child failed a math test and needs a tutor, that our blood pressure is high and we need to watch our salt intake. Feedback is when the GPS tells us we've missed our exit and have to turn around. Feedback is the stuff we don't necessarily want to hear but that makes our lives better when we let it in and deal with it. Stuff that's so important that doing it right—by following these rules—just might save the relationship.

You've presented this whole idea as if you need both partners working together to put the 1, 2, 3 Method into operation. But my husband is very skeptical about these kinds of therapy things, as he calls them. Can I use this method on my own? Will it still work?

Short answer: Yes!

Let's assume that your partner isn't a sabotaging asshole. They're just wary. They need evidence. So you give them the evidence.

What you do—and I've seen this work and coached people to help make it work—is let your partner know that you're going to be doing things differently from now on. You're going to change. You hope your partner will change, but in any case you will change.

So you don't make power moves. Note that this will *not* make you less effective. It will actually make for fewer occasions when your partner feels disempowered and needs to make power moves on his own. You can even note when your partner makes a power move without trying to get him to change. And if possible, try not to get disempowered by his power moves.

If he says, "Don't be ridiculous," don't get your hackles up. Instead, show understanding: "I know this is hard for you to take in," you might say.

In fact, show understanding at every moment you can. People melt in the face of feeling understood (although they may not melt immediately, but just wait!). Down will go his resistance. Up will go his desire to cooperate.

You try to come up with options beyond the ones you've started with. Maybe his competitive juices will start flowing and he'll come up with more options on his own.

And you can start the process of exploring your options. In fact, you can get him to do some exploring by asking him to expand on his *no* and his *yes*. "Okay, so you say that's what you want to do. Talk to me about why it's a good idea." Let him go on and on. Ask questions. Then ask if there's any downside, if he has any reservations about his idea. After all this, ask him if he's interested in hearing your thoughts about his idea, and begin by sharing the ways you agree with him. Then say, "Okay, we've explored your preference. Now can we explore mine?" Unless he's a pretty unfair person, he'll say *sure*.

Here's how all this will play out.

It will go better than your attempts to deal with a conflict have usually gone, *if* you can manage not to pop your cork at your partner's power moves.

And you will be frustrated that you're doing all the heavy lifting.

My hope is that afterward you'll be able to *say*, "Now didn't that go better? I was using the method in that Kirshenbaum book."

And he'll grudgingly admit, yeah, it was better.

Don't push it. Just do the same thing again, when you face your next issue. If you get the same more-or-less positive result, then maybe you can suggest he try it too. Maybe just the no-power-moves part.

You can't lose. You'll either demonstrate that this **1, 2, 3 Method** really works and slowly gain a convert. Or you'll confirm a dark suspicion you've been having for a long time anyway about your partner. Either way, you'll be on the path to things being much better in your life.

Conclusion

"I'm so glad we've had this time together"

I truly believe the odds are overwhelmingly on the side of things being good between you. The feedback I've gotten from countless people I've helped get back on track is—surprise!—how easy it is. You just have to *decide* to do the **1, 2, 3 Method**, something that's a hell of a lot easier than struggling!

The only hard part is letting go of power moves, and if you help each other and are patient with each other and don't expect perfection, even *that's* a piece of cake.

Suppose you and your partner have lived a long and fruitful life and now one of you is dying and it's time to say goodbye to each other and you want to speak the truth. It would kind of suck if your truth at that moment would be, "I love you, but let's face it, we really screwed up a good thing."

I think you'd want your truth to be, at that moment, "I'm so glad we've had this time together." It's certainly what I'd want.

This book is my gift to your future . . . Together.

Why I Wrote This Book

For as long as I can remember, empowering people who've been disempowered has been just about the most important thing in the world to me.

It goes way back to when I was a little refugee girl in a displaced person's camp near Munich, a child of Holocaust survivors, not knowing what the future of my family would be. Outside the gates of our camp were the very Germans who'd tried to destroy us—who'd killed every one of my grandparents, aunts, uncles, cousins . . . pretty much my whole family—now in their own homes, their own lives already almost back to normal. How unfair!

Nazi Germany was a prime example of power run mad, leaving so many without any power at all.

My awareness of how little power I had was driven into me over and over. In those very early years, my brother, four years older, got more food than I did. Why? I wondered. I was told: because he's a boy. I was to understand that girls are expendable. I guess in a mass of hungry people, I was. When I finally arrived in America, a distant male relative saw me standing there and burst into tears because I was so skinny.

Despite my poor upbringing, my family valued education, and I was always encouraged to read whatever I could get my hands on. Books gave me power and, boy, did I know it. In the sixth grade, I was so far ahead of everyone else they took me out of class and gave me a job going through files looking for people's Social Security numbers. For the entire year. At the end of the year, one person was selected to get into the special classes for advanced students for the next year. I was supposed to be that kid. But a boy, Martin, was chosen even though his grades and test scores were below mine. Why? I wondered. But I heard the answer as I listened to two teachers talking. I was a girl. All I'd ever do was work as a file clerk anyway. Again, something about who I was as a human being utterly disempowered me.

Skipping ahead, when I was about to graduate from college, there were three of us in my major. I was the one with the best grades. We all wanted to go to Yale for grad study. The two guys were recommended for a Woodrow Wilson Fellowship. I wasn't. Why? I wondered. I needn't have wondered; I was told *outright*. "You're just going to get married anyway. Why worry about grad school? You're pretty. Why not be a model?"

So let me ask you: Do you think that after being clobbered with disempowerment like that, just because I was a woman, I would ever have any interest in disempowering any woman anywhere?

I also had my own #MeToo moment, to say the least! While I was still in high school, I came home late one day because I had activities after school. It was probably about eight o'clock. As I got into the elevator of my building, a man in his early twenties slipped in after me. Why? I wondered. He told me. He was going to rape me. We were going to stop on a higher floor and he was going to rape me in a stairwell. He had a huge knife at my throat.

What's more disempowering than such a very credible threat of violent rape? But I would not let him take my power away from me. I told him, hey, if we're going to have sex, why do it in a stairwell when we could do it up in my apartment. My mother wasn't home, I said.

Luckily he wasn't all that bright. He bought it! Up we went to the tenth floor where, as I knew she'd be, my mother was waiting for me at the open door to our apartment. I started hollering, my mother started running toward us, and the guy fled.

Speaking of my mother, she was one tough woman. She'd brought two babies through the horrors of the Holocaust and of Stalinist Russia, then through terrible poverty in the slums of the Lower East Side in Manhattan, all on her own.

In her marriage to my stepfather, whom she married after we got to America, I saw a completely different side of the power issue. I saw her going toe to toe with him through the most vicious fights you could possibly imagine. She took no shit. Neither did he. And neither of them accomplished *anything* but scorching the earth of their marriage, leaving not a scrap of warmth or caring.

The power that meant everything to me was sheer poison in that marriage. I was to later learn that power dynamics had the ability to poison my own marriage and the relationships of all the people who came to me for help over the forty-five years of my professional life.

And so here I am believing at the very heart of my being in two contradictory things:

On the one hand: We need all the powerful women we can get. Our society, *every* society, needs women's potential.

So I champion, as I always have, our right to elbow our way to the table of power and to break through all the glass ceilings that are in our way. To take no shit from anyone. And I want the same feeling of enablement for men.

And I believe in women having our full voice in our relationship, in our not giving our power away to our partner, in our being able to get our needs met, and in our being in a relationship that allows full room for all of who we are.

But on the other hand: In the intimacy of a committed relationship, where it's so important to keep love alive, it's essential for both people to work together to resolve their conflicts without resorting to power and attempts at gaining control. And the reason is that these result NOT in people getting their needs met but in escalating power dynamics taking over, damaging and ultimately destroying the relationship.

A contradiction? A dilemma?

Not at all. Women, and men, can and should have full empowerment, full and strong voices in the world and in their relationships. And women and men can, and should, have total ability to get their needs met in their relationships, along with the ability to keep those relationships alive and thriving in the process.

I want you to know how much I honor you. I know you—as a woman or a man or however you identify yourself in terms of gender—have already struggled to empower yourself in the face of forces that have attempted to disempower you. I know—and that's why you're listening to me now—that you've struggled as I have with the incredibly difficult balancing act between fighting for your own needs in your relationship and working for peace and love and harmony between the two of you at the same time.

And I know that balancing act may have seemed impossible for you, as it did for me. But it isn't. That's why I've written this book.

Acknowledgments

Oh, my gosh, I am so grateful to so many people for so much it's hard to know where to begin.

But begin I must, and so let me start with Dr. Charles Foster. My husband *and* my life partner. More to the point, since this is a book about how to make room in a marriage for two whole people, I have to tell you that he is my full partner in the making of this book. From the incredibly difficult process of turning the germ of an idea into a viable proposal and then into a completed book, this has been not a 50/50 collaboration but a 60/60 collaboration, which is crazy but totally true. Every word in this book is as much his as it is mine. Really.

And because of him, this book about love has been a labor of love. Proof? After writing a book together, we're not only still on speaking terms, we're closer than ever.

So now you know.

And I'd like you to know how grateful I am to my agent Howard Morhaim. I've been with him for every one of my books except the first. Howard has been there for me when things have been great and when they've been not so great. And at every step Howard's told me the truth, helped me along, supported me, encouraged me, and pointed me in the right direction. Howard, you're just great

I am endlessly grateful to my greatest teachers: my

333

patients. There have been thousands of you over the years, but I want you to know that each of you, and each of your lessons, are vividly etched in my mind. I remember you and I treasure you. And, dear reader, I hope you will find a place in your heart to thank all these people who've suffered and struggled just the way you have but who have worked to make things better and in the process have taught me how to make things better for you.

Not that my *teacher* teachers were chopped liver. And let's be clear what we're talking about here. These were people who re-wired my brain in real time without anesthesia. To learn is to change, and to change is to throw your old self out the window. And that's what my teachers helped me with, not because it was what I needed—the hell with my needs!— but because it was what YOU needed. So a huge embrace of gratitude to Paul Watzlawick, Jay Haley, Roger Fisher, Chloe Madanes, Father Bill Richardson, Pepper Schwartz, Gitta Sereny, Gregory Bateson, Martin Buber, Don Jackson, Jules Henry, Alfred Kazin, Rabbi Harold Kushner, Richard Stuart, Paul Goodman, Allan Kaprow, Salvador Minuchin, Harold Zyskind, and Herbert Berghof. And a particular thanks to the Rev. Kate Kress for some crucial support and encouragement just as I was starting to write this book.

This is the first book I've written in Los Angeles and the first not in a house but in a high-rise. So you need to know how grateful I am to the manager here, Craig Settimo, for doing everything he can to take care of us, a job that's all the more difficult with the pandemic raging around us. And big thanks to Aaron Gonzales and Lawrence McDonald and Juana for all their wonderful work. And big thanks to Aaron

Gonzales, Lawrence McDonald, Felipe Velez, Tom Roy, and Juana for all their wonderful work helping us make our lives better.

Now writing a book is a funny thing. Just when you think you're bringing your baby up just fine, thank you very much, and when it reaches the difficult teen years, you suddenly find you have a co-parent. Your editor. In my case, this book's co-parent is Denise Silvestro. I can't imagine having a better editor or a better experience with an editor. Let's look at things from Denise's point of view. She wouldn't be publishing my book unless she liked it, but let's face it: it's not unconditional love. Her job is to represent the reader, to make my book better, to tell me that my precious child isn't perfect. And Denise does that with incredible sensitivity, honesty, integrity, and a wealth of intelligence and experience. It's been a joy to work with her.

I also want to thank other folks on the Kensington team. Ann Pryor—how over-the-top lucky we are to have you leading the marketing and PR team. Your energy and understanding are so special. And hey, I'll do whatever I can to help, dance naked in the middle of Times Square, you name it. And a wow and a thanks to your team, Ann, the folks helping with marketing, social media, our web presence, and all the other pieces crucial to launching this rocket. Kristine Noble, I LOVE the cover—I can't thank you enough for that miracle of elegance and impact. Arthur Maisel and Susan Higgins—copyediting is such an odd combination of the technical and the personal, requiring both vigilance and sensitivity, and I just loved what you did. Thanks also to designer Joe Gannon. Lynn Cully, Jackie Dinas, Steve

Zacharius: I know that your being behind *Why Couples Fight* makes a huge difference, and heartfelt thanks for the difference you make now and in the future.